To Keane
with love
on reachin

CW00586995

'To Me To Live Is Christ'

A Biography of Peter H. Barber

Commendation

It is right that during this centenary year of the Baptist World Alliance we remember those great leaders of the past who have inspired and led us. We are grateful to Edward Burrows for his book on the life of Peter Barber who was not only a great Baptist leader in Scotland, but in the European Baptist Federation and the Baptist World Alliance. His life was a shining example of life in Christ as a pastor, administrator, leader and friend who inspired a generation of Baptists in East and West during crucial years.

His outstanding leadership was felt, especially during three crises for European Baptists: the fall of communism and the re-establishment of freedom in Eastern Europe; the crises of the Baptist Seminary in Rüschlikon being defunded; and the election of the EBF's first woman president.

The lives of thousands of Baptist youth worldwide were changed by the Baptist Youth World Conference held in Glasgow, Scotland, in 1988. It was Peter Barber's leadership that made this conference an outstanding success.

I am eternally grateful for having known Peter Barber as a friend and counselor. For those who did not experience personally his Christ-like life, this biography now makes it possible to know him. This book reminds us of how God has blessed Baptists in Europe with leadership for which we should all be thankful.

Read this book and you will be inspired by seeing how living in Christ made all the difference in Peter Barber's being a servant leader!

Dr Denton Lotz
General Secretary
Baptist World Alliance
January 2005

'To Me To Live Is Christ'

A Biography of Peter H. Barber

Edward W. Burrows

Foreword by James Taylor

Paternoster is an imprint of Authentic Media
9 Holdom Avenue, Bletchley, Milton Keynes, MK1 1QR, UK
and
P.O. Box 1047, Waynesboro, GA 30830–2047, USA

11 10 09 08 07 06 05   7 6 5 4 3 2 1

British Library Cataloguing in Publication Data
A catalogue record for this book is available from the British Library

ISBN 1–84227–324–8

Typeset by A.R. Cross
Cover design and illustrations by Lyn Sneddon, Potion 9 Design, Glasgow
Printed and bound in Great Britain
for Paternoster
by Bell & Bain Ltd, Glasgow

In grateful memory of Peter,
for Isobel, Fiona, Susan and Colin

Contents

Chapter 12

Chapter 13

Chapter 14

Chapter 15

Foreword

To have known Peter Barber was to have known a careful student of God's Word, a more than able preacher, a faithful pastor, a man of visionary leadership, a good friend and, above all, a man of God. As a bonus it was to encounter, but never suffer from, a rich sense of humour and a warm and generous heart. He was a big man in almost every sense of the word. That is why his passing from us, in God's mysterious purpose, has left a huge void in many of our hearts, certainly in the Baptist family in Scotland and also in the wider Baptist scene.

It is because of the stature of the man and what many of us owed to him that I welcome Edward Burrows's excellent biography. It succeeds in showing Peter as many of us knew him, a warm human being, who was a good friend and a congenial companion, but who left no doubt that his passion was Jesus Christ, the desire to communicate him to men and women and to build up his church.

I read Edward Burrows's work at a sitting. When I put it down my reaction was 'Yes, that's the Peter we knew and loved!' It certainly describes his roots in great detail and how God prepared him for what lay ahead. The story of East Kilbride continues to thrill. His 'secret' courting of Isabel will bring a smile. His ministry 'down south' is well documented and his outstanding leadership as Secretary of the Baptist Union of Scotland well described. What you are about to read also points to his wider ministry and the vision and wisdom he was increasingly bringing to the European Baptist Federation.

Many who knew Peter will read this book and their sense of thanksgiving for him will be renewed. Many, who didn't know him, will hopefully also read what follows and realise that a giant was among us—and many of us knew it.

James Taylor
Former Minister, Stirling Baptist Church, 1970–95
President of the Baptist Union of Scotland, 1971–72

Preface and Acknowledgements

When Peter Barber died at the age of sixty-four on 1 September 1994 many Christians in Britain and around the world shared with Isobel and the whole family in suffering a great loss. From our human perspective it was decidedly a premature death.

The intention of this book is to preserve something of the message and the example that God gave us through Peter. For this reason there are extensive quotations from his own writings.

It has been most natural to refer to Peter as 'Peter' rather than 'Barber', though he was, of course known as 'Mr Barber' in his pastorates and as General Secretary.

I am very grateful for all the help and information given by Isobel and by the other members of Peter's family, in particular by his daughters Fiona and Susan, his son Colin, his brothers and sisters-in-law, Joe and Mary, Wilf and Dorothy, his sister Helen, and his aunt, the late Mrs Jessie Sutherland. Peter was a hoarder: much of the information comes from his own memorabilia.

My thanks, also, to others who supplied information, including the following. For Peter's family and early life: Mr Adam Burnett, Lieutenant Colonel (Retd) A.A. Fairrie (Archivist of the Highlanders), the late Mr John S. Fisher, Mr Angus Ferguson, Miss Linda Murison (Librarian of Boroughmuir School, Edinburgh), the late Miss Mamie Ross, Mrs Helen Sneddon and the Rev. James Taylor. For the East Kilbride period: the late Mr Peter Blackwood and Mr Alex Calder. For the Upton Vale period: Mr Howard and Mrs Elaine Bishop, Mr Aubrey and Mrs Heather Cutts, Mr Ken and Mrs Beth Cutts, Mr Ivor Gane, the Rev. David Hewitt, the Rev. Keith and Mrs Lynne King, Mrs Kath McBride, the Rev. Nick Mercer, Mr Michael Quantick, Mr Reg Sage, Mr Rob Shaw, Mr Edwin and Mrs Joyce Taylor, Mr Reg Vigurs, Mr David and Mrs Margaret Voyce, Mr John Walker, the Rev. Graham White. For the General Secretary period: the Rev. Alf Peck, the Rev. Karl Heinz Walter and the Rev. Eric Watson.

I am also most grateful for those who read a late draft, encouraged me and made helpful comments: Prof. David Bebbington, the Rev. Douglas J. Hutcheon, the Rev. Dr Andrew D. MacRae, the Rev. Dr Derek B. Murray, the Rev. Alf Peck and the Rev. James Taylor.

I am most indebted to the Paternoster Press and in particular to Jeremy Mudditt and the Rev. Dr Anthony R. Cross for their part in the publication of this book.

Edward W. Burrows

Abbreviations

BMS   Baptist Missionary Society (now BMS World Mission)

BUGBI   Baptist Union of Great Britain and Ireland

BUGB   Baptist Union of Great Britain (name changed in April 1988)

EA   Evangelical Alliance

Focus   *Focus on East Kilbride Baptist Church* (published from August 1969 onwards)

Record   *East Kilbride Baptist Church Record* (published from January 1957 to June/July 1969)

SBM   *Scottish Baptist Magazine* (monthly; ceased publication after December 2000; referred to in some chapters as the *Magazine*.)

SBN   *Scottish Baptist News*

SBYB   *The Scottish Baptist Year Book* (published annually by the Baptist Union of Scotland, Glasgow)

Vision   The bi-monthly magazine of Upton Vale Baptist Church, Torquay before, during and after Peter Barber's ministry there.

The 'Union' refers to the Baptist Union of Scotland.

Our roots go deep into our past.
Much of what we are is what our past has made us.
Not to know our past, or to sever our connections with it
in the name of modernity, can result in a loss of
identity, understanding and stability.

I am not saying that we should live in the past (that is escapism)
or on the past (which is idolatry)
but we should build on it, learn from it
and keep of it that which is timelessly valuable.
We need to 'remember all the way the Lord our God has led us'.

Peter Barber, *Scottish Baptist Magazine* (June 1991), 10.

Illustrations

1. Vacation work in a road gang, July 1951. Peter Barber is third on the left.

2. The student evangelist.

3. Andrew MacRae, Ronnie Scott and Peter Barber as young men.

4. Joe, Jean, Wilf, Peter, Ronnie and Helen early in the 1980s.

5. An early deacons' court at East Kilbride. Peter Blackwood is on Peter's right.

6. Deacons' court at East Mains, 1973. Alex Calder is on Peter's left.

7. Wedding day: Friday 13 August 1965.

8. Preaching from the East Mains pulpit.

9. Peter and Isobel with Fiona and Susan shortly before leaving East Kilbride in 1973.

10. Evangelist at Downfield (St Kilda Road), Dundee, during the simultaneous evangelism of 1970. Those seated: Lord Provost, Rev. Douglas Hutcheon (minister), Rev. Jim Powrie (Church of Scotland).

11. Ordination and Induction of Jim Hamilton at Calderwood, 7 August 1971. Principal R.E.O. White, Rev. Alex Hardie, Mr James McDonald (secretary), Peter Barber, Pauline and Jim Hamilton, Rev. Jim Murdoch.

12. With the deacons of Upton Vale, Torquay, 1973. Ken Cutts is in front of the window.

13. In the pulpit of Upton Vale, Torquay, with members of the team from the Movement for World Evangelisation, 1977.

14. Peter and Isobel at the EBF Congress in Budapest, July 1989, when he became President of the Federation.

15. In Glasgow's George Square with an Argentinian couple who were delegates to the BWA Youth Conference, July 1988.

16. With Mrs Irmgard Claas at the Brandenburg Gate, Berlin, Sunday 13 April 1991.

17. The leaders of the Foreign Mission Board and the EBF meeting in Hamburg, Germany, September 1992. The result was the 'Hamburg Agreement' on the Rüschlikon Seminary.

18. Karl Heinz Walter (standing, extreme left) and his wife Traute (seated, third from left) with the leaders of the Baptist Union of Scotland and their wives in the Barbers' home, Summer 1990.

19. With his son Colin (about 14) and a dog called Peg on the hill above Kiloran Bay on the island of Colonsay, around 1990.

20. Portrait taken by Stephen Younger at the first ministers' prayer day at Perth, 1 September 1993.

21. With granddaughter Zoe at Kiloran Bay on the Island of Colonsay, July 1994.

CHAPTER 1

Family Background

Birth, Name and Infant Baptism

Peter Horne Barber was born in the Slateford district of Edinburgh, in his parents' home, 10 Hermand Terrace, on 25 August 1930. He was the fourth child of Wilfred and Helen (Nellie) Barber.

They named him Peter Horne, which was the complete name of Nellie's father. When his second name was abbreviated to 'H.' Peter was sometimes asked what it stood for. His standard reply was 'Itch is for scratching'—an Edinburgh pronunciation of the letter!

His parents belonged to the Glanton Party of the Brethren, who practised 'household baptism'. Peter was, therefore, baptized as a baby at home in a large bath. Later, when he had come to hold Baptist convictions, he had lengthy and lively discussions on the subject of baptism with relatives in the Glanton Brethren!

Peter's father was born in London and his mother in Inverness. It was Wilfred's career in the army that brought them together.

Father's Father

Wilfred was the only son of Joseph William Barber, who also had one daughter, Winifred. Joseph was born in Mottingham, Kent, in March 1873, the son of Charles and Emma Barber. He was a butcher by trade, but in November 1891 he enlisted for the Queen's Own Cameron Highlanders. After a short period at their Depot in Inverness he served with the 1st Camerons in Malta, Gibraltar, Egypt and the Sudan. He fought in the Boer War at Atbara and Khartoum, and was awarded the Redvivus Medal, the Atbara clasp and the Sudan medals (Khedive's and Queen's). He led a Bible Class in the regiment.

He was invalided back to England in September 1898 and discharged in the November. He married Hannah Elizabeth Bloomfield at Mottingham on 14 February 1899. For the next thirty years he worked as an insurance agent with the Prudential and then bought a farm in

Rayleigh, Essex, on which he worked until his death in December 1946.[1] Peter, who had a great love of animals, remembered visiting his grandfather's farm as a boy and being fascinated by it.

Father's Mother

A distant relative of Peter, Jack Bloomfield, has done a great deal of research into the Bloomfield/Blomfield family, which came originally from France. The genealogy he has produced goes back as far as Robert de Blomeville, who was living in 1190 in Norfolk. One of his sons became Bishop of Norwich. The family tree features many clergymen of the Church of England, including other bishops, and many high-ranking officers in the forces, including two major-generals and an admiral.

Hannah Elizabeth is remembered as 'a lovely person, a real lady'. She was the fourth child of William and Eliza (née Askew) Bloomfield. She had three sisters and five brothers. Another brother had died in infancy. A younger brother, Arnold Wilfred, was a colourful character. He was ordained as a presbyter in the Presbyterian Church in the USA and was awarded the DD degree. During both World Wars he served as a padre in Britain. In the Second World War he saw a plane crash in a field in England. It blew up and the crater revealed a hoard of Roman coins. He kept one to use as an illustration. He married twice, the second time at the age of eighty-nine! He was ninety-eight when he died in 1978.

Father

Peter's father, Wilfred Reginald Charles, was born to Joseph and Hannah Barber on 29 November 1899 in Plumstead, London, Kent. He enlisted in his father's regiment, the Queen's Own Cameron Highlanders in 1917. His previous trade was described as a fitter. He served in the 3rd Battalion and after training at Invergordon saw action with the Machine Gun Corps in France. On 10 October 1918, very near the end of the war, he sustained a serious gunshot wound while crossing a river. He managed to crawl out and was admitted to the General Hospital in Rouen. He was demobilised on 8 February 1919. His physical wound caused him little trouble in his later years, but the memories of his experiences while serving in the Machine Gun Corps remained through his life, as was the case with many men who fought in the trenches in the First World War.

Despite these experiences he enlisted again in the same regiment on 5 January 1922. This time he was sent to Cameron Barracks in Inverness and was soon befriended by a Brethren couple, Peter and Mary Horne,

---

[1] Most information in this and the previous paragraph was supplied by Lieutenant Colonel (Retd) A.A. Fairrie, Archivist of The Highlanders.

whose daughter he was to marry. How he came to meet them and whether he had any previous connection with the Brethren we do not know. The 'religion' of his father Joseph is given as 'Wesleyan' in his army Account Book.

Wilfred served with the 2nd Battalion of the Camerons at Aldershot (1922–23) and Cologne (1923–26) before being transferred to the Redford Barracks, Edinburgh, in 1926. The family moved to 10 Hermand Terrace at this time. Wilfred was a fine looking soldier and perhaps for that reason was chosen to be one of the four men standing at the corners of Earl Haig's coffin when he lay in state in Edinburgh in 1928. He served until 1929, when he was released to the Reserve and took up employment as a motor mechanic in a garage in the Morningside district of the city.[2]

During the Second World War he joined the RAF Medical Corps and was stationed at Kinloss, while his wife stayed on in Edinburgh. Reacting against his previous experience in the Machine Gun Corps he wished to save life rather than kill.

Great-Grandfather Horne

On his mother's side one of Peter's great-grandfathers (his mother's paternal grandfather) was Peter Horne, who moved from Huntly in Aberdeenshire to Inverness to be employed in the workshops of the Highland Railway.

Huntly was a centre of evangelism and saw the 1859 Revival, when there were great meetings in the park. These took place in Peter Horne's boyhood. When he came to Inverness he was already a Baptist and had been baptized as a believer. It is likely that he became a member of a 'Scotch Baptist' church in the town.[3]

Believers may have been baptized in the River Ness early in the 1800s, but it was not until around 1820 that the first Baptist church (of the 'Scotch Baptist' tradition) was formed. Its first pastor was Walter Munro and when he died in 1837 the Baptists worshipped with the Independents. It seems that some years later a 'Scotch Baptist' congregation was formed again, one of its leaders being Dr Duncan Mackay, a general practitioner.

---

[2] Much of the information in this and the previous two paragraphs was supplied by Lieutenant Colonel (Retd) A.A. Fairrie, Archivist of The Highlanders.

[3] The 'Scotch Baptists' arose in the eighteenth century in Scotland and spread to parts of England and Wales. Some of their churches in Scotland that were willing to change joined with the Baptist Union of Scotland early in the twentieth century. A few still exist in North Wales. A distinctive feature is leadership by a plurality of lay elders rather than by an ordained minister.

For the last period of his life he was its part-time pastor. It was of this church that Peter Horne probably became a member.[4]

A young woman called Jane, who became Peter Horne's wife, was baptized, together with another young woman, in the River Ness on a cold January Sunday in 1865. The report in the *Inverness Advertiser* was factual and fair in its reporting but disapproving in its comment, no doubt from a Presbyterian perspective:

> 'BAPTISMS' EXTRAORDINARY.—About the hour of one o'clock on Sunday last, church-goers returning from the different places of worship were attracted by the unusual sight of a pretty large crowd gathered on the banks of the river at Ness Walk, a little below Ardross Street. Two gentlemen residing in town, of much respectability and noted for their Christian zeal, engaged in devotional exercises, which were joined in by the majority of those present with great propriety and order; and, at a given signal from the leaders, two females dressed in a kind of bathing costume emerged from a cab, which was in waiting on the road, and were in succession guided into the water by a reverend gentleman belonging to the Baptist persuasion in the country, and twice plunged head over ears in the stream. The unfortunate creatures were then led out, shivering with cold and the water dripping from their garments, and in this state made their way back to the cab with considerable difficulty, and were driven off—let us hope to the house of some good Samaritan, where they would get, along with a change of attire and something to restore natural warmth to their systems, a bit of plain friendly advice. The day on which this extraordinary ceremony took place was cold although seasonable; and the curiosity of the crowd was intense, many parties witnessing the proceedings from the Castlehill, and a good deal of speculation being rife as to who the victims were to this revival of a custom which on Sunday last was neither in keeping with the time nor place in which it was made public, and indeed in the present day seems positively indecent and inhuman.[5]

After his death on 3 June 1886 Dr Mackay's congregation dispersed. The present Inverness Baptist Church was formed in January 1898. Peter and Jane Horne were founder members of the new church, which continues to flourish today (Castle Street).[6]

---

[4] Information from John S. Fisher, and from George J. Mitchell, *Guidance and Gumption: A Hundred Years and More of Inverness Baptist Church* (Centenary 1898–1998; Inverness: Inverness Baptist Church, 1998), 16-23.

[5] *Inverness Advertiser* (10 January 1865). I am indebted to John S. Fisher for this quotation, also to be found in Mitchell, *Guidance and Gumption*, 17.

[6] Mitchell, *Guidance and Gumption*, 21-23. The period of the church's history in which the Castle Street building was planned and erected is covered by John S. Fisher, *From Friars Lane to Castle Street: A Fragment of Inverness History* (Inverness: Inverness Baptist Church, 1983). It was opened in 1933.

Grandfather Horne

Peter and Mary had a son and they gave him his father's name—another Peter Horne. He was born in Inverness on 3 May 1873.

When he grew up, he went away from his parents' faith for many years. He had a consuming passion for football and served as a referee. His dramatic conversion came when, at the age of thirty-six, he was deeply distressed and challenged by two tragic bereavements within a week. In March 1910 his sister Mary and his son Bertie (Robert Ellis Horne), who was only five and a half years old, died within a few days of each other. He often told later of the struggle he went through, of the way he paced up and down in the front room of the house, before he yielded his life and knew peace with God, and of John Fraser, from an Independent Brethren Meeting in Inverness, who helped him come to the Lord. His wife had become a Christian ten years previously.

Once converted there was for him no turning back: he gave up refereeing football (such games being regarded as worldly pursuits) and became a zealous Christian worker. He had just received a list of appointments for referees, including the Scottish Qualifying Cup, but he was sure he must give it up. Much later he wrote in a private letter: 'I sent my resignation to the secretary of the Associations and confessed him my excuse. Jn 3:16, Rom 10:9—a decision I never regret.'

He made contact with the Baptist church in Inverness and asked for believer's baptism, but the minister would not baptize him unless he intended to become a member of the church. He turned to the Brethren. At first he worked in a mission in Shoe Lane, in a poor part of the town. Later he served in the Glanton Hall Mission and then for many years in the Gospel Mission in Swan Lane, off Wells Street, where he was Superintendent. His remaining seven children, three boys and four girls, including Nellie (Helen), Peter's mother, were brought up in the Brethren.

Grandfather Horne was tall and distinguished in appearance, a strong man physically, mentally and spiritually. His robust faith and bright Christian witness made an impact on all. Early in his working life he was a compositor with the *Northern Chronicle*. Later he took up insurance and for many years was an agent and latterly manager with the Scottish Legal Insurance Company in Inverness, proving himself to be a good friend to many families in times when there was much unemployment and hardship. Peter's brother Wilf remembers cycling with him when he was in his early seventies from Inverness to Nairn (sixteen miles) to collect insurance money. On the way he picked up medicine that had been prescribed for a client.

For the last twenty years of his life he lived in Kyle of Lochalsh on the west coast of Scotland at the home of his daughter Jessie and her husband

Donald. For several years, until he was over ninety, he ran a children's Bible Class there.

He died in his ninety-seventh year on 9 February 1970, having been confined to bed for little more than a week. After a short service at Kyle his body was taken to Inverness, where his grandson Peter Barber (in his year as President of the Baptist Union of Scotland) conducted the funeral service and burial. His wife Mary Dewar (née MacDonald) had died on 6 March 1941 at the age of sixty-eight. Both were buried in the same grave as their infant son Bertie.

Writing in the East Kilbride Church magazine soon after his grandfather's death Peter paid this tribute:

> There are many things I remember about him, many little things that mean so much. The twinkle in his eye when he was teasing—the erect way in which he walked—his unbounded affection for children. But two memories remain that nothing will erase.
>
> I remember the night when he said to me, 'Peter, never make the mistake of thinking the Christian life gets easier as you get older. The opposite is the case. It is a battle right to the end.' And he certainly fought his 'good fight' right until the 'hour of his departure' was at hand.
>
> Then there was the other occasion when he said, 'We are not all carpenters, but when the occasion demands we can all do the work of a carpenter. Yes, and we may not all be Evangelists, but we can all do the work of an Evangelist.' He did, even in his nineties, when he went with pockets full of tracts to give to pensioners sitting in the summer time on park benches.
>
> Now Granddad is no longer with us—or is he?[7]

Grandfather Horne's Family

At the time of Grandfather Horne's death three of his four sons had already died, but his four daughters were all living; he had twenty-four grandchildren, many of whom were in full-time Christian work, and thirty-five great-grandchildren.

One of his sons, also named Peter Horne (Peter Barber's uncle), was a well-known pioneer missionary with the Christian Brethren. He went to Bolivia in 1922, where he met and married Mima Campbell of Irvine, who had begun her missionary service two years earlier. They served in Santa Cruz (Bolivia), Iquitos (Peru) and Montero (Bolivia). Peter died in Montero on 7 January 1964 and Mima continued with the work there. They travelled many hundreds of miles in pioneering endeavour and had

---

[7] *Focus* (March 1970), 1.

the joy of seeing assemblies firmly established.[8] One of their sons, Robert, who lives in Ayrshire, is a preacher with the Brethren. He is a shepherd, a poet with publications to his credit, and a preacher. Peter Barber was great friends with his cousin Robert and was best man at his wedding: he learned a lot from him about shepherding and shared with him a love of poetry.

One of Grandfather Horne's daughters, Carrie, married Duncan Chisholm, who was a popular Brethren preacher and teacher with a special interest in the fulfilment of prophecy and in particular the book of Revelation. He was in great demand to give Bible studies in Brethren circles in Scotland and the north of England. He had a deep influence on his nephew Peter, who greatly admired him.

Another daughter, Mollie, married the Rev. David Gill, who left Scotland to become pastor of Evangelical churches in the Bournemouth area. Their only daughter, Rhoda, qualified as a nurse and studied at the Faith Mission College, Edinburgh. She served in the Congo with the Regions Beyond Missionary Union and there met and married John, missionary son of the Rev. and Mrs David Gordon-Roberts. He taught mathematics and science. After further service they had to return to Britain because of Rhoda's ill-health. Tragically Rhoda and John were killed in a car crash on 24 February 1976 on the way from Bournemouth to Cardiff. Their two little girls Sharon (five) and Esther (three) lay injured in hospital as the funeral of their parents took place in Heath Evangelical Free Church, Cardiff, where the family had worshipped and served for three years.

Rhoda had a rich contralto voice and had sung in the Youth For Christ Choir. The last solo she sang just before her death was:

> Face to face with Christ my Saviour,
> Face to face — what will it be,
> When with rapture I behold Him,
> Jesus Christ who died for me?

Sharon and Esther were brought up by John's twin brother, the Rev. Peter Gordon-Roberts, and his wife Catherine. Together with the whole family Peter Barber was deeply affected by the death of his cousin and her husband.

Grandfather Horne's last surviving child was his youngest daughter Jessie (known to the family as 'Jay'). He stayed with her and her husband Donald in Kyle of Lochalsh for the last twenty years of his life. When Jessie and Donald returned to Inverness they became members of Castle

---

[8] W.T. Stunt *et al.*, *Turning the World Upside Down: A Century of Missionary Endeavour* (Bath: Echoes of Service, 2nd ed., 1972), 203, 205, 566; *The Irvine Herald* (Friday 8 September 1967), 4.

Street Baptist Church, where Donald served as a deacon. He died on 8 September 1991 and Peter Barber took the funeral service in the Church. Jessie remained an active member until her death on 28 August 2001.[9]

Peter and the Family

Peter came from a large family that kept in close touch. He learned much from his relatives about Christian faith and service and was very ready to pay tribute to their influence upon him. He was also very interested in the occupations and pastimes of the various members of the family. He looked for God to reveal himself through any experience of life and drew illustrations for his preaching and teaching from a wide range of knowledge, much of it gleaned from being in a lively extended family.

---

[9] Much of the information in this chapter was supplied by Mrs Jessie Sutherland.

CHAPTER 2

Early Life

Peter had a happy childhood in a Christian home that laid the foundation for his life of Christian service. His mother and father were quite different from each other in personality. Andrew MacRae, who knew them well, described Peter's father as 'gifted, artistic, quiet, unassuming' and his mother as 'bustling, energetic, loving and wonderfully welcoming'.[1]

Mother

Nellie Barber had a sure and practical faith. She was a woman of prayer and an example to her family of joyful Christian living. Bringing up six children obviously involved a lot of hard work, but she carried out her duties cheerfully. She generated a lot of fun and was the hub of the family, which was a great joy to her. When the children grew up she kept in constant touch with all of them, and with all the grandchildren.

She encouraged Peter in his studies and supported him in his ministry, both spiritually and practically. In his early days at East Kilbride, while he was still a bachelor, she travelled by bus from Edinburgh once a week to do his laundry, clean the house and cook him some good, nourishing meals.

Physically Nellie was dark haired, like her mother before her, but smaller in stature. She was quick-thinking and quick speaking, as were all the family. Peter was notable for his speed of thought and rapid delivery. Jessie Sutherland described her as a strong and capable character: 'She could have entertained the Queen.'

Nellie died on 16 November 1974, soon after suffering a stroke. The funeral took place on 20 November at Stenhouse Baptist Church, Edinburgh. In his address the Rev. Donald McCallum called her 'a mother in Israel' and said:

> One of the chief glories of the Gospel is its recognition of the place of women in the home, in society and in the church, and all down the centuries women

---

[1] Thanksgiving Service address, 9 September 1994.

have given generously, sacrificially, gladly of themselves in the service of the
Saviour to whom they owed so much...

She was the answer to a well known child's prayer: 'Lord make the bad people
good and the good people nice!' In the sense in which the child meant it, Mrs
Barber was 'nice'; her goodness was attractive and practical and joyful. She was
happy and holy, natural as well as spiritual—a fine Christian woman for
whose life and service we give hearty thanks to God.[2]

Peter by this time was minister of Upton Vale, Torquay, and in its
magazine he wrote a remarkable pastor's letter in which he thanked the
church for their support in his bereavement, expressed the renewed
conviction of the Christian hope that had come to him through this
experience and paid tribute to his mother's faith and service:

My mother loved the Lord Jesus from her earliest years; despite daunting
difficulties she was to be found with her husband and six children every Sunday
in God's house; she was selfless in her service of other people.

I suppose, from one point of view, a mother's lot is a mundane and tedious
one—what with shopping, cooking, mending, washing, cleaning and dusting.
And the trouble is, it means going through the same routines again and again
without let up and with little appreciation. She must sometimes be tempted to
ask herself, 'Is it worth it all?'

As a great crowd gathered round my mother's grave-side for the service, I know
that among the crowd were seven very full and grateful hearts that would have
said resoundingly, 'Yes, it IS worth it all!' A husband and six children who
had been served and cared for unstintingly by a devoted wife and mother all
knew that for so much they were indebted to her. I know that, as my mother's
son, I can say with Teilhard de Chardin, 'To my mother I owe the best part of
my soul'.

It was she who taught me Christian values by living true to her own Christian
principles, and it was she who established for me Christian priorities by herself
seeking first the kingdom of God. She was my best teacher, and her life the
most convincing argument I have every met for the Christian virtues of
unselfishness, industry and trust. What she has invested in my life just by
being a Christian mother is beyond calculation and beyond price.[3]

---

[2] Sermon script in Peter's papers.
[3] *Vision* (January–February 1975), 3-4.

Father

Wilfred Barber was creative, artistic, intelligent. He had an enquiring mind and was an avid reader, always seeking to increase his knowledge right up to his death at the age of eighty-three. He was always curious to find out how things worked. He not only played organs but taught himself to tune them. He was a gifted man who could turn his hand to anything.

One of his skills was painting, both water colours and oils. He started painting when he was sixteen. He painted his wife's face on the ceiling of their bedroom so that he could lie in bed and look up at her! He was delighted when at the age of fifty he had a painting accepted by the Royal Academy in Edinburgh to be hung in an exhibition in the National Gallery there. Four of his children took up painting: Joe, Wilf, Jean and Peter.

He was strict with the children, as were many fathers of his generation. As a young man Peter cycled with his father from Edinburgh to Taunton and back. This took two weeks and led to a deeper understanding between them.

He was quieter and more serious than his wife, but had a great sense of humour and sometimes did the unusual. His wife used to tell the following story against him. One night, when they were in bed, some cats were howling in the garden. Wilfred got out of bed, got a squib out of a drawer, opened the window and lit the squib, intending to throw it in the direction of the cats. It went in the opposite direction and he made the funniest sight chasing it round the bedroom! It eluded him and exploded!

Another story was told of how one Sunday when he was playing the organ at Stenhouse Baptist Church, Edinburgh, the service was proceeding so slowly that he felt it appropriate to play the funeral march for the offering voluntary. He was highly amused at his own joke, but no-one else made any comment.

He was a man of few words, but one letter that Peter kept reveals his personal faith and his love for his wife. It was written, while she was away for a break, to the two boys still at home: Peter (twenty-four) and Ronald (twenty). Helen was sixteen.

Dear Boys,

Having due respect to Mum's near return home, we, i.e. Helen and I, hope to have the house nice and clean. Mum has had a perfect holiday and I would like to add to its pleasure by giving her a surprise in finding the house clean. You two can co-operate in this if you tidy your room on Friday so we can clean it at night, also to tidy it on Saturday. You will be giving the greatest assistance if you do this.

I expect Mum home by noon, Saturday. If you see any other way to help it will be much appreciated. It is just another way of saying thanks to Mum for her unceasing love and devotion to us as a family.

My one prayer is that she may be spared for a long time yet, to spend and be spent, for she loves to serve, not looking for reward. I am sure her labours of love have at all times been appreciated by you all. To-day is our Wedding Anniversary, 30 years of happiness. During these years you have only added to our happiness beyond the power of the pen to interpret.

I am glad to record that our ties that bind are stronger than earthly ties and for this reason our sojourn here has been most happy. I only hope you experience the joys that Mum and I have experienced, for which I return thanks to God for all these temporal blessings, of the past and present, and look forward to the time when our happiness will be complete when we are at home with Him no more to roam. In the meantime I trust Him to lead us on from strength to strength.

POP

In their later years Wilfred and Nellie changed denomination and became members of Stenhouse Baptist Church, where Wilfred served as deacon and organist. He was not a preacher but late in life he prepared and conducted Bible studies for Grandfather Horne's Bible Class at Kyle, which revealed his ability to interpret the Scriptures.

Nearly two years after the death of Nellie in 1974 Wilfred married again on 7 October 1976. He died on 13 November 1982, a few days after suffering a heart attack. The funeral was in Charlotte Chapel, Edinburgh. His second wife, Mima, survived him for a few years.

Brothers and Sisters

Peter had three brothers and two sisters. Joe was five years older, Jean three and a half years older, Wilf twenty months older. Later came Ronnie, three years and two months younger, and Helen, seven years and nine months younger. It was natural that Peter was closest to Wilf. They were great friends and their mother described them as being 'like twins'.

Jean died of cancer at the age of fifty-eight on Christmas Eve 1985, nearly eight years before Peter died. She bore a strong physical resemblance to Peter. She was a deeply spiritual woman and had a big influence upon him. When she moved to East Kilbride during his ministry there and became a member of the church, she gave pastoral care and guidance to many in the congregation and became one of Isobel's best friends. She encouraged people to pray for Peter's ministry both there and when he moved on to Torquay. He was deeply fond of her and gave a moving tribute to her at the funeral. For the last three months of her life she lived with Peter, Isobel and the family in Glasgow. Her husband Douglas had predeceased her. They had three children: Elaine, Miriam and Iain.

The Home

Peter grew up in a close and happy family. His younger sister Helen remembers their situation: 'Father worked as a garage mechanic, and there were six children, so we hadn't a lot materially, but we had enough because my mother was an industrious woman and a good manager. In the things that really matter we were rich in abundance: we had plenty of love and a wonderful faith. We had great fun and we grew up having a pride in each other and in our family.'

At 10 Hermand Terrace, Edinburgh, the family lived in the ground floor apartment of a Victorian tenement. There were three rooms, plus a bathroom and scullery. The parlour was to the front of the house and contained, among other things, a wonderful wind-up gramophone, which gave the family enormous pleasure. The middle room was a bedroom with a fireplace in the corner. At the back of the house was the kitchen and off this was a small scullery. In the kitchen the big black grate shone where the steel parts had been burnished with steel wool. It contained an oven with large doors and was a source of heat and comfort to all the family. The bathroom was a most intriguing room as in it their father Wilfred painted various murals, including the ship which Joe sailed in while in the Navy.

It was an open house. At teatime on Sunday evenings there were always lots of people around the table. Many lively and interesting friends came to the home. They broadened the horizons and stimulated the minds of the children.

Childhood Activities

Wilf recalls some of the pastimes of their childhood. When he was five and a half and Peter was four they both contracted scarlet fever and had to stay in hospital. When they returned home their mother was so pleased that she bought them a train-set. One day, as they were playing Peter asked his mother his first theological question: 'If I throw these balls up into the sky, will Jesus catch them?'

He was a great reader. At bedtime he read stories to Wilf, particularly the adventure stories in comics like the *Hotspur* and the *Rover*. These were passed on to them second hand by a boy at school. Wilf believes that Peter's talent for description was nurtured as he read those stories.

He suspects that their mother must have turned a blind eye to some of their childhood activities of which the Brethren disapproved. There was a cinema at the end of their street and they would sometimes slip away to watch a cowboy film. They showed great enterprise by chopping and selling sticks to get sixpence (two and a half pence) for the admission fee. On one occasion the children were amazed when their mother gave them money, sent them to the cinema and told them to stay there for the whole afternoon. When they returned home they found that their cousin Rhoda had been born there.

Helen remembers that as a teenager Peter enjoyed the radio comedy programme *The Goon Show*, which no doubt appealed to his sense of humour, and the detective serial *Dick Barton—Special Agent*. All the family would listen to the radio in the same room—there was no central heating and there were no transistor radios or headsets. She also remembers playing 'church', with Peter leading the services, obviously showing early talent.

Wilf recalls the excitement and interest of the 'back yard' in the street, which was like the country in the town, as people kept in it their chickens, bulldogs, spaniels, finches and horses. Peter's love of animals was nurtured there. It was a fascinating place for children to play and afforded them much freedom.

A favourite family spot for holidays was Inverness, partly because of the beauty of the town, partly because of family connections. Peter later recalled the enjoyment of playing with his brothers by the banks of the Caledonian Canal, throwing stones at floating tins, sailing rough bits of wood that became magnificent liners to their inventive minds, and fishing—though they caught little! They would listen out for the deep-throated engine of a boat, for that would herald the excitement of seeing it pass through the lock. The canal-man would come out with a long pole, insert one end into a capstan-like lock and they would help him push it round and round so that the gates opened and the water burst through.[4]

As a boy Peter had blond hair, unlike the rest of the children. He was quieter than the others, at ease in company he knew well, but shy with strangers. He was 'the dreamer'. He would sit whistling and be miles away, lost in a world of his own.

Schooldays

Peter attended Craiglockhart Primary School and passed the qualifying examination to go to Boroughmuir Secondary School at the age of twelve. After a year or two he was getting results near the top of the class. He set the highest standards for himself and was always anxious before exams: he never believed he had passed an exam until he got the result.

---

[4] *Record* (April 1962), 2.

At the school he met two boys who were to become Baptist ministers and close friends of his: Andrew D. MacRae, who was to be his predecessor as General Secretary of the Baptist Union of Scotland, and W. Ronald (Ron) Scott, who served the Union as an Assistant Secretary (overlapping with Peter's Secretaryship) until his untimely death in 1982. He also met two other boys he later had fellowship with at Charlotte Chapel: Gilbert Kelling and Angus Ferguson.

The motto of Boroughmuir School is an apt description of Peter and may have had its influence upon him: *Justus et Tenax* ('Upright and Constant').[5] In his last year (1948-49, the sixth year) he served as a prefect and as captain of the boys' hockey team. A report in the school magazine commented: 'P. Barber at right-back is a reliable, hard-hitting player, whose untiring efforts give confidence to the team.'[6] In the same year he led the Scripture Union together with Gilbert Kelling and Andrew MacRae. They were supported by Miss Betty Graham, Head of the Geography Department, who was a member of Charlotte Chapel.[7]

It was at the school that he became acquainted with Handel's *Messiah*. He sang in the school choir and was in it when it made two '78' records of pieces from the work. Later, in his student years, it was his custom to attend the performance of the *Messiah* in Edinburgh's Usher Hall at mid-day on New Year's Day.[8] He mentioned his love of the work in a sermon at Upton Vale: for him listening to a large choir singing it was an 'intensely emotional experience' as it presented the incarnation, life, death and resurrection of the Lord. The climax of the *Hallelujah Chorus* thrilled him beyond all telling.[9]

Peter had seven subjects on his Senior Leaving Certificate: the paper in Arithmetic that everyone had to take; two 'lowers'—History and German; four 'highers'—English, Mathematics, French and Science (Chemistry and Physics).

Nurtured by the Brethren

The Barber children were brought up in the Brethren Assembly of the Glanton Party at Shandwick Place. The Glanton Party, named after a village in Northumbria, was a moderate group that split from the Exclusive Brethren in 1908. It spread quite rapidly in Scotland, though

---

[5] It is a quotation from an ode by the Roman poet Horace.
[6] *Boroughmuir Magazine* (February 1949), 27.
[7] Information from Angus Ferguson.
[8] Appointments diaries: 1951, 1953.
[9] Tape-recording of sermon preached at the morning service, 10 July 1977.

there are only a few assemblies today.[10] Its policy towards other Christians is between 'closed' and 'open' — some describe it as 'door ajar'.[11]

Peter's brother Wilf remembers that Sunday was no rest day: they had a 'murderous programme of activity' going round the Brethren meetings. First they went to the Morning Meeting at Shandwick Place, then to the Sunday School at Gorgie (Open Brethren) before dinner back at home. In the afternoon they attended Sunday School at the Old School House (also of the Glanton Party) in Morningside. At 6.30 they went back to Shandwick Place for the Evening Meeting, after which they went canvassing at a Soldiers' Meeting. Sunday was strictly observed: they *walked* to the meetings and never used the trams. Shandwick Place was a mile and a half from their house.

Ian Leitch, the evangelist of the Heralds Trust, was also brought up in the Shandwick Place Assembly. He was the son of Arthur Leitch, a great Christian worker. The two families shared friendship and hospitality. Ian recalls that there were numerous copies of *The Believers' Hymn Book* with football teams written in the back cover comprised of elder Brethren worthies, all selected by Barber boys! Four young men from the Shandwick Place Assembly became Baptist ministers: Peter, Andrew MacRae, Arthur Leitch (Ian Leitch's brother) and Norman Sinclair.

In his address to the Scottish Baptist Ministers' Conference in March 1994, a few months before he died, Peter recalled:

> My earliest experiences of worship were as a very young child in the morning meetings of a Glanton Brethren Assembly in the West End of Edinburgh. We used to sit in four sections all round a table; those of us not allowed to participate had to sit behind a row of chairs, one of which had a board attached indicating we could not come any further.

> There were certain things I learned from this experience of worship which live with me still: the beauty of unaccompanied part-singing; the significance of silence (it could live); the value of lay/congregational participation; the limits of worship theory (even as a child I saw that spontaneity did not guarantee inspiration and that a 'Spirit-led' service could be utterly predictable).

Apart from his mother and father, one of the people who influenced him most during his childhood was David Ross. He was the Superintendent of the Old School House Sunday School in Morningside where the Barber children went on Sunday afternoons. His daughter, Miss Mamie Ross, remembered teaching Peter and also Ian Leitch in her Sunday School class. David Ross loved preaching. During the school holidays he was often away from home on preaching tours. He went to

---

[10] T.C.F. Stunt and N.T.R. Dickson in Nigel M. de S. Cameron (eds): *Dictionary of Scottish Church History and Theology* (Edinburgh: T.&T. Clark, 1993), 94.

[11] Information from Dr Derek B. Murray.

Ireland, Germany and Switzerland. He had a ministry particularly among young people.

Peter also met him as a teacher at Boroughmuir School. He was on the staff there from 1905 to 1943.[12] His subjects were History and Scripture and he threw himself into the whole of school life, being involved with sport and with the establishing of the Scripture Union Group, which he used to attend regularly even after his retirement.[13] There was great sorrow when he died of a heart attack at the age of sixty-six on 21 March 1949. He was described in the school magazine as 'a great teacher and a man greatly loved by all, young and old, who knew him'. He was affectionately known as 'Daddy Ross' because of his paternal nature. Peter often spoke of the encouragement he had received from him and the deep impact he had made on his life.[14]

Another Brethren teacher who influenced him was A.J. Pollock, a member of the Glanton Brethren, whose Bible studies he attended in Edinburgh. He often said that he got a good foundation in his Brethren upbringing. There were distinctive Brethren features that remained with him. Sometimes after preaching he was met with the question: 'Were you ever in the Brethren, son?'

Peter's Upbringing

Peter owed a good deal to the circumstances of his upbringing. He was raised in a busy, caring, Christian home, with a mother devoted to the welfare of her children and a father inventive and unconventional. He was close to his three brothers and two sisters and the family kept in touch. For many years they held a picnic annually, when forty to fifty family members would get together to enjoy themselves with a lot of good natured banter, fun and teasing.

Peter had the opportunity of developing his academic skills at a good school, which had high standards and encouraged creativity. From his Brethren experience he derived a love for and a detailed knowledge of the Bible. He was influenced by Brethren folk who were not narrow in their sympathies but had broader horizons. Peter's horizons were to grow broader and broader.

---

[12] *Boroughmuir Magazine* (June 1944), 30.

[13] *Boroughmuir Magazine* (June 1945), 30.

[14] Information from Miss Mamie Ross and *Boroughmuir Magazine* (June 1949), 26 (in Peter's files).

CHAPTER 3

Youth

Full Commitment

In his teenage years Peter had rapidly widening horizons. Edinburgh presented him with many choices and opportunities. When he was fourteen and Wilf was sixteen they made a break from the Glanton Brethren Assembly, feeling that it was too restrictive, and began attending Carrubers Close Mission. This Mission had a deep influence on all the Barber children. It held a Saturday night meeting that was very popular and attracted Christians from across the denominations. The pastor was Dr David Laurie and he was assisted by Professor Norman Hunt (whose own subject was Economics).

A week or two before he died Peter told his brother Joe that David Laurie was the one man he had set out to emulate in his preaching. Laurie later went to minister in the USA, but died in Scotland on a visit home.

Peter's friends had taken it for granted that he was already converted, but it was in August 1948, when he was eighteen, that Peter committed his life fully to Christ in the quietness of his own bedroom. He sat up in bed and read a book by Oswald Smith on the Holy Spirit. After each chapter he formed a prayer from its theme. It was a rational conversion: he had been thinking it all through and had come to the conclusion that the Christian faith made sense. As he expressed it in his Ordination Statement:

> It was my immeasurable privilege to have been born into a Christian home, so that from my earliest years I was conversant with the message of the Gospel. However, it was not until August of 1948 that I first realised the full personal implications of that message and fully yielded my life to Christ. From that month onwards I have had the inner assurance of Christ's presence and guidance in my daily walk.

Soon afterwards he sensed that he might be called to ministry and confided in his mother. He experienced great joy as he dedicated his life to God and began to give his testimony and other talks at various meetings and open-air services. He was soon in great demand as a speaker.

He attended, with various groups of friends, a variety of places of worship on Sunday and a variety of young people's meetings during the week. He went out on Saturday afternoons to different locations with a tract band and found it a privilege to be able to point needy people to Christ. In Edinburgh he had the opportunity of hearing many well-known speakers, including evangelists such as Jock Troup, Roy Hession, James Stewart and Bob Jones, Jr.

'The Team'

One group that he soon became associated with was the Mound Open-air Fellowship (known more conveniently as 'The Team'). The Mound in Edinburgh was like Hyde Park Corner in London: a place where speakers could address crowds in freedom on all sorts of subjects. Some enthusiastic young people saw that there was no gospel meeting there on Sunday afternoons and formed the Fellowship to fill the gap in July 1948. The leaders were Hamish MacRae (brother of Andrew MacRae) of Charlotte Chapel and Joe Barber (Peter's brother) of Carruber's Close. Johnny Lawson played the 'squeezebox' (accordion). He had been an Amateur Middleweight Boxing Champion and his presence was sometimes helpful when there were rough scenes at open-air meetings! Other members of the team were Ron Scott, Andrew MacRae and Angus Ferguson. They got a good site for their meeting on the corner of Princes Street. They also supported other open-airs on Saturday and Sunday nights on the Mound. Sometimes they were up until the early hours of morning commending the faith to enquirers. Their activities were not confined to the Mound: they travelled widely, taking services and conducting evangelistic crusades.

Peter's baptism as a believer took place at Gorgie Baptist Church, Edinburgh, on Sunday 20 March 1949, in the evening. 'The Team' took the service. Five others were baptized with him, including his brother Joe and his sister Jean. He had given his testimony at one open-air service in the afternoon and attended another after the evening service.

Preaching Experience

On one occasion Peter and his brother Joe were part of a group taking a meeting in a church in Leslie. Joe was leading it and Peter was the preacher. When Peter put his notes on the lectern they fell down on the floor. He tried twice more and the same thing happened, so he concluded that this was the wrong sermon and preached another without notes. Around thirty people made decisions for Christ in the church that night and it was in the small hours of the morning when the team got home.

Angus Ferguson[1] remembers the first church services that he and Peter took. At very short notice an evangelist who knew Peter phoned to ask him to take the Hogmanay Weekend at Pittenweem Baptist Church, Fife, at the end of 1950. This included a Saturday evening social as well as the two services on the Sunday, 31 December. Angus agreed to go with him. Both were well skilled at open-air preaching and deputation work, but neither had taken a church service before. They worked out their sermons on the train from Edinburgh's Waverley Station. They decided to share one text, Philippians 3:13b-14: 'But this one thing I do, forgetting those things which are behind...' Angus was to speak on the first part at the morning service and Peter the second part in the evening. They made notes in the train but there was no light in the carriage and when they got to their boarding house they found that the notes for point two were on top of those for point one!

Singing Opportunities

Peter was a good singer in four part harmony. As a young man he had opportunities of singing in various groups. He sang in the youth choir at Carruber's Close and for two or three years was a member of a Quintet, which included Angus Ferguson and Gilbert Kelling. Later on, had he not been so busy, he would have loved to sing regularly in a choir or even to lead one. He would also have liked to go to musical concerts more frequently, but felt this was an indulgence.

One year the Quintet performed in an unusual setting at the Charlotte Chapel Young People's Meeting Halloween Party (in the days when these were regarded as innocent fun). They obtained a skeleton from a medical student in the University Christian Union and arranged it on the hall platform so that the skull floated above folded arms against a green background, illuminated by a red floodlight. Behind the stage were milk bottles with different levels of water. Angus played on these while the other members came in dressed as ministers, with walking sticks, singing 'Dem bones, dem bones, dem dry bones...'!

Charlotte Chapel

Peter had to make a decision about his future church allegiance. Gilbert Kelling and Angus Ferguson talked him into going to Charlotte Chapel and its Young People's Meeting. His mother was worried that he was 'being caught up in the system' — as indeed he was. He began attending the Chapel regularly in 1949 but did not become a member there until Sunday 3 June 1951.

---

[1] Much of the following information in this chapter was given by Angus Ferguson.

In his address to the Scottish Baptist Ministers' Conference in March 1994 Peter contrasted the worship at the Chapel with his earlier Brethren experience:

> It was an immense change when...I became a member of Charlotte Chapel—a congregation of around 900 people with a traditionally Scottish Baptist style of worship. There I learned: the inspiration of great preaching and the place it had within the context of, and as a contribution to, worship; the meaningfulness and beauty of dignified order, especially in the communion service; the peril of passivity in a large congregation with too much left to, and dependent on, the minister.

His gifts of leadership were soon recognized. He was appointed Evangelistic Convenor of the Young People's Meeting in 1950, his duties being to organize the open-airs and the monthly prayer meetings. He then served as Vice-President (the minister is always President *ex officio*) for the maximum term of three years from 1951–54, when he was succeeded by Andrew MacRae. The secretary of the meeting for one of his years as Vice-President was Dorothy Stark, who married his brother Wilf.

Wilf had been called up into the Army when he was eighteen and Peter was sixteen. He was away for two years in Palestine and North Africa. When he left, Peter was still a boy, but when he came back he saw Peter as a man, leading the Young People's Meeting (YPM). He recognized then Peter's outstanding gifts of leadership and was not surprised when he rose later to the leadership of the denomination. In particular he had a great way with the YPM committee: he let others have their say, but he had his own ideas and knew the direction in which he wanted to guide them. The meeting flourished under his strong leadership and he took a fatherly interest in the younger members. It was a remarkably gifted group of young people: many went on to full-time Christian service; others continued their Christian witness in their careers in education or business.

The aim of the YPM, which was open to young people from the age of fourteen, was 'to deepen the spiritual life of its members, and to discover and develop their abilities for Christian Service'. It met on Wednesday evenings from September to April for a varied programme of speakers, missionary evenings, visiting groups and open-air meetings. Among the speakers were scholars such as Dr Norman Hunt, Professor Thomas Torrance, the Rev. Dr G.S. Gunn and the Rev. Dr G.W. Bromiley. They held a Saturday Night Fellowship once a month, including testimonies, an informal item and a speaker. After the evening service on Sundays they held a prayer meeting once a month and an open-air meeting once a month.

Peter's papers relating to the YPM reveal his methodical approach, a mind fertile with ideas and his interest in history: there are detailed notes

of 'Y.P.M. Historical Research Tour'. A favourite text that he often
quoted was Colossians 1:18: '...that in all things He might have the pre-
eminence'.

But as well as finding out more about their faith and engaging in
earnest service the young people had plenty of fun, including outings and
social occasions. On one such occasion a member of the group, hiding
under the pseudonym 'E.H.T. TORRAP' (try reading each word
backwards!) wrote a scurrilous poem entitled 'The Trials of Peter', which
began:

> Along in Charlotte Chapel, you will meet our Y.P.M.
> A fine young man in charge of it—Pete Barber is his name.
> The fragrance of his presence is as sweet as lilies fair,
> Especially if you're standing near his collar or his hair.
>
> His rotund, jolly personage ne'er fails to make us smile,
> While 'mischief' gleaming in his eye declares him full of guile,
> The words which pour forth from his lips in torrents loud and long
> Are listened to expectantly by all our noisy throng.

The rest cannot be printed here!

The minister of Charlotte Chapel while Peter was there as a young man
was the Rev. J. Sidlow Baxter and Peter always acknowledged the great
influence he had been upon him. During his ministry some fifty
members of the Chapel were called to full-time Christian service. He was
very much a pastor to Peter and he served as a fine example of what a
pastor should be. The Chapel had a book fund for those training for the
ministry and missionary service. Peter, like others, was given a set of
Sidlow Baxter's six volume work *Explore the Book*,[2] which he treasured.
An entry in his diary for one Sunday in January 1951 reads: 'At night
Mr Baxter excelled himself on text "His name shall be called
Wonderful". 1 soul saved.' He regularly recorded the number saved at
meetings.

After seventeen years Sidlow Baxter felt called to wider ministry and
preached his last sermons as pastor of Charlotte Chapel on 1 February
1953.[3] Towards the end of the following year he left Edinburgh for
Dukinfield, Cheshire, and was seen off by many friends on Caledonian
Station. Peter (in his final year of study before his ordination) had written
a letter of appreciation to him and the great preacher replied, with a
Christmas card, on 21 December 1954:

---

[2] London: Marshall, Morgan & Scott, 1951-1955.
[3] *SBM* (March 1953), 13.

For what you say, I can only thank God from my heart; for only Heaven knows how much of failure I have felt at times—though I have undeviatingly adhered to that princeliest of all purposes in a preacher, the exalting of our dear Master. Many new and wonderful doors are wide-opened before us. Oh, to be humble, to be 'clothed with power from on high', to give Christian hearts new vision of Christ, and to capture unsaved ones for Him!

Pray for us dear Peter; we shall oft remember you. I have a pledge in my heart that God will do (in the best senses) 'big things' through you. Keep low at Jesus' feet. It is the highest of all altitudes. We shall be only too happy to send you a note of our doings from time to time—and shall be especially interested to know how your own career is providentially patterning out.

The influence of Sidlow Baxter's emphases here on Christ-exalting preaching, humility and prayer are plain to see in Peter's ministry.

Just over thirty-eight years later Peter, as General Secretary, wrote to congratulate his former pastor on his forthcoming ninetieth birthday (25 February 1993). In his reply Dr Baxter wrote: 'I am honoured to think that two of our Y.P.M.ers have been elected in turn as secretary of the B.U. in Scotland.[4] I know from occasional reports how you have "adorned" that office, and how you have influenced the churches.' He died in Santa Barbara, California in 1999 at the age of ninety-six.[5]

University Career

When it came time to choose a university in 1949 Peter found it most natural to stay in his home city and attend the University of Edinburgh. Earlier in the year the family had moved to 39 Broomhouse Place South in the Broomhouse area of the city, about two miles from the city centre and further west from their previous address in Slateford.

Like many Scottish ministers of his and preceding generations Peter first obtained an Arts degree and then a Divinity degree. However, when he began his Arts course in the autumn of 1949 he was not yet fully convinced of his call to ministry and was tending towards a teaching career. It was in his second year that his conviction became certain.

Among the subjects he took for his Arts degree were British History, French, Economic History, Moral Philosophy and Geology. He graduated MA in 1952 and won a prize in Political Economy. The traditional breadth of this Scottish degree stood him in good stead later as he brought his Christian understanding to bear on a wide range of subjects.

He then transferred to the Faculty of Divinity (New College) for the three year BD course. Sidlow Baxter encouraged young men like Peter to

---

[4] The other was Andrew D. MacRae, General Secretary 1966–80.
[5] Obituary: *Baptist Times* (9 March 2000), 13.

go to New College rather than go away to a Bible College, because he had confidence in the teachers and believed it would provide the highest standard of theological education, which would be a solid foundation for a lifetime's ministry. Among the well-known names on the staff were the Rev. J.G.S.S. Thomson and the Professors J.H.S. Burleigh, John Baillie, Norman Porteous, Matthew Black, Thomas F. Torrance and James S. Stewart. The last two in particular influenced Peter. He enjoyed the lectures of Tom Torrance on Christian Dogmatics and student discussions with him. James Stewart, who taught New Testament studies, was perhaps the greatest influence upon Peter in his student days. Peter admired him tremendously. He was known as 'the Prince of Preachers' in the Barber home and there were echoes of his style in Peter's preaching.[6] On the subject of miracles Peter wrote in 1984: 'With all my heart I echo the words of Professor James Stewart, shared with our New Testament Class in New College in the middle of a lecture, "If Jesus Christ be God, we must expect anything to happen".'[7]

Among his fellow BD students were Gordon W. Martin, who was to become Principal of the Scottish Baptist College in Glasgow (1979–88, overlapping with Peter's years as General Secretary, 1980–94) and Andrew MacRae (from Peter's second year). Peter graduated at the same time as John Balchin, who became a lecturer at the Bible Training Institute in Glasgow and London Bible College, and later became minister of a Presbyterian Church in New Zealand.

Jim Taylor[8] was also a student at the same time as Peter and recalls his first meeting with him, on the Mound in Edinburgh, when he was confronted at once with Peter's humour: 'He rhymed off a couple of verses from the Greek N.T. and asked me, with a straight face, if I was happy with the A.V. translation of the passage.'[9]

Peter was a distinguished student. In his second year he was awarded the Second (Equal) Hope Prize for Church History and the Second Waterbeck Prize for Systematic Theology. In his third year he specialized in Systematic Theology and won the First (Equal) Waterbeck Prize. He graduated BD on Friday 8 July 1955.

Before he began his BD course Peter had been recommended for ministry by the Baptist Union of Scotland and accepted by the Baptist Theological College of Scotland[10] as a ministerial candidate. In fact he

---

[6] Keir Spiers wrote a recollection of J.S. Stewart a few weeks after his death, in which he notes his influence upon Baptist preaching: '...you only need to listen to people like Peter Barber and Andrew MacRae...to hear the echoes' (*SBM,* September 1990), 11.

[7] *SBM* (December 1984), 15.

[8] The Rev. James Taylor, now retired, was minister at Helensburgh 1956-60, Ayr 1960-70 and Stirling 1970-95.

[9] *SBN* (October 1994), 1.

[10] Re-named the Scottish Baptist College in 1981.

was interviewed by the College Committee first, on 6 May 1952, and then met with the Baptist Union Ministerial Recognition Sub-Committee on 3 June. The College was then at 113 West Regent Street, Glasgow, where it shared premises with the Union. As an ordinand Peter was able to claim exemption from National Service (the two years of training in one of the Armed Services that was compulsory for young men after the Second World War until 1960).

Like other students who studied for the BD at Edinburgh or Glasgow, Peter was required to attend Summer Sessions at the Baptist College during his long vacations. He attended the Sessions in 1952, before his BD course began, and in 1953. His lecturers in both years were the Rev. J. Allan Wright (Old Testament), the Rev. R.E.O. White (New Testament), the Rev. R. Guy Ramsay (Philosophy of Religion and Christian Ethics) and the Rev. Dr A.B. Miller, Principal (Church History and Biblical Theology, Pastoral Theology and Homiletics). In the second year he came top in all subjects except one, in which he came second, and he was awarded the Jervis Coats Prize for the Best Student. Dr Miller wrote to congratulate him and commented:

> I think you now realize more clearly the position in which, as Baptists, we have to work. I would say that we must first be true men of God, secondly men with adequate culture and thirdly men of loyalty to one another and the Denomination. If we could keep these ideals before us our teaching and our learning would turn instinctively in the right direction.

Peter received the College Diploma at the Valedictory Service in June 1955.

Student Missions

During his three years as a Divinity student at New College, Edinburgh, Peter employed his gifts as an evangelist in special missions. One was a fortnight's campaign in Newton Church (to the east of Edinburgh) in June 1953. Over fifty young people from the 'Edinburgh Youth Witness Team' (very largely the Charlotte Chapel YPM) took part. Peter was the speaker and he gave evangelistic talks on fourteen consecutive evenings. His photograph featured on a printed publicity leaflet and on the programme.

The front of the leaflet was a 'teaser': 'Who is he? Why is he coming? When?' Inside the answer was given:

> Just an ordinary young man. PETER H. BARBER, M.A. Graduate of Edinburgh University. He has a wide and varied experience—having worked with factory hands, shop assistants, engineers, office clerks, farm workers,

postmen and road labourers. He is thus well acquainted with the problems perplexing men and women to-day. Please come and meet him.

Each evening featured a testimony. The programme mentions only the occupations of the persons concerned. 'A University Student' was Andrew MacRae; 'Ex-member of R.A.F.' was Ron Scott; 'An apprentice electrician' was Peter's brother Ronnie; 'A railway fireman on the Royal Train' was his brother Wilf. There were to be four 'question nights', 'when Mr Barber will try to answer any problems you care to give to him'. The confidence of youth! In a follow-up prayer letter it was reported that '19 people responded to God's call and many more were quickened into new life', while church attendance was growing steadily.

Peter was the leader of a team of five young men (including Andrew MacRae and his brother Hamish) who led a 'Prove God Now' campaign in Tynecastle (Church of Scotland) Parish Church, for a week in January 1954. The church was situated in an industrial area of Edinburgh, not far from where Peter had been brought up. He wrote a letter for the Parish Magazine, which reveals that his evangelistic approach, structured outlines and pungent, concise writing style were already fully established. He had three alliterative headings: 'The Opportunities We Face', 'The Obstacles We Expect', 'The Outcome We Await'. Under the first heading he wrote:

> There must be few more challenging parishes in Scotland than that of Tynecastle. Containing, as it does, well over four thousand homes; large factories and works, and a thronging shopping centre it is truly a fertile field for the preaching of the Gospel. And throughout the parish there are hundreds of men and women who long to know Christ. Many are baffled, others are disillusioned and others are in despair. But this they have in common—they want to know God. This Campaign is our opportunity to help them to find the very way they seek.

The team gained access to four of the largest local factories. Three thousand leaflets were distributed and a personal invitation given to each home in the Parish. The church was close to the Heart of Midlothian Football Ground and on the Saturday before the campaign, with the ready assistance of the Manager, Tommy Walker, who was a well known Christian, an announcement of the campaign was broadcast to the 30,000 crowd.

Peter shared the preaching with the MacRae brothers. His brother Wilf still remembers Peter's sermon on the opening night, from Malachi 3:10: 'prove me now, herewith, saith the LORD of hosts, if I will not open you the windows of heaven and pour you out a blessing, that there shall not be room enough to receive it'.

There is an interesting link between that mission and Tynecastle Parish today, for another Peter Barber is now ministering there. Wilf and

Dorothy called their second son Peter after his uncle. 'Young Peter' entered the Church of Scotland ministry and served first at Tollcross in Glasgow, but in 1995 moved to the Gorgie church, which, as 'Cairns Memorial', united with the Tynecastle church in the 1980s. The Tynecastle church was demolished.

Student Pastorate: Bo'ness

As part of his ministerial training Peter had the opportunity to serve as student pastor of Bo'ness Baptist Church. Bo'ness (a contraction of Borrowstounness) is a small town on the Firth of Forth, seventeen miles west of Edinburgh. The age of steam began in Bo'ness, for it was in a cottage on the estate of Kinneil House that James Watt developed the condensing steam engine in 1764. Today the town is well known for the Bo'ness and Kinneil Steam Railway. In the nineteenth century it was an important port, but lost trade in the twentieth century as Grangemouth was developed, seven miles further west.

In the 1950s the population was around 14,000. The industries were mining and dock work. The mines have all closed and the dock has gone. Today the population is around 20,000; there are some local factories, but most working people are employed in the refineries in Grangemouth. When Peter was student pastor almost everyone in the congregation would have been regarded as working-class. There are more professional people today.

The church was constituted in 1906 with six founder members. In the 1940s there had been student pastorates but James Graham served as full-time pastor from 1949 to early in 1954. Soon after he left to go to Lerwick Baptist Church[11] the Bo'ness church enquired of the Baptist Theological College of Scotland for a student pastor. Dr A.B. Miller, the Principal, met the deacons in May. Of the three students available he recommended Peter, particularly because he lived in Edinburgh. At first the appointment was for three months, but there seems to have been some confusion about the nature of it, because on 4 August 1954 Dr Miller wrote to Peter asking him to consider becoming student pastor of Peebles and stating that he regarded the Bo'ness appointment as 'normal supply' with no written agreement.

In his reply Peter must have made a good case for continuing at Bo'ness. Dr Miller wrote back on 28 August pointing out the official position and the normal rules for student pastorates, but he was obviously open to persuasion:

---

[11] He later served as minister of Pollokshields Congregational Church, Glasgow, and is now retired.

I am very glad that you have been happy in the work and I would not judge Peebles by the conversation of other students. The whole point is that responsibility in the end rests with me. That is your safeguard and I reach decisions in these matters along various lines.

As I say, however, I am not unfriendly to the suggestion but it will need a week or two to get all aspects into line. Meantime I need hardly tell you that the secret of work lies in ourselves—it depends what a man is after. If it is God's kingdom we can safely rely on all things working together for good.

With kind regards

A. B. Miller

Peter won the argument and was properly appointed as student pastor for a further six months. He travelled out by bus from Edinburgh on Sundays and Tuesdays and sometimes on other days. He usually took both Sunday services and spoke at the open-air service before the evening one. On Tuesday evenings he led the prayer and Bible study meeting. He was given hospitality in various homes and did pastoral visiting. He became great friends with the church secretary, Duncan Spowart.

The membership was around thirty, but there were also many adherents. Peter attracted people to the congregation and had the joy of baptizing and receiving into membership a married couple, Margaret and William Malarky. These were his first baptisms.

Two members of the Bo'ness church, Mrs Helen Sneddon and her brother Mr Adam Burnett, remember how mature Peter was for his age (twenty-four on 25 August 1954). He had a tremendous depth, way ahead of his years. He was a good mixer and made people feel at home with him. The congregation learned a lot from him: he was an effective teacher as well as a winsome evangelist. He had thought through his faith and was equally able to discuss it at an academic level and to commend it to ordinary folk. He told of how when doing a labouring job in Edinburgh he had explained the faith to a workmate, who had responded: 'Well, that makes sense!'

His humour was appreciated, as there was no malice in it. One Tuesday evening he announced that the subject of his talk was to be 'The Devil'. Mrs Burnett (mother of Helen and Adam) couldn't help smiling. With a mischievous twinkle in his eye Peter said: 'You smile, Mrs Burnett? Do you think I am not capable of speaking about the devil?' His pastoral skills were evident. He could sense unrest in the congregation or friction between members very quickly and dealt with the situation at once.

He got alongside folk in all kinds of need. James Melville did not know that he had cancer until he was given an appointment for the hospice at Cupar, some forty miles away. He had to go by bus. Peter went

with him and a month after the end of his pastorate received a letter from
him expressing deep appreciation of the love and comfort he had given
him and putting into words the thought of the whole congregation: 'Oh
that the Lord had just led you to Bo'ness, but he has another place for
you and his way is best.' Peter had already accepted the call to East
Kilbride.[12]

The pastorate finished officially with a farewell social on Tuesday 29
March 1955, but his appointments diary reveals that Peter went back to
Bo'ness at least twice in the following weeks, once to speak at the Parents'
Night of the Girls' Guildry and once for an important pastoral visit.
Contact between Peter and the Bo'ness people continued in his early
years at East Kilbride: a busload of people from the church used to attend
the East Kilbride church anniversary.

During his pastorate Peter was often supported by his Charlotte Chapel
friends. In particular the Bo'ness folk often saw Hamish and Andrew
MacRae. It was on Peter's recommendation that Hamish was appointed
lay-pastor of the church from August 1955, a ministry he fulfilled for six
years.[13]

Ready for Ministry

The years of Peter's youth were packed with activity. Many people who
can look back to an active youth have to admit that they have
increasingly eased up! Peter's energetic programme lasted all through his
life.

Important decisions were made in those years. Peter regarded his
decision to become a fully committed Christian at the age of eighteen as
the key one. It had been prepared for by his upbringing by parents of a
sure and practical faith and by the influence of the Brethren assemblies
he had attended as a boy and of the other fellowships, including
Carruber's Close Mission, that he attended in his early teenage years.

His decision to attend and then become a member of Charlotte Chapel
was crucial, because it led to the opportunity of full-time ministry, in
which his gifts could be used to best advantage. In that church and in
other fellowships he mixed with many committed young people who
enjoyed themselves hugely, but also became more fully established in the
faith and reached out in evangelism.

Peter's preparation for future ministry was deep and wide. It began
with personal evangelism and open-air preaching. Then he received
invitations to conduct church services and to lead church missions. His
academic preparation covered a full range of arts subjects and theological

---

[12] Information from Melville's letter.
[13] Information from Helen Sneddon and Adam Burnett.

education of the highest standard. By the time he served as student pastor at Bo'ness it was clear that he was well fitted and prepared for his calling.

CHAPTER 4

Pioneering at East Kilbride

The Expanding New Town

The location for Peter's first full-time ministry was East Kilbride, a New Town eight miles south-east of Glasgow city centre.[1] It is on high ground, on average 550 feet above sea level, and often experiences fresher winds and more snowfall than the city. From the large number of roundabouts in its road system it is sometimes known as 'Polo City'!

Soon after the Second World War the New Towns Act of 1946 authorized the designation of New Towns to receive population from nearby congested cities. The Secretary of State for Scotland designated East Kilbride as a New Town in 1947. The Clyde Valley Plan of 1946, which had proposed a green belt to surround the main towns of Clydeside, made New Towns almost inevitable. At the public `enquiry Glasgow Corporation objected to the proposed designation, but by the early 1950s it changed its attitude because it was becoming difficult to find sites for rehousing within the city boundaries.

In its detailed physical planning East Kilbride incorporated most of the contemporary New Town features, including a town centre, residential neighbourhoods, separation of traffic, separation of land uses, industrial estates, low and medium density housing.

At first the target population figure was 40,000, but in 1960 this was raised to 70,000 and in 1965 to 82,500 in response to the increasing needs of the Glasgow overspill. In 1947 East Kilbride was a village of 2,500 people. By the end of 1952, when the first services of the new Baptist fellowship were held, the population was 3,250. The following year it rose to 5,000 and in 1955, when Peter Barber began his ministry, to 11,800. In 1973, when he left for Torquay, it had reached 66,900. Over 60% of those who moved to the new town in 1966–71 came from

---

[1] Information in this section from: G.C. Cameron, J.D. McCallum, J.G.L. Adams, *An Economic Study Conducted for the East Kilbride Development Corporation* ([East Kilbride]: [The Corporation], June 1979); *East Kilbride* (a promotional booklet published by the East Kilbride Town Council and the East Kilbride Development Corporation, undated); *East Kilbride Development Corporation Newsletter* (August 1957). The last two are in Peter's own files.

the city of Glasgow and over 75% from the Central Clydeside conurbation as a whole. Around 7% came from other parts of Scotland, around 9% from England and Wales, and around 5% from other parts of the world.

The most distinguishing feature of those who moved to the town was their relative youth. The town had a relatively low population of older people, especially older women, and the people who moved from Glasgow were younger and more highly skilled than the overall population of Glasgow.

Many new firms came into the town, though only a few from Glasgow industrial overspill. The Scottish Office influenced factory and office location. In particular, the Mechanical Engineering Research Laboratory (later re-named The National Engineering Laboratory), Rolls-Royce and Inland Revenue Centre 1 located there. At a time when the economy of Strathclyde as a whole was declining, East Kilbride was a growth point of employment. There was large scale commuting of professional men to Glasgow.

The Beginnings of the Church

East Kilbride Baptist Church arose from a very small and discouraging beginning.[2] The Rev. George Hardie, Secretary of the Baptist Union of Scotland, wrote to the Lanarkshire Baptist Association raising the question of Baptist witness in the New Town. At the suggestion of the Association Executive an ad hoc committee was formed, with representatives of the Association and the Union, and also one member from the Rutherglen church and one from the Cambuslang church. The committee called a meeting for all interested in the formation of a church to be held in June 1952 on the very day when Peter Blackwood moved to the town. The Rev. John Dines of Hamilton invited him to the meeting. Few people attended and only two were local: an elderly lady and Peter Blackwood, who found himself appointed secretary of the intended fellowship.

Blackwood had been brought up in Ayr. His mother was Episcopalian and his father Presbyterian, but he was attracted to the Baptist church in the town by the preaching of the Rev. James McGregor Tosh at an open-air beach service. He yielded his life to Christ in October 1937, was baptized and became an active member of the Ayr church. In 1950 he qualified as a chartered quantity surveyor and a year later moved with his wife Isa and daughter Myra to Gateshide near Kilmarnock and then in

---

[2] Much information in this chapter was given by Peter Blackwood. Some details are derived from the *Souvenir Brochure to commemorate the Opening of East Kilbride Baptist Church* (9 April 1960), hereafter: *Souvenir Brochure*.

less than a year to East Kilbride, where he had been appointed as a senior surveyor with the Development Corporation.

That first meeting in June 1952 decided to find out the number of Baptists in the town who might support a new Baptist church. Two surveys were carried out by the Lanarkshire ministers and young people from various Lanarkshire churches. The results were disappointing. Another meeting was held in the YMCA hall in Kittoch Street, attended by thirty-four people. A third meeting was arranged for further discussion, but it was a very frosty and foggy night and only seven people came. Nonetheless it was agreed to start evening services. The first one, held in the YMCA hall in Kittoch Street on 23 November 1952, was conducted by the Rev. George Hardie. It was fairly well attended, mainly because Baptists from other churches came to support it.

Progress was very slow for the first year and many disappointments were faced. Sunday services were held only in the evenings and were attended by an average of eight adults and six children. It was not surprising that office bearers of the Union were not persuaded that the new cause was going to get off the ground. But four people continued to meet, in a different home each week, for prayer. They believed that a town expected at that time to have a population of about 45,000 could support a Baptist church.

In September 1953 an evangelistic campaign was held, with the help of the Lanarkshire Association. The attendances were very disappointing and there were no visible results, yet progress began immediately after it. The following Sunday was the September holiday weekend and some of the regulars were going away, so the service was almost cancelled, but some who had been present at the campaign meetings came along. Attendances increased to around fifteen adults and ten children. From that time onwards the work went steadily forward. All the time more Baptists were moving into the town and giving their allegiance to the group. The prayer meeting was growing.

At this time the Church of Christ was having a building put up in the town and George Hardie wanted the Baptist group to join them. Peter Blackwood, however, sensing that growth had now begun, kept pressing him to arrange for the appointment of a student pastor from the Baptist Theological College of Scotland. He even hinted that a student from the rival Evangelical Baptist College (also located in Glasgow)[3] might come and this provoked George Hardie into asking Principal Miller to go out and meet the group. He went out with his wife on a cold, wintry evening in January 1954 to attend the prayer meeting and have discussions. He

---

[3] The Evangelical Baptist Fellowship Bible College was founded in 1949 by some who distrusted the Baptist Theological College of Scotland and regarded its teaching as 'liberal'. It existed for a few years.

went with the full intention of refusing their request but was so impressed that he promised to do all he could for them and soon arranged for James R.G. Graham (Jim) to be their student pastor.

Jim, who was a member of the Airdrie church, was welcomed at a social evening on Saturday 3 April in the Willow Café Tea Room in East Kilbride.[4] The following day for the first time there were two services. The Lanarkshire Association urged churches within easy travelling distance to provide at least six worshippers on a rota basis to attend the services.[5] The first morning service was quite an experience for the pastor. It was held in the recreation room of the YMCA hall, a timber building badly in need of repair. During the service there was a hailstorm and the deficiencies in the building became more apparent as hail started to fall on members of the congregation.[6] An umbrella was an essential piece of equipment for members of the congregation in those days![7]

Numbers grew under Jim Graham's ministry and on 31 May the church was constituted in the presence of Union and Association representatives by twenty-one baptized believers, who signed the Declaration. A deacons' court of eight men, most with previous experience in the office, was elected and office bearers were appointed; Peter Blackwood as secretary and D.F. McLeod as treasurer.[8]

Jim Graham had the joy of conducting his and the church's first baptismal service in the High Blantyre church, Hamilton, on Wednesday 23 June, when he baptized three people,[9] one of whom, Mrs Doris Liddell, is still a member. He recalls that he got completely wet in the process and contracted flu as a result of driving all the way back to Glasgow on his motorbike in that condition. He served for six months, as had been agreed, and then went on to be student pastor at the Port Dundas Church, Glasgow. By the time the fellowship said farewell to him at a social on 5 October in the Lesser Village Hall, there were twenty-eight members.[10]

---

[4] SBM (May 1954), 14; Souvenir Brochure, 7-8.

[5] SBM (February 1983), 11.

[6] Souvenir Brochure, 8.

[7] Silver Jubilee: East Kilbride Baptist Church 25, 1954-1979 (published by the church, 1979), 21, hereafter Silver Jubilee booklet.

[8] Silver Jubilee booklet, 6, 19; SBM (July 1954) 13. The number of signatories varies in the sources, but the minutes give twenty-one.

[9] SBM (August 1954), 13.

[10] SBM (November 1954), 22. After his ordination Jim Graham served as pastor at Dumbarton (1956–60), Viewfield, Dunfermline (1960–68) and from 1968 at Gold Hill, Buckinghamshire. In 1996 he retired into a wider ministry, still based at Gold Hill.

The Call to Peter

Services were now quite well attended. A Women's Auxiliary, a Girls' Life Brigade Company and a Life Boy Team were all formed during the autumn. The new church began to press for a full-time minister and for help with a building. The Church Extension Committee of the Union agreed to make East Kilbride its next priority.[11] The Sunday services were being held in the YMCA hall, but the rapid growth of the New Town made the provision of more adequate facilities urgent. The Committee hoped to settle a minister and erect a building as soon as funds were available. The second hope was to be deferred, but the first was fulfilled very swiftly.

In January 1955 a vacancy committee was formed. Principal Miller telephoned Peter Blackwood with a suggestion: 'You know, Blackwood, I believe I have the very young man for you—his name is Peter Barber—he has quite a reputation too as an evangelist—in fact, Blackwood, you better watch out: he might even convert you!' It was arranged for Peter to lead the services on Sunday 13 February in the YMCA hall.

Peter Blackwood wrote to him with the orders of service and to invite him to be considered as pastor. He explained the church's situation: the membership had risen to thirty-two and there were prospects of others joining.

That the Church will grow I don't think there is any doubt—1,000 houses are being built every year and this rate of building will continue for another 8 years. This means that the population is increasing by approximately 3,500 people every year. The Church has been admitted to the Baptist Union and is also federated under the settlement and sustentation scheme. The Union has promised that East Kilbride is the next on the list for the building of a new Church. Plans are at present being prepared and we hope the building itself will get under way in the early summer.[12]

Peter and Isa Blackwood gave the young student hospitality for what proved to be a very cold weekend in February. The church members took to him immediately and found him 'such a homely lad': they felt from the beginning that they had a friend in him. He had obviously had wide preaching experience and was a very mature young man. Everyone felt that Peter Barber was God's man to lead in the building up of a new church in a New Town with a population predominantly in the under thirty-five age group.

The church business meeting on Friday 11 March agreed unanimously to issue a call. Peter received a letter from Peter Blackwood and also, as it

[11] *SBM* (February 1955), 5.
[12] Letter dated 30 January 1955.

was an aided church, an official letter from the Union informing him of the call and offering a stipend of £335 per annum, £70 of which would be paid by the church and £50 by the Lanarkshire Association.

Peter accepted and George Hardie announced with enthusiasm in his report on Church Extension with regard to East Kilbride in the *Scottish Baptist Magazine*: 'Most interesting item of all, Mr P.H. Barbour [somebody got the wrong spelling, as often happened], M.A., of the Baptist Theological College of Scotland has had the honour to be called to be the first pastor of the church and will commence his ministry in June, a fact which it is confidently anticipated will give added impetus to a new cause already alert and vigorous.'[13] George Hardie's optimism was well founded.

The induction took place as soon as was possible, on Saturday 4 June. Over 300 people filled the assembly hall of the Murray Primary School. They came from Edinburgh, Ayrshire, Bo'ness, Dalkeith, Lanarkshire and Glasgow. The service of ordination and induction in the afternoon was conducted by Principal Miller. As the church was just over a year old a combined anniversary and public recognition meeting was held in the evening, addressed by the Rev. Gerald B. Griffiths, Sidlow Baxter's successor at Charlotte Chapel.[14]

It was not long before Peter had the joy of conducting his first baptismal service for the East Kilbride fellowship. This was held in the Hamilton church on Wednesday 14 September, when five people were baptized. By this time there were over fifty members and the congregations were growing.[15]

Despite these encouragements Peter did not have an easy start. There was controversy in the fellowship at the very beginning, with clashes of views arising from previous experiences of different church traditions. Two families left the church, though they were to return some years later. The experience was useful for Peter as he developed his leadership gifts in the face of adversity.

With regard to worship, Peter reflected in his address to the Scottish Baptist Ministers' Conference in March 1994:

> In East Kilbride, first as a small congregation in very uncongenial surroundings, I discovered the difficulty of generating a sense of worship in such an environment. But with a young church without traditions I was able to discover the useful place new elements could have in worship such as mime, song, responsive readings, etc.

---

[13] *SBM* (May 1955), 5.
[14] *SBM* (July 1955), 7-8.
[15] *SBM* (December 1955), 12.

At the Home Mission Meeting of the 1956 Assembly in Edinburgh Peter pointedly confronted the denomination with the challenge: twenty-five new homes a week were being built, bringing 3,500 people annually to the town. The church had totally inadequate resources and its major problem was accommodation: scattered places of meeting were a hindrance to integrating effectively the work of the church. The membership had increased from twenty-one to eighty-eight in two years and the church was suffering from 'growing pains', but the fellowship was of a high standard.[16]

The Building Problem

The church experienced much frustration before it was able to get a building of its own. Early in 1955 the Church Extension Committee of the Baptist Union authorized the erection of a building on a site at the junction of Kirktonholme Road and the proposed West Mains Road at an estimated cost of £8,000-9,000.[17] At Peter's induction on 4 June Peter Blackwood reported that the plans were well in hand.[18] It was expected that building would begin in the summer and be completed by June 1956, but the project came to nothing.

Early in 1956 the Moncrieff Church of Scotland building was put on the market because its congregation was due to move to Calderwood, another part of the town. It was in Maxwell Drive, in a central area of town and a most suitable situation. With the approval of the Baptist Union Council the church acquired the building late in 1957, but unfortunately they had a long wait before they could use it. The Church of Scotland congregation was unable to move out at the expected time because the building of their new church was delayed.

By March 1957 the membership was ninety-four and the congregation had outgrown the YMCA hall. From 5 May the Sunday services and Sunday School were held in the Public Hall. This was much more expensive to hire, but was felt to be inevitable for the growth of the church and the effectiveness of evangelism.[19] The church had a good relationship with the Moncrieff church and was also able to use the Moncrieff manse for various meetings. On Sunday 12 May members of the Moncrieff church joined with the Baptist congregation for a united service in the Public Hall, in which both ministers took part. The Church of Scotland minister, the Rev. Andrew R. Morton, preached.[20] Later in the

---

[16] *SBM* (November 1956), 9.

[17] *SBM* (May 1955), 5.

[18] *SBM* (July 1955), 8.

[19] *SBM* (May 1957), 10.

[20] *Record* (May 1957), 4; (June 1957), 3.

year a united evening service was held in the Moncrieff church, with Peter Barber preaching.[21]

Meanwhile good progress had been made in accumulating a building fund: the immediate aim of £1,500 was achieved by the third church anniversary on 2 June 1957.[22] These anniversaries were great occasions. People came to support them from nearby churches such as Cambuslang, Cathcart and Hamilton, and from places further away, such as Edinburgh, Bo'ness, Irvine and Ayr.

At the third anniversary the church was greatly encouraged by the large and representative attendance at the meetings on the Saturday, which were held in Duncanrig Secondary School, Westwood. The speaker for the weekend was a well-known Scottish Baptist who had gone South: the Rev. Henry Cook, MA, DD, who at the time was based in London as the European Secretary of the Baptist World Alliance.

The theme of the Saturday was church extension. There was an exhibition of Baptist extension work in Scotland, in which photographs, slides and films were shown. Information was given about the work of all the churches in East Kilbride. At the afternoon rally 300 people heard a panel of ministers (Donald McCallum, George McNeill and J. Hope Scott) ably answer questions on Baptist life and belief and Dr Cook gave a lively survey of Baptist churches in Europe and 'behind the Iron Curtain', which he had visited during a recent tour. At the 'social' in the evening, at which 400 were present, Dr Cook gave a summary of Baptist history and Peter Barber, in the chair, spoke of the challenge and opportunity for the gospel of Christ in this New Town.[23]

Peter's imagination and breadth of vision can be clearly seen in the planning of that occasion. There was nothing parochial or self-centred about it. While the claims of the East Kilbride situation were persuasively advocated, other church extension schemes in Scotland were advertised. While instruction in Baptist principles and history was given, the exhibition included the work of other denominations in the town. Peter had an awareness of the widening circles of Baptist witness in the work of the Baptist World Alliance and especially in Europe that he wanted to share. No doubt his later journeys for the European Baptist Federation were to take him in the footsteps of Dr Cook and he had the joy of visiting those places 'behind the Iron Curtain' after that barrier had been demolished.

Soon after the third anniversary the church produced a booklet giving the history of recent church extension work in the Union. It gave brief accounts of Granton (Edinburgh), Glenrothes, Pollok (Glasgow),

---

[21] Sunday 17 November 1957; *Record* (November 1957), 7; (December 1957), 3.

[22] *Record* (July 1957), 7.

[23] *SBM* (September 1957), 13; *Record* (July 1957), 4.

Glenburn (Paisley), Bathgate, Broxburn, Downfield (Dundee; later renamed St Kilda Road) as well as East Kilbride. It was featured by Rae Gowley, the religious affairs reporter of the Glasgow newspaper, *The Bulletin,* who introduced it as having 'all the ingredients of a best-seller—heartbreaks, set-backs, difficulties, and ultimately success'. She had been to see Peter, whom she described as 'a young minister with a tremendous concern for church extension'. She quoted Peter's explanation for the booklet: 'We decided to find out how other extension charges were progressing, and what difficulties they were facing. We are convinced that when people know the needs they will respond.'[24] It was typical of Peter and of the church to research their projects thoroughly and to see their own cause in a wider perspective.

By October 1957 the accommodation problem had become so acute that it was decided to erect behind the Moncrieff church a timber framed prefabricated building, known as 'the Back Hall', which is still in use at East Mains.[25] The Public Hall was very cold and heavy rain caused its roof to leak, so for a few months from March 1958 services were held in the Masonic Hall.[26] The church members felt that Hebrews 13:14 ('Here we have no continuing city') was an apt text for them at that time![27]

The cost of the Back Hall was £3,300. The Union gave a grant of £1,000 and a loan of £1,500 towards the building and also paid the total of £332 for the furnishings.[28] As much work on it as possible, including all the painting and joinery, was done by members and friends. So many took part that it was completed in a remarkably short time: ten and a half weeks. Work began on 17 June 1958 and it was opened on Saturday 30 August. It was described as 'restful and comfortable, with a good vestry, kitchen and cloakrooms'. The intention was to use it for the organizations when the Moncrieff church became available for Sunday worship.[29]

Over 200 people were present for the opening. At the service of dedication in the afternoon John Grant, President of the Union, turned the key for the congregation to enter the building and gave a stimulating address. At the thanksgiving social after tea Peter stressed in his chairman's remarks that what mattered most to him was not simply the structure of the building but rather what it symbolized: the unity of purpose experienced during its construction and greater opportunities for the church in its use.[30]

---

[24] *The Bulletin*, Monday, September 10, 1957, 10.
[25] *Record* (November 1957), 5.
[26] *Souvenir Brochure*, 9.
[27] *Record* (March 1958), 8.
[28] *Record* (October 1958), 7.
[29] *SBM* (October 1958), 11.
[30] *Record* (September 1958), 3.

The Priority of Witnessing

Witnessing had been a high priority of the church from the beginning. Peter was superbly skilled at planning programmes of mission and the members responded readily to the challenges he gave them. In 1958 he led the church to launch 'a fourfold attack upon the Community in an all-out effort to reach men and women for Jesus Christ'.

Phase one was the delivery by the young people of hundreds of tracts and invitations to the services. Phase two was the visiting of all newcomers to the town. Phase three was an open-air crusade (involving cars with loudspeakers and tract distribution) in the last fortnight of August while the Back Hall was being built. Phase four was a mission of visitation for a fortnight in September, immediately after the opening of the Back Hall, followed by a weekend of evangelistic meetings, including the showing of the Billy Graham film *Souls in Conflict* on the Saturday evening.[31] Eighty of the 110 members were actively involved in the visitation fortnight, fifty-six of whom did the visiting: 2,146 visits were made.[32]

Such a hectic programme would have exhausted the energy and enthusiasm of most churches very quickly, but it was only a small part of a sustained evangelistic endeavour that lasted throughout Peter's eighteen and a half years of ministry.

The open-air loudspeaker campaigns continued for several years. They took place in various areas of the town on weekday evenings and were later extended to Saturday mornings in the shopping centres. The September visitation mission also continued, together with constant visitation of newcomers to the town. Many came into the church following these contacts. There were also open-air meetings for children on Sunday afternoons in July and August.

In a special 'Church Extension' issue of the *Scottish Baptist Magazine* in May 1959 Peter Blackwood wrote about the history of the East Kilbride church and its current situation. The membership had risen to 121. Since the formation of the church thirty-one people had been baptized at services held in the High Blantyre, Hamilton, and Cambuslang churches. Twenty-one people had joined on profession of faith (formerly baptized) and the remainder had transferred from other churches. The town now had a population of 25,000. He acknowledged that much of the success of the church was due to the devotion of the pastor, who had never spared himself and whose preaching was very much appreciated.[33]

As a follow-up article in the next issue of the *Magazine*, Peter Barber contributed a passionate appeal for the denomination to accept the special responsibility of supporting evangelism in new towns and areas. It is a

---

[31] *Record* (April 1958), 12.
[32] *Record* (October 1958), 5.
[33] *SBM* (May 1959), 7-8.

piece of red-hot rhetoric and speaks more than any facts, figures or tributes can about the drive, energy and burning convictions of the twenty-eight year old minister of East Kilbride:

Just Houses?

When the countryman sees the city he is repulsed by it. To him it is a jangling confusion of bustling traffic jostling between shadowed tenements. When the Industrialist sees the city he is attracted by it. To him it is at the same time a compact labour-force and crowded market—employee and customer in one. When Jesus sees the city He weeps.

And why does He weep? He weeps, because for Him the city is not simply a conglomeration of grey roofs and red chimneys. Beneath these roofs and chimneys there are men and women, and within these men and women hearts haunted by fear, harried by temptation, vibrant with yearning. These are men and women who, when the chimneys have toppled over, and the roofs caved in, will live on forever. The city may serve its hour, then crash to dust, but these are shaped for eternal destinies. How Christ fain would gather them to the place prepared, to the city which has foundations unshakeable, whose Builder and Maker is God.

Have we caught the vision of Jesus? Especially when we look at new towns and new areas, what do we see? Are these to us simply an interesting post-war development, a regrettable encroachment upon the green countryside, an unimaginative offshoot of mass-production? If that is all they are, we shall be inclined to tolerate, or ignore, or despise them.

But if we see these areas with the Master's vision, they will be for us an inescapable call for Christian concern, an urgent opportunity for eternal investment, a mission-field on our doorstep.

But why should these areas have priority? Are not the needs of an established area just as great? The answer, of course, must be in the affirmative. The needs of men and women in all areas are the same for 'all have sinned' and 'He died for all.' But the fact remains that those in the established areas have their opportunity to hear the Gospel. They are as answerable as Nineveh.

In the new areas this is not so. Sometimes it is one Church serving 20,000 people. These areas are to a larger degree than is realised unevangelised fields where opportunity abounds. Those who live there now have no flimsy Church connection with which to parry an invitation; they are characterised by insecurity and loneliness, and long for fellowship; they have set up a new home, and with it are ready to seek out a new Church; they long (at very least for their children's sake) for a Church that cares. And it is imperative that we act quickly. Experience of Visitation Evangelism amply proves that the more recently a family has settled, the more easily that family is won. Also, there is this—if we do not go, others will, others who are bent on turning men and women from the true Faith.

These are the factors which give Church Extension such priority—the need is so great; the opportunity is so limitless; the call is so urgent.

What we need is vision—Christ's vision—a vision which nought can blur save tears of compassion and concern. Can we honestly say that we as a Denomination have such a vision, when, in response to the five-year Appeal for Church Extension, we gave less than a penny a week per member? And still our contributions lag far behind our openings and undertakings. This is the Church's unfinished task. Dare we fail in this? 'Where there is no vision, the people perish.'[34]

In promoting visitation evangelism Peter was inspired particularly by the vision of the Rev. George Young, minister of Adelaide Place Church, Glasgow,[35] as were other ministers in Scotland.

The Opening of the Church Building

The new Moncrieff Church of Scotland in Calderwood was at last opened on 18 September 1959 and their previous building was vacated and made available to the Baptists. However, before it could be used some areas had to be treated for dry rot, an open baptistry was installed and other improvements were made.

Addressing the church business meeting on 2 December Peter emphasised to his people the need of flexibility in their minds and wills as they faced the changes that were bound to emerge with the occupation of their new premises. He warned against worshipping the sacred idol of the status quo and urged them to be prepared for experiment and adaptation.[36]

The opening of the building for Baptist worship on Saturday 9 April 1960 was an exultant occasion when the long-deferred hopes of the congregation were at last fulfilled.[37] About 500 gathered to witness the ceremony as the President of the Union, D.S.K. MacLeay, having been handed the key by Peter Blackwood, opened the door. The people streamed in and admired the renovated interior. There were too many to accommodate. Some stood in the aisles, others listened in the committee room and others heard the service in the hall relayed by loudspeaker.

The pastor chaired the service and the Rev. William Whyte, Vice-President of the Union, preached a stirring message on the words 'I will build My Church'. The preacher at the evening social was the Rev. Jim

---

[34] *SBM* (June 1959), 4.

[35] George Young served with the BMS in China 1924–52 and at Adelaide Place 1952–68.

[36] *Record* (December 1959), 6.

[37] *SBM* (May 1960), 2. Also: *Souvenir Brochure*; *SBM* (April 1960), 7; *Record* (May 1960), 1-3.

Graham, their previous student pastor, who was then minister of the Dumbarton Church.

Congregations were well above average on the Sunday and during the services the members brought as a thank offering their gifts of one-third of a week's wage. The total given was £221,[38] compared with an average of around £24 on a normal Sunday. Many may well have given much more than a third. It was Peter who had challenged the members to this sacrifice, a challenge accepted by a special business meeting in January. In the *Record* he persuasively countered all the objections any might have against such a high target. He listed the major ways in which the Lord had hitherto helped them and went on:

> East Kilbride Baptist Church, I know, has come to mean a tremendous lot to us. We have watched it totter from an uncertain infancy to face a road beset by hardships and setbacks. Often disappointed but never downtrodden; often opposed, but never overwhelmed, the Lord has carried us through, and obstacles have only served to bind us the more closely together. This has been the Lord's doing. We praise Him for it. On this occasion we want, I know, to give to <u>our</u> Lord and <u>our</u> Church, a thank offering worthy of both.[39]

The church was nearly six years old as it took charge of its own sanctuary. Undoubtedly its acquisition was not regarded as an end in itself but as a base from which to extend its witness in the town. The purchase of the nearby manse was included in the deal with the Church of Scotland, and it became known as 'the old manse'. The church allowed various groups to use it for social and welfare purposes. In the summer of 1962 work started on the basement of the old manse to convert part of it into a coffee room to be known as the 'Grotto'.

Further Evangelism

One co-operative evangelistic endeavour that the church fully supported was the all Lanarkshire 'Christian Challenge Crusade'. The evangelist was Victor McManus of the Movement for World Evangelisation. Evening meetings were held for a fortnight in April–May 1960, in the Hamilton church. People were bussed in by the surrounding churches and the response was good. It was an unusual enterprise for a county association and had taken two years to plan. Victor McManus was impressed with the efficient organization when he visited the area in January. He noted that 'The Rev. Peter Barber, of East Kilbride, publicity convener, had the publicity end of the campaign really tied up.'[40] That comes as no

---

[38] *Record* (May 1960), 8. The total given to the Building Fund over the whole weekend was £300.

[39] *Record* (February 1960), 1-3.

[40] *SBM* (March 1960), 9.

surprise! For the church Peter held training classes in counselling in preparation for the Crusade.[41]

A few months later, in October 1960, the church volunteered to be the 'guinea-pig' for an experiment in youth evangelism. The idea came from the committee of the Glasgow Baptist Youth Rallies, under Dr Charles Anderson's chairmanship. Peter was on the committee and provided a liaison between it and the church. More than forty young people from various churches took up residence for a weekend on the premises—the church, the hall and the old manse. After a great deal of hard work the old manse was made ready for their occupation.

The aim was to reach the 'cafe-crawling, coffee-drinking' young people of the town. Some of the team went 'street fishing' and others went into cafes (with the proprietors' permission) and used the census form technique to get into personal conversation. A shuttle service of cars brought more than 150 teenagers to the church hall for the 'Late Night Special' on the Saturday evening at 9.30. Many young people from the town attended an 'after-church canteen' on the Sunday evening, which became a regular feature for the next few months and led to at least ten professions of faith.[42]

Victor McManus returned to Lanarkshire in April 1961, this time to the East Kilbride church to lead a 'Turn to Christ' campaign for a fortnight. In the *Record* Peter stressed that the Campaign was not Victor McManus' Campaign: 'It is our campaign. The responsibility of all of us and each of us.' He gave a warning from the disturbing words of the risen Christ to the church in Ephesus: 'Repent and do the first works', and presented the alternative: 'When the Church is truly met in His name He is present in the midst. That Church is nothing short of His body and He the Church's life. Such a Church he animates and empowers and uses beyond the dreams of men and hopes of saints... If Christ is to use us in this Campaign as He fain would do we must all engage in a frank and ruthless examination of our hearts before Him.'[43]

The publicity was intensive: handbills were delivered to every house in the town, posters were placed in buses, shops, house windows and on billboards, loudspeaker announcements were made and special news articles were placed in the local newspaper. In addition to the evening meetings there was a series of 'At Homes', visits were paid to two old people's clubs so that many pensioners attended the meetings, and a youth 'squash' was held. Twenty-seven people indicated their desire to

---

[41] *Record* (March 1960), 5.
[42] *SBM* (November 1960), 16; (December 1960), 6, 10; *Record* (November 1960), 6.
[43] *Record* (February 1961), 1-2.

follow Christ, most between the ages of fourteen and nineteen. The campaign raised public awareness of the church considerably.[44]

Stewardship Campaigns

East Kilbride was the first Baptist church in Scotland to organize a stewardship campaign. It was Peter's idea. He had formed a friendship with George McNeill, when he was minister of the Cambuslang church, and they kept in touch after George went to Canada in 1958. It was through George that Peter got information about the stewardship campaigns being held in Canada.[45] Many features of the East Kilbride campaign were adopted from literature used by the Canadian Maritime Convention. One reason for the timing of the campaign was the decision of the church to be self-supporting financially from 1 December 1961, which required a great increase in giving.[46]

It was decided that responsibility for the campaign should be upon the lay folk, so Peter Blackwood acted as chairman of the executive. The pastor's main contribution was to preach five sermons on the subject: 'Stewardship of Time', 'Possessions', 'Talents', 'Money' and a final one on 'the Priorities of Stewardship'. These set the tone for the campaign. The emphasis was not on giving to meet a budget figure to cover domestic needs but on giving as stewards to the Lord himself, so that they could reach out beyond the church in evangelism and church extension. Despite the expense it was decided to have a free meal as the focal point of the campaign, as in the Canadian model. Two hundred and thirty people enjoyed the dinner in the Public Hall, immediately opposite the church, on Saturday 10 March 1962. Eighteen hostesses had visited every home connected with the church to give the invitations. Afterwards eighteen visitors went out in pairs to gather the responses, collecting 152 'Stewardship of Money' cards and 211 'Stewardship of Time and Talent' forms.

The success of the campaign surprised everyone concerned. In the month before the campaign the average weekly giving was £39. This went up to over £60 immediately afterwards. The church was able to pay off a loan from the Union much sooner than expected. The enthusiasm generated was considerable. Unity of purpose and efficient organization had led to wider and deeper commitment to Christ and to practical acts of service. Many had learnt a vital principle of Christian living.[47]

---

[44] *Record* (February 1961), 6; (March), 2, 4-5; (April), 1-3; (May), 1-2, 7; *SBM* (June 1961), 2.
[45] Information from Peter Blackwood.
[46] *Record* (November 1961), 6.
[47] *SBM* (May 1962), 8-9; *SBM* (April 1962), insert.

The experience reminded Peter of occasions when as a boy he had been on holiday in Inverness and helped the canal-man to open the lock gates on the Caledonian Canal to allow a boat to pass. He wrote of this in the *Record*:

> During these past days I have felt the same excitement again, and not a little pride. Again I have seen gates open and a flood bursting through—only this time the gates have been a Church's surrender, and the flood a Church's generosity. The results of this Stewardship Campaign have far and away exceeded all expectations. Your willingness and generosity it has been a tremendous thrill to witness. No wonder I feel so excited and so proud of you...
>
> And now the ship can come through and set sail for wider seas and broader horizons. The tide is rising. Let us launch into the deep![48]

From that time all who became members of the church were given stewardship forms to fill in, indicating the gifts they had that they could use for the church and how they felt the church could help them. A further campaign took place in 1964, with the dinner being held in the Rolls Royce factory on 1 June as part of the tenth anniversary celebrations.[49] This was effective but, as was to be expected, did not have quite the same impact as the first one.

All Age Sunday School

Another idea that came from across the Atlantic and was taken up by churches in Scotland was the All Age Sunday School. Andrew MacRae, as Convener of the Sunday School Committee of the Union, invited Clifton J. Allen from the USA[50] to come to Scotland to promote the scheme. He preached at East Kilbride at an evening service in September 1962 and addressed a meeting afterwards on the subject.[51]

At the Assembly in October Andrew MacRae strongly advocated the all age system of Christian education as the answer to the drift from church of those in their early teens. Baptists in Australia and New Zealand had adopted the scheme and the reason for their growth and expansion was attributed to it. Peter reported this in the *Record*.[52] The subject was one of the three chosen for discussion at the church 'Get Together' on 24 November (the others were stewardship and church unity).

---

[48] *Record* (April 1962), 2-3.

[49] *SBM* (April 1964), 14.

[50] The Rev. Clifton J. Allen was the Editorial Secretary of the Sunday School Board of the Southern Baptist Convention and came over from Nashville, Tennessee.

[51] *SBM* (October 1962), 14.

[52] *Record* (November 1962), 2.

This was a time when Peter was keen to lead the church into further growth. Under the headline 'Let us go on', he wrote in the *Record*:

> In our present Church situation here in East Kilbride, it would be easy to become complacent. The membership of our Church is growing, the auxiliaries are flourishing, our fellowship together is enriching. Glanced at superficially, we might be tempted to conclude that our Church life is complete and satisfactory. Indeed we might be tempted to echo with the Church of Laodicea, that we are 'rich and increased with goods, and have need of nothing'. Such an attitude is, of course, perilous. The kingdom of heaven will only be perfected when Christ comes.
>
> During these recent days, we have been made to think again about many features of the Church's life. Perhaps God has been gently pushing open these doors, challenging us to go further with Him in the fulfilment of His will.[53]

A special church business meeting in May 1963 decided to adopt the all age system.[54] Dr John Moore, a Southern Baptist who was the Director of the European Baptist Press Service, was unexpectedly able to be present and helpfully clarified the issues.[55]

The opening session on Sunday 6 October 1963 (10.15–11.15 a.m.) was very successful. Classes were bulging at the seams in the adult section. The church was packed to capacity for the service that followed the Sunday School at 11.30 a.m.. Attendance at Sunday morning worship continued to increase. Many more people found they had to sit in the balcony![56]

In the October *Record* Peter rejoiced in the enthusiasm so many had shown and explained the value he saw in the provision of this teaching. Firstly, 'It means that in these days when there is so much confusion and haziness in the thinking even of God's people, we shall have the opportunity to learn what the Bible says. Opinion is interesting but truth is fundamental—and such truth as we may know is only to be found in the Word of God.' Secondly, it would greatly improve the quality of their witness: 'A well-informed Scripture-taught witness is a mighty weapon in the hands of God.' Thirdly, meeting in class each week would bind them together: 'To share the things of Christ is to be drawn into a fellowship which is not only strong, but deep.'[57]

---

[53] *Record* (February 1963), 2.
[54] *SBM* (June 1963), 13.
[55] *Record* (May 1963), 'Pastoral Letter' insert.
[56] *Record* (November 1963), 7; *SBM* (November 1963), 13-14; (December), 12.
[57] *Record* (October 1963), 2.

Fruitful Partnership

There is no doubt that Peter Barber was the right man at the right time
when he was called to East Kilbride in 1955. Despite its small and
discouraging beginning the church was able to take up the opportunities
of the expanding New Town. Peter was seen as the pastor of the whole
congregation. He was young, but no one saw him as being concerned
only for the younger members. Derek Murray recalls that as he was
setting out on his ministry Peter advised him always in his preaching to
think of the older Christians in the congregation and not always to exhort
everyone to greater effort. 'Think of the hurt people', Peter told him.

Peter himself was the first to acknowledge that the congregation
worked as a team. He recognized the commitment of the church members
to the vision of a constantly growing, witnessing Baptist community in the
New Town. The average age of the membership was lower than in most
churches, but young and old worked in harmony. It is a tribute to their
zeal that so much energy was expended on the many regular and special
activities that they embraced. But the congregation in turn paid tribute to
the quality of ministry they received, to the imaginative leadership, the
pastoral care, the stimulus to evangelism, the constant encouragement to
go forward and make yet more progress.

CHAPTER 5

Planting the Westwood Congregation

Missionary Vision

As the number of members was growing and as the Westwood area of the town was expanding rapidly, the next step of faith became clear: to form another congregation in that area. Careful thought was given to the relationship there would be between the congregations. Peter Barber got in touch with the Rev. Jack Brown, Senior Minister of the Dagenham Group of Churches, in which five fairly small churches had been linked together, with a team of ministers. He came and spoke to the church.

As a result Peter Blackwood put forward the idea of having *one Church with two Congregations*. The pastor was persuaded of the idea, the church agreed unanimously, and so did the Union, by a majority: some disapproved because of their understanding of the independency of a local Baptist church.

So the church sent out fifty-six people to Westwood who became the nucleus of a new congregation but remained part of the church. There was one East Kilbride church, with one membership, but there were two congregations: at East Mains and at Westwood. They were convinced that it was valuable to do as many things as possible together: to share in visitation and evangelistic campaigns, to discuss budgets, to have one magazine. Each centre of worship would be the particular responsibility of one minister, but the ministers would form a team and consult regularly together, as well as exchanging pulpits. There would still be quarterly business meetings, two for the whole membership, and two for each congregation. Later the combined meeting became an annual event. There would be occasional united deacons' meetings.

Peter Barber wrote later: 'The United Church Scheme was not easy to establish nor is it costless to maintain, but as an alternative to Baptist churches in the same town either ignoring or competing with each other it has so much to commend it. I believe it sets a model for others to follow...'[1]

The development proceeded in a very similar pattern to that of the original church. A Westwood Extension Committee was formed at the

---

[1] *Silver Jubilee* booklet (1979), 9.

quarterly business meeting on 4 December 1963[2] and action followed rapidly. Morning services with a crèche were started in Canberra Primary School, in the newest part of Westwood, on Sunday 12 January 1964. Visitation had been carried out in the area near the School during the previous week.[3] Peter wrote in the *Record*: 'It is God who is calling us to enter our Macedonia. If He calls, He also can equip. Let us go forward in His strength and to God be the glory!'[4]

Peter took the inaugural service, but the following week Alex Rodger, a first year student at the Baptist Theological College in Glasgow, was received as student pastor. Alex was a member of Queen's Park Baptist Church, Glasgow, and President of the Youth Fellowship there. He had gained a first class honours MA in Philosophy at Glasgow University. He was married to Joan and they had recently had a son.[5] On Saturday 18 January Alex and Joan had the opportunity of meeting the church members and adherents from the Westwood area who formed the nucleus of the new congregation. The deacons of the church and their wives were also there and the gathering was addressed by Principal A.B. Miller. Alex Rodger preached the following morning in the Westwood Congregation.[6]

Peter was keen to stress the bonding together of the two congregations, to be involved in Westwood himself and to give his student assistant opportunities at East Mains, so it was arranged that on the second Sunday morning of each month he would preach at Westwood and Alex at East Mains.

In the early weeks about fifty adults and thirty children were attending regularly.[7] A Sunday School was begun on 5 April at the same time as the morning service.[8] A Fellowship Meeting for prayer, Bible study and discussion was held monthly at first, but later fortnightly and then, after Alex Rodger's ordination, every week. Evening services were started on 6 September 1964 and a building fund was opened in that month.

Peter Blackwood Moves On

In recognition of his work as a surveyor in East Kilbride, Peter Blackwood was appointed Principal Surveyor in the New Town of Livingston on 1 March 1963, but he did not need to move immediately. He laid down the office of secretary in June 1964, just after the tenth anniversary of the church. When Peter, Isa and their daughter Myra

---

[2] *SBM* (January 1964), 14.
[3] *SBM* (February 1964), 13.
[4] *Record* (January 1964), 2.
[5] *Record* (January 1964), 5.
[6] *SBM* (February 1964), 13.
[7] *SBM* (March 1964), 14.
[8] From January 1965 its time was changed to 3 p.m..

finally had to move to Livingston in April 1965 it was a great wrench for them and for the church.

The partnership of the two Peters had played a crucial role in the dynamic growth of the East Kilbride church. Alike in many ways, they were complementary in others. They remained very close friends and with their families they took holidays together at Kippford and Strathpeffer.

It so happened that each was given the opportunity to pay tribute to the other, for Peter Barber wrote the profile of Peter Blackwood for the *Scottish Baptist Magazine*[9] when Blackwood became President of the Union in October 1967 and *vice versa* in October 1969. We shall come to Blackwood on Barber later, but Barber wrote of Blackwood, having referred to his arrival in East Kilbride:

> The next thirteen years in this new town were to be as busy as they were rewarding. His tenacity and vision were of tremendous help to the little Baptist fellowship that was just being formed, and as their secretary he gave the kind of leadership needed in these early discouraging days. The fact that there is a Baptist Church in East Kilbride today is in no small measure due to the hard work and wise guidance of Peter Blackwood.

He then wrote of Blackwood's work for the Union and continued:

> All of this, however, would hardly have been possible without the understanding and support of his family. Nobody in the East Kilbride Church was more hospitable or hardworking than Mrs Blackwood whose warmhearted concern for others remains exemplary. She has certainly been her husband's helpmeet. Their daughter, Myra, now a fourth-year medical student, has inherited her parents' mantle, and is active in the service of Christ.

He mentioned Blackwood's appointment in Livingston and service as deacon in the Broxburn church, reported that Blackwood with others was (in 1967) just starting services in Howden House, Livingston, so as to build up another Baptist church in a New Town, and concluded:

> Peter Blackwood is an avid reader who thinks deeply and courageously. Restless by nature, he is intolerant of tradition for tradition's sake and eager to see the Church face the challenge of today with methods suited to today. Yet withal he is compassionate. He has a burning concern for the welfare of our Baptist ministry and for the social involvement of the Church in practical caring.

These are apt descriptions of Peter Blackwood, but this profile reveals a lot about Peter Barber too: about his talent for expressing appreciation

---

[9] *SBM* (October 1967), 9.

for the work and gifts of others and about his own nature and ideals. In a personal letter to Peter Barber immediately after moving Peter Blackwood expressed his gratitude for the years they had worked together: 'All I can say is I enjoyed every minute of it and it was wonderful to work with someone who wasn't afraid to try something new...'.[10]

The Calder Brothers

The new secretary, who took up his duties in June 1964, was Alex Calder. He had served as a deacon for several years. He was not from a Christian home, but had been sent as a boy to a Baptist church and was involved in the Sunday School, Life Boys and Boys' Brigade. At the age of twenty-four he was the first in his family to be converted, becoming a member of Victoria Place Baptist Church, Glasgow. His wife Martha was brought up in the Church of Scotland but attended Victoria Place with Alex and was converted a year after their marriage. They moved to East Kilbride in 1957 and transferred their membership to East Mains in 1959. Alex worked as a senior social worker as one of a team serving a community of 50,000 in the Pollok area of Glasgow. It was an exacting job with the demands of frequent overtime, but he somehow found time and energy to be secretary of a growing, active congregation.

Alex's younger brother, David, served as treasurer from 1965–78, having been a deacon from 1961. He was converted at the age of eighteen and became a member of the Victoria Place church. He and his wife Cathy had become members in 1957.

Developments at Westwood

When the Westwood Congregation was constituted in 1965 the original church became known as the East Mains Congregation. Fifty-six members transferred their membership to Westwood. The two congregations held their first united business meeting on 3 March. Peter reflected on it in the *Record*:

> Here was the sharing in fellowship of which the New Testament speaks. The interests of the one congregation were the interests of the other, and the development of the whole Church the concern of both. For instance, as each Sunday School Superintendent gave his report we were all able to share in the difficulties and achievements of the other congregation's Sunday School. Yet, when the matter of filling the pastoral vacancy in Westwood was under consideration, this was the concern of the whole Fellowship. Bearing one another's burdens, we found the joy of fulfilling the law of Christ.

---

[10] Letter dated 18 April 1965. Peter Blackwood was born on 26 October 1918 and died on 8 March 2001. Isa died in February 2004.

If that meeting showed us the advantages of the Scheme, I am certain that the next few months will indicate just as clearly the responsibilities to which we are all now committed. As members of each congregation we have chosen not to live for ourselves, a choice which cuts across the grain of human nature. Yet for the Christian it is always the right choice. After all, was not the very purpose of our Lord's cross that we should die to the self-centred life?[11]

Alex Rodger was called to be the first full-time pastor of the Westwood Congregation on the completion of his college course. He was ordained and inducted in the Canberra Primary School on Saturday 3 July 1965 in a service conducted by Principal Miller. Appreciating the problem of finding one's way around in New Towns the church had signposts erected to show the way from East Kilbride Cross to the School.[12] Later Alex Rodger described the experience of becoming pastor of Westwood as 'more like boarding a moving bus than pushing a car to get it started'.[13]

On special occasions such as anniversaries the East Mains Congregation joined with the Westwood folk for the evening service. On the second anniversary of the Westwood Congregation in January 1966 it was an impressive communion service attended by over 200.[14] The membership of Westwood was sixty. Such was the solid support that the first congregation gave to the second.

A Building

Lack of premises was a problem at first, but plans for a building soon became a reality. On the first weekend of June 1967 there was a memorable joint celebration of the thirteenth anniversary of the East Mains Congregation and the stone-laying ceremony of the new Westwood building. Andrew MacRae, as General Secretary of the Union, laid the foundation stone on Saturday 3 June and the impressive ceremony was followed by a service of thanksgiving in Canberra School at which Peter gave a challenging address. The church was required to pay one fifth of the cost of the building and at the Saturday evening meeting a cheque for £1,000 was handed to Mr J.A. Dick, former Treasurer of the Union, as a first payment. On the Sunday evening the congregations united at Westwood in Canberra School for a communion service.[15]

Peter headed his pastoral letter in the June *Record* with the motto of East Kilbride: 'Forward!':

---

[11] *Record* (March 1965), 2.
[12] *SBM* (June 1965), 11.
[13] *Silver Jubilee* booklet (1979), 14.
[14] *SBM* (March 1966), 14.
[15] *SBM* (July 1967), 15.

The motto of our town was certainly the keynote of our Anniversary Weekend. Time and again the Word of the Lord came to us as once it came to Israel—'Speak unto the children of Israel, that they go forward!'

When you reflect on the weekend, there was much that might have caused us to look back. It is quite amazing (a tribute to God's goodness) to think that so much has been achieved in just thirteen years. For it was only thirteen years ago that some twenty-five [actually 21] believers met in the YMCA hall to constitute themselves as a Baptist Church. Many outside the town wagged their heads and whispered that a Baptist Church would never be established here. Others advised these believers to join in with another local Church and give up the whole wild dream. But these men and women believed that this was no wild dream but a divinely imparted vision, and in the light of the vision they prayed and witnessed and worked. Thirteen years later there we were gathered to lay the foundation stone of a second building in the town, now a company of some three hundred believers bound together as two congregations in one Church. Yes, we might well have looked back with wonder, and cried out, 'Ebenezer', 'Hitherto hath the Lord helped us'. Thanks be to God![16]

While the building was under construction members of the church guarded the site during the night and at weekends. The volunteers were able to use the builders' hut for this purpose. This saved about £500 on the cost. The builders were amazed at how well the site was watched: nothing was known to have been stolen or destroyed during the whole period.

Nearly a year after the stone-laying, on Saturday 25 May 1968, as part of the celebrations of the fourteenth church anniversary, the new Westwood building was opened.[17] The membership of the Westwood Congregation was now eighty-five. Peter Blackwood was again involved in the opening ceremony, as he had been at the East Mains opening, but this time as President of the Union. On the Sunday morning a large number of Westwood residents attended morning worship and in the evening the building was filled to capacity for a united service of the Westwood and East Mains Congregations. Peter Barber wrote:

It was a moving sight, and humbling in the extreme to realise that this congregation of over 300 people of all ages, many of whom had come to Christ through the Church's witness, had arisen from that small group of 21 people who, on 31st May, 1954, had signed the Constitution and formed themselves into a Baptist Church. Here was faith rewarded. Here too was opportunity granted. What could such a Church not do for East Kilbride if everyone were 'all out' for Jesus Christ? Following the service a man received

---

[16] *Record* (June 1967), 2-3.
[17] *SBM* (July 1968), 9; *Record* (June–July 1968), 2, 11.

Jesus Christ as his Saviour. How better could a building be hallowed on its first Sunday?[18]

About 250 people attended the anniversary 'At Home' on the Monday evening, when the guests of honour were Peter and Isa Blackwood. It was an evening of humour that Peter Barber thoroughly enjoyed:

> If anyone were to tell you that you would laugh for over two hours at a Church Social, I suppose you would find it impossible to believe. Yet that is what we did. Without exception those who took part in the programme had us rocking in our chairs with their amusing anecdotes, poems, songs, etc... It was a night of memories, of friendship, and of fellowship. It was a night when we felt our oneness as one family in Christ.[19]

James Murdoch

Three months later Alex Rodger concluded his pastorate to take up a lecturing post in religious education at the Dundee College of Education. The congregation had been surprised and disappointed when he had announced this two months before the opening of the building, but they understood his desire to use his gifts to further the effective teaching of religious education in schools. A gathering of members of both congregations and other churches said farewell to Alex and his wife and family on Saturday 17 August. His ministry of four and a half years as student pastor and then full-time pastor had been greatly appreciated. He was presented with the robes he would be required to wear in his new appointment.[20]

During the vacancy of seven months the Rev. J.G.G. Norman served as interim moderator and Peter Barber also gave the congregation pastoral care. The Rev. James Murdoch, a lay-preacher from the Cathcart church who had been accepted for ministry by the Union, was ordained and inducted on Saturday 26 April 1969.[21]

The ministry of Mr and Mrs Murdoch gave a considerable impetus to the work in the new area.[22] When they had been there for a year Peter commented in *Focus* (the new name of the church magazine) on the way they had adapted to their new roles and the encouragements they had already seen:

---

[18] *Record* (June–July 1968), 11.
[19] *Record* (June–July 1968), 11.
[20] *SBM* (October 1968), 14.
[21] *SBM* (June 1969), 6.
[22] *SBM* (July 1969), 12.

Transitions are never easy—not least when they involve a change of career—and no doubt there were many who wondered at the wisdom of God's servant in moving from the directorship of a large business to the totally different life of a Baptist Pastorate.

As one who has stood as near as any to God's servant following this transition I can only say that the seal of God has most certainly been upon it. It is hard to conceive of Mr. Murdoch now as anything other than a pastor—they must have schooled him well in Cathcart! And how we have rejoiced in the many signs of God's approval on the ministry of the Word in Westwood. Several times the 'waters have been troubled' in the Church as candidate after candidate has come forward for baptism. The attendances both at the Sunday services and the midweek services have grown. The giving of the people has multiplied. The Women's Auxiliary, so ably led by Mrs Murdoch, has effectively reached out to others. The spirit of love within the Fellowship is there to feel, and there is a strong sense of oneness with the Congregation in East Mains.[23]

Peter's Marriage to Isobel Taylor

It came as a great shock to the East Mains Congregation when in February 1965 it was announced that their pastor was engaged to be married—and to a girl who was one of their members! No-one had guessed and the dreams of others in the 'band of hope' (as it was called) were shattered! Peter Barber's eligible bachelor status had been a talking point for years. A report in the *Record* of the Sunday School trip to Kilsyth in 1959 indicates the kind of fun the church derived from the situation:

The highlight of the day was undoubtedly the Single Men's Race. This was run over a long and arduous course and the winner was our own Mr Barber (only 1 ran!).[24]

In 1963 the *Record* announced the forthcoming marriage of Mrs McKie and Mr George Kerr of Edinburgh and commented:

We understand that a very eligible bachelor in the Church once remarked to Mrs McKie, 'When you take the step so will I'—Mrs McKie has taken the step—we now await further developments from the other airt.[25]

It was another two years before he finally succumbed to all the pressure!

His bride-to-be, Miss Isobel Taylor, was born in Fife and moved with her family to East Kilbride in 1953. The school to which she transferred

---

[23] *Focus* (May 1970), 1.

[24] *Record* (June 1959), 5.

[25] *Record* (April 1963), 4.

was Hamilton Academy. By the time Peter became the pastor of the church in 1955 she had left school and was working in the office of the CID in Hamilton. One of the girls who worked with her was Janette Wilson, a member of the Motherwell church, who told her about the new pastor and attended the induction. Isobel did not attend it, but she later went to a church anniversary in Murray School and after that began attending the Sunday services.

In 1958 she became convicted of the need for change in her life and during one of his vestry hours Mr Barber led her to the Lord. The following year, on Wednesday 17 June, he baptized her at the Cambuslang church, together with five others, two ladies and three men. One of the men was Edwin Gunn, who was to enter the ministry, serving at Drumchapel, Ayr and Queen's Park, Glasgow, where he is at present the senior pastor. The six were received into church membership on the following Sunday.

Isobel became fully involved with the life of the church, becoming secretary of the Young People's Fellowship (with Edwin Gunn as President), Superintendent of the Primary Department of the Sunday School and Secretary of the Missionary Committee.

Eight years after her baptism she found that friendship and respect for her pastor had become a strong romantic attachment. She went away with the young people to Crieff for a weekend conference in January 1965, when she prayed a lot, becoming convinced that a decision had to be made. She had been considering leaving her job with the police and working with children. Believing it would be best for her to get right away, she wrote an application for a suitable job in the south of England. The letter was in her pocket as she returned from Crieff on the Sunday afternoon of 24 January. She had been due to go elsewhere that evening, but one of the boys had asked if she minded her place being taken by his girl-friend. So she went to the Youth Fellowship in the church and found herself alone with Peter after the others had left. They chatted a long time, until finally Peter said, 'You know, I think we should see more of each other.' To Isobel it was the stuff that dreams are made of!

It was a whirlwind courtship. During the next two weeks they met again four times, well away from East Kilbride. They went for a whole day to Inverary, where they talked and prayed. They were quite sure of their feelings for each other and in no doubt that God had brought them together. They became engaged on Saturday 6 February.

Peter had a speaking engagement with the Aberdeen Evangelical Union on the Friday evening. On his way back from that on the Saturday morning he called in to see Andrew and Jean MacRae. Andrew recalled the event vividly:

I still remember that breathless day when Peter arrived at the Ward Road manse in Dundee to tell us his well-kept secret—he was on his way back to East Kilbride to get engaged that evening to Isobel. We flatly refused to believe it! We knew Peter and although he used to breeze into our home singing, 'I dream of Jeannie with the light brown hair', he had, from time to time, extolled to us the merits of the celibate life in enabling a person to do the work of the Kingdom without distraction. That day it was different! He had to produce the engagement ring to convince us! Whereupon our young son set to with his dad to clean 'Uncle Peter's mini-minor', which, according to young Findlay, was 'filfy'! And during this process my wife Jean sewed back on his waistcoat a button he'd screwed off in his excitement![26]

Later that day Peter and Isobel were able to share the news with the Blackwoods in Livingston. Isobel recalls that Peter Blackwood put both his arms on her shoulders and anxiously asked, 'Are you absolutely sure you know what you're doing, my dear?' She didn't, but never regretted her decision!

On the following day Peter announced the news to the congregation. In the February issue of the *Record* he thanked the church for sharing in their joy—once they had recovered from the shock!

If there was one thing both Isobel and I regretted it was that the news had to be broken to you so suddenly and unexpectedly. However, as the matter was prayerfully considered we knew there was no other way. We knew beyond all doubt how we felt towards each other; we knew beyond question that it was the Lord's will that we should be together; we recognised the talk and the trouble that would be created if we took any other course of action. Therefore, both for our own sake and for the sake of the Church we felt the honourable thing to do was to make publicly known that of which we were both personally certain.[27]

Inserted in the magazine was a folded sheet of four pages entitled 'Free! Special Valentine's Day pull-out Supplement or "The Taylor 'suits' the Barber" or "What's a Collar without a leash!"' It included a letter of congratulation from Alex Rodger on behalf of the congregation and poems of various kinds including:

O Kirk! sae staid an' settled doon
Sae calm, sae lang wi'oot a froon—
Whit's happened noo wi' fearsome clatter
Tae cause sic muckle fuss an' chatter?

---

[26] Thanksgiving Service address, 9 September 1994.
[27] *Record* (February 1965), 2.

O Toon! your phones are hummin' still
(The wifies dinna get the bill!)
They're ringing lood o' love an' passion—
They're a' engaged—for that's the fashion.

O man! the source o' sic commotion!
Ye've caused an unco' lood explosion!
Its blast has shook an' thrilled us a'
(Methinks the wifies maist of a'.)

O lassie! whitna muckle cry!—
An ye were aye sae prim an' shy!
We never heard ye mak' a cheep—
But then, still waters aye rin deep.

O Baptist Spinsters!—far an' wide
Hoo mony o' ye lang hae tried –
Whit will ye dae wi' hearts sao sair?
Fash not—The College aye mak's mair.

O Happy Pair!—an end o' jest—
We pray God's love will on ye rest—
May He who joined your several ways
Still bless an' keep ye a' your days.

It was big news in the wider denomination too. At a youth rally shortly afterwards a minister's daughter said to Isobel: 'Did you know about Peter Barber's engagement?' Isobel showed her the ring and she was covered in confusion!

Peter and Isobel were married on Friday 13 August. She was twenty-five years old and he was thirty-four. They were surrounded with kindnesses by the church. Some members helped in the redecoration of their home. The more usual wedding presents were not needed as Peter's mother had furnished his first manse, but many fine presents were given and they were put on display overnight in the church hall. At this time Isobel was working in the finger-print department of the police in Glasgow: there were two police officers on guard at the door of the hall all night.

According to the Rev. James Taylor (no relation to Isobel), who was one of the guests, it was a warm day and the consumption of orange juice was so great that Isobel's father (a baker) could be heard complaining that the price of rolls in East Kilbride would have to be increased![28]

---

[28] *SBN* (October 1994), 1.

The music and hymns at the service were standard for the time: Isobel and her father came down the aisle to the Bridal March from Wagner's *Lohengrin* and the procession at the end was accompanied by the *Wedding March* from Mendelssohn's *Incidental Music to A Midsummer's Night's Dream*. The hymns were: 'Praise to the Lord, the Almighty, the King of Creation', 'O God of Love, to Thee we bow' and 'O Thou whose love has brought us here', which ends with a trustful rededication:

> With hope we face the paths untrod
> Which none can see;
> For Thou wilt guide our stumbling feet
> And near us be.
> May each year's service find us still
> Nearer to Thee.

The honeymoon was spent at Ballater for a week and St Andrews for a week, after which Peter returned to the busy round of ministerial life and his young wife experienced it for the first time, learning to give him her support and adjusting to a quite new relationship with the church. After his settled bachelor routine the pastor took some time to adjust: there were times when he went home after a service without his wife and had to return with abject apologies to fetch her! They had a complementary relationship in marriage and in ministry. Isobel did not seek the limelight and wanted just to be there for Peter. She did not see herself as a speaker, but she did serve as President of the Lanarkshire District Union of the Women's Auxiliary.

Their first child, Fiona Christine, was born on Thursday 28 July 1966. The manse at 60 Kelso Drive proved to be inadequate for the growing family. Peter, Isobel and Fiona moved to a new manse at 1 Glen Bervie in the St Leonards area towards the end of 1967. It was better situated for privacy and quietness, more centrally placed for visitation, and warmer as it had central heating with a gas boiler. A second daughter, Susan Elizabeth, arrived on 10 January 1969. It was now a time when fathers were encouraged to be present at the birth: Susan's was the first birth Peter had witnessed and he said it was the most amazing thing he had ever experienced.

The close partnership of their marriage brought great enrichment to Peter and Isobel. Despite all the hectic activity of ministry their children became central to their lives. Fiona and Susan have memories of their early years at East Kilbride. Fiona remembers her father's patience in helping her to ride a bike: the many times he ran with her, holding on to the bike, before she achieved balance for herself. She also remembers the day when she fell over on ice at school and broke her right wrist. It was the same day that her father accidentally cut into tendons on his left hand while doing one of his odd job good turns. Both had arms in plaster for six weeks.

Both girls remember well the Sunday morning that the baptismal pool at East Mains had been filled and the water heated. Polystyrene tiles had been placed on top to keep the heat in. Fiona wondered whether she could walk on them, but was not too sure, so she coaxed Susan to try—and she fell in. Fortunately their mother had an inkling that something was wrong and came and fished Susan out.

Drive-In Church

A novel and ambitious method of evangelism that the church used was the Drive-In Church. Peter's brother Ronnie had emigrated to the United States. While on a visit to him (with their brother Joe) in 1963 Peter had seen drive-in services and believed the idea would work in East Kilbride. The church had tried normal open-air services, but they had not been successful in the East Kilbride situation, where people were usually out with an aim in mind and were not inclined to stand and listen. In the late 1960s the town had one car to every two families, a high proportion at that time, and large car parks had been laid out for the shopping-centre area. The Development Corporation gave permission for one of these car parks, which had accommodation for 250 cars, to be used for the purpose of the Drive-In Church experiment.

Months of planning, preparation and prayer preceded the first drive-in service to be held in Scotland on Sunday 6 August 1967.[29] Many willing helpers came forward and the organization was very efficient. A large truck brought the equipment. A platform was constructed by the men of the church that was capable of being erected and dismantled quickly and solid enough to carry the weight of an electronic organ and four people. Loudspeaker equipment was built suitable for carrying voices from the platform to every part of the car park. Stewards directed the cars into the best formation in front of the platform and gave the occupants a leaflet that welcomed them and gave them information.

Publicity materials to direct car drivers were posted on all the entrance routes to the town. Four thousand leaflets were placed under the wipers of cars. A great deal of interest had been aroused by the press, radio and television coverage. Press photographers and reporters were present.

Before the service tape-recorded music was played until the organist took over for a voluntary. The service began at 7.45 and lasted forty-five minutes. Peter was chairman and the programme comprised solos, prayer and Scripture reading by a church member, a five minute testimony from

---

[29] *SBM* (September 1967), 10-11; *Record* (August 1967), 7.

George Sharkey (a converted alcoholic) and an evangelistic sermon by Alex Rodger.

About 100 cars came and there were pedestrians standing at the sides. The total number of people was about 500, of whom about 100 were from the two congregations. The services continued over the next five Sundays and the number of cars remained about 100. A census at the last two services showed that between a quarter and a third of those present had no regular church connection.[30] About 50% came because of the media publicity, another 40% came because they had heard about it from friends. Reporting to a Conference on Experimental Evangelism at the Assembly in October Peter commented that two of the things that appealed to the folk were the anonymity and the informality.[31]

The church did not regard the drive-in service as a substitute for the evening service in the church building, but 'as an effort at outreach, whereby the Church emerges from her hideout to confront people with the gospel who would never be seen dead in a church building'. They recognized that those present formed an audience rather than a congregation and that congregational participation was impossible. The only means of involving people was by making sure the service relayed was so relevant that their attentive interest was sustained.[32]

Following the first experiment the church was convinced that these services were meeting a need and had a future as a means of outreach. They continued for four or five Sundays in the summer each year until the Barber family left for Torquay in 1973.

In 1972 the services were brought forward from August to June 'in the hope of better weather and longer evenings'. Peter shared in a tour of publicity with 'Drive-in' leaflets to some of the seaside towns. Other churches took up the idea. Under the headline 'The Drive-In Disease' the September issue of *Focus* was happy to report:

> This relatively new disease is highly contagious. Since our church pioneered Drive-In Services in Britain these are now being held in various parts of the country, e.g. Godalming, Bishop Auckland, Johnstone, Dundee. The most recent to catch the smit [Scottish word for 'disease'] is Perth. An enthusiastic letter from the secretary of the Baptist Church there speaks of a remarkable response to this open-air venture.[33]

---

[30] *SBM* (October 1967), 13.
[31] *SBM* (November 1967), 4.
[32] *SBM* (September 1967), 11.
[33] *Focus* (September 1972), 12.

Church and Personal Development

And so in this middle period of his ministry at East Kilbride Peter Barber had the joy of leading the East Mains people as they formed a new congregation in Westwood, a growing area of the town. He was gratified to see it develop quickly, call its own pastor and erect its own building. It took courage to send out fifty-six members to plant another congregation in faith. Westwood was regarded as a sister congregation rather than a daughter. Because of his experience Peter was bound to be seen as the 'senior pastor', but this was not his official description and he made sure he related to Alex Rodger and Jim Murdoch on equal terms. The congregations responded to his lead in establishing a relationship of co-operation rather than competition.

Peter Blackwood played a key role in the founding of the church and its growth and it was he who established the idea of the one church with two congregations. A new era began when he and Isa moved to Livingston. This was a great wrench for the church and for Peter and Isobel Barber, but there was a good succession of key workers who were provided as the East Mains congregation continued to consolidate its own witness as well as give effective support to the Westwood folk.

Peter's own life was radically changed for the last eight years of his East Kilbride ministry, because he married and became a family man. For some years he had not considered it at all likely that he would take on these roles, but suddenly his life was transformed and enriched. Isobel's support became crucial to him and they devoted themselves to their young family.

CHAPTER 6

Planting the Calderwood Congregation

Further Expansion

Alongside the development of the Westwood Congregation the East Kilbride church committed itself to outreach in the east of the town in the areas of Long Calderwood (later shortened to Calderwood) and St Leonards (south of Long Calderwood).

The annual business meeting in September 1965 unanimously decided to start a Sunday School in Long Calderwood. There were more than 500 homes there, but no Sunday School at all. Following visitation and leaflet distribution the Sunday School began in Long Calderwood School in the afternoon of 24 October. The response was good: sixty-five children attended on the first Sunday and eighty-one on the second.[1]

At the end of August 1966 the East Mains and Westwood congregations combined for a week of intensive visitation in the Long Calderwood area, leading up to the showing of a Billy Graham film on the Sunday evening in Long Calderwood School. House meetings started in October.[2]

In June 1967, just after the thirteenth church anniversary, which incorporated the stone-laying of the Westwood building, Peter issued a further challenge:

> The areas of growth in the town are now in the South (Westwood) in the North (Calderwood) and in the East (St Leonards). The first area is obviously on the doorstep of the Westwood Congregation. The other two areas are equally obviously on the East Mains side of the town. So that each congregation is surrounded with a growing mission field 'white unto harvest'.

> Which means one thing. East Kilbride Baptist Church cannot afford the luxury of touch-line Christians. There is far too much to do for anyone to opt out of the work. Whether it be by prayer or by giving or by visitation or by teaching or by leadership—we need YOU.

---

[1] *Record* (October 1965), 11; (November), 9.
[2] *Record* (October 1966), 5.

So whenever the call goes out for your help, have done with every excuse, and for the sake of Christ and the souls of men and women and young people, come forward immediately and join in the greatest adventure and most rewarding task that this life affords.[3]

The East Mains business meeting in March 1968 decided unanimously to begin evangelistic morning services in Allers Primary School, Long Calderwood. The deacons and representatives of the areas had made a careful survey of the work at East Mains and at Westwood and the potential of the Long Calderwood and St Leonards areas. A further £2 a week was required to pay for these services, but the members accepted that God was calling the church to this work and they must make it a viable proposition. However, they decided 'not to plan to build in the foreseeable future in either Long Calderwood or St Leonards but rather to redecorate, improve and, if need be, extend present premises at East Mains'.[4]

James McKendrick, a deacon at East Mains, led the first services and shepherded the work. There was heavy, persistent rain all day on the first Sunday (5 May), but to everyone's surprise and delight sixty-five people came, fourteen of whom were children and twenty-three of whom were newcomers to the church services. In the afternoon forty-four children attended Sunday School.[5] A separate Sunday School continued at Long Calderwood School.

More than two years later, on the evening of Wednesday 19 August 1970, at 83 Warwick, the Calderwood Fellowship was formed. Twenty-eight people signed the commitment to become the nucleus of the third congregation in the United Church should the work so develop over the next two years. Within those two years the church planned to clear the debt on the Westwood building, to make the Westwood Congregation self-supporting and to advance the work in Long Calderwood sufficiently to be able to call a third full-time minister.[6]

James Hamilton

At the meeting a Calderwood Committee was formed with Peter as chairman. Its first task was to function as a vacancy committee, for the immediate intention was to appoint a student pastor. With this in view two students took services and one of them, James Hamilton, was approached. Jim was a final year student at the Baptist Theological College of Scotland. His home church was King's Park, Glasgow. He and his wife

---

[3] *Record* (June 1967), 3.
[4] *Record* (April 1968), 3, 7.
[5] *Record* (May 1968), 14.
[6] *Focus* (September 1970), 11.

Pauline were welcomed by the Calderwood Fellowship on Wednesday evening 21 October 1970. The preacher was his Principal, R.E.O. White.[7]

The Calderwood Fellowship—and the two congregations—immediately appreciated the gifts that Jim and Pauline Hamilton brought to East Kilbride. They visited the homes of members and of the Sunday School scholars. The work made good progress: attendances at the morning service increased to around seventy and the Sunday School grew to around 150. The meetings of the committee and the fellowship were characterized by a sense of unity and expectancy. Pauline's talents were well employed in the leadership of meetings for women, called 'KUMAZUARS', which were held twice a month in the Allers School on Wednesday evenings and took the form of demonstrations followed by a gospel epilogue. The average attendance was eighty.[8]

It became so obvious to the church that Jim Hamilton was God's man for Calderwood that their previous timetable was scrapped. At a united church meeting on 3 March 1971 Peter Barber 'gave a lucid exposition of the beginnings of worship in Calderwood' and explained that 'the deacons courts of both congregations and the Calderwood Fellowship had recommended that Mr Hamilton be called to a full-time pastorate as a third member of the East Kilbride team', adding 'that the Baptist Union were now willing to support such a pastorate'. He urged the church to 'catch the vision of those who saw this as God's call'. The church voted unanimously in favour and had no doubt that its decision was led by the Spirit.[9] On 7 August Jim Hamilton was ordained and inducted to the pastorate of Calderwood and to the church's team ministry.[10]

Among his reflections on the occasion of the seventeenth anniversary of the church Peter wrote: 'Which of us will ever forget that it was during this past year that God so unexpectedly hurried forward the work in Calderwood, making His people willing in the day of His power?'[11]

When the new congregation was constituted in 1972 over fifty members transferred from the East Mains Congregation. A building fund was opened and because of the rapid development of the work Calderwood was given priority by the Church Extension Committee of the Union. The new building was opened in 1976.

Jim Hamilton, who continued as pastor until October 1982, is deeply appreciative of his time with Peter and has offered these reflections:

Peter was essentially a very humble man who was always positive, would see the best in people and would inspire them to fulfil their potential. He worked incredibly hard—I was always amazed at the way he would be able to fit in pastoral visits before, between and after meetings, and people felt totally cared for. He was a true visionary, never satisfied with things as they were, always thinking and planning ahead, and always believing that God could do more than we could imagine. He was very patient with me and I benefited so much from his wisdom and insight.

I will always remember Peter as a great enthusiast, not only in his work for the church and the wider Christian family, but in everything he did, whether it be on the golf course (where to be honest he was pretty average), playing table tennis at the Youth Club, or waxing eloquent about the way his beloved dog Darroch could jump up and open the door! I remember him also being bowled over when he got his first new car—a Volkswagen Beetle with the registration number MYJ. He called it 'Midge' and to say the least, drove it with enthusiasm! Peter had a very quick and sharp sense of humour, and he wasn't averse to practical jokes, but it was never cruel or designed to humiliate.

In some ways Peter was a pastor of the old school, doing many of the things like regular visiting that many pastors, especially in large churches, no longer do. Yet in other ways he was ahead of his time, seeing the value of co-operation with Christians and churches of other denominations and seeing the need to try new and innovative methods of evangelism like the Drive-in Church experiment in East Kilbride.

Three Congregations

Peter was delighted that the East Mains Congregation was able to form another congregation with a good base of members. The original plans were laid with due caution, but to Peter's surprise the development of congregation, pastor and building followed rapidly. Jim Hamilton fully appreciated the advantages of working alongside Peter in the early years of his ministry, just as Alex Rodger and Jim Murdoch had.

Some consideration was given to two other areas of the town, but no further plants were made. The three congregations, although distinct, continue to work in co-operation as one church today.

CHAPTER 7

Wider Ministry

Preaching, Teaching and Learning

The East Kilbride folk were well aware that their pastor was in great demand for ministry in other churches and groups, both within the denomination and beyond it. They were happy to support and encourage him in this, because they knew his capacity for work was phenomenal and they themselves received the benefit of his wider experiences.

He was much sought after for preaching at church anniversaries, evangelistic meetings and other special services. He spoke at conferences and conventions. In April 1959 he was one of the speakers at the Christian Endeavour National Convention in Hamilton.[1] In June 1965 he spoke at the Portstewart Keswick Convention in County Londonderry, Northern Ireland, shortly before his wedding. Other speakers included Paul Rees and George Duncan.[2] He was invited back as one of the speakers in 1989, when he was in office as General Secretary of the Union. He contributed a page-long message to the leaflet that gave details of the programme and began with reminiscence:

> It was in 1965, a memorable year for me, since it was the year I married, that I was last one of the speaking team at Portstewart. Though 23 years have passed since that Convention, many memories of it still remain vivid and fresh. I can still recall the packed tent, the flapping canvas and the sense of eager expectancy as we gathered day by day to hear the Word of the Lord. I still have treasured transparencies of the Giant's Causeway and waves beating on the rocky shore line. Stirred by these memories I am looking forward to returning to your island, your warm hearted fellowship and to our sharing together in the Word of the Lord.

Peter came across as a confident, accomplished speaker. People were not aware of just how nervous he was when addressing such gatherings, but when he went to Portstewart for that first time he now had a fiancée and was able to confide his real feelings to her.

---

[1] *Record* (April 1959), 8.
[2] *Record* (June 1965), 4.

He was guest speaker at Capernwray Hall, the residential Bible School in Carnforth, Lancashire, for a week in July 1968[3] and a week in September 1969.[4] In August 1972 he spoke at two meetings of the Strathclyde Christian Council Convention at Kilmacolm[5] and in September that year he returned to Ireland, to Portrush, to speak at the Convention of the Ballymena and Coleraine Christian Endeavour Union.[6] In May 1973 he addressed a conference of the extension ministers of the Church of Scotland at Pitlochry on the subject of 'Mission'.[7]

His teaching skills were used in theological education. He gave a course of lectures for an evening class at the Bible Training Institute in Glasgow in October–December 1963. The following year he wrote and marked a correspondence course for the Institute. He served on the College Committee of the Baptist Theological College of Scotland from 1970 to 1973 and preached at the Valedictory Service in June 1972.[8]

He continued, however, to be a learner. His keenness to extend the skills of ministry for himself and others is shown by his arranging a residential course at the Crichton Royal Infirmary in Dumfries in September 1968 for Baptist ministers in the West of Scotland. The Infirmary was a famous mental hospital. The matron was a keen Christian and was happy to administer the course on the subject 'Understand the needs of the mentally sick'.[9]

In February 1973, knowing that at the age of forty-two he was not too old to learn more about evangelism, he attended a 'WIN School', with fourteen other Baptist ministers. The Rev. Ervin Hastey from Mexico led it in Granton Baptist Church, Edinburgh. Peter wrote in the *Scottish Baptist Magazine* with enthusiasm about his experience and the potential of the method under the headline 'Peter Barber's Schooldays'.[10] WIN stood for Witness Involvement Now and was a method of training for lay evangelism developed by Dr Bill Stanton, the first school being held in Atlanta, Georgia in 1970.

Young People

Peter had many opportunities of working with children and young people. He served as chaplain of three local schools: Jackton Primary

---

[3] *Record* (June–July 1968), 8.

[4] *Focus* (August 1969), 7.

[5] *Focus* (August 1972) Prayer Focus insert: Friday 25th, Monday 28th August; *SBM* (August 1972), 15.

[6] *Focus* (September 1972) Prayer Focus insert: Friday 22nd September.

[7] *Focus* (April 1973) Prayer Focus insert: Tuesday 1st May.

[8] *Focus* (May 1972), Prayer Focus insert: Tuesday 13th June; *SBM* (August 1972), 13.

[9] *Record* (September 1968), 3.

[10] *SBM* (April 1973), 8.

School, Claremont School and Hunter High School,[11] visiting each for
one period each week. He addressed Scripture Union groups in schools
and Christian Union groups in colleges. In 1960 he was joint speaker with
the Rev. Eric Alexander at the Scottish Inter-Varsity Fellowship
Conference (for students) in Largs.[12] In the summer of that year he was
padre at the Crusaders' Camp (for young people) in Aviemore.[13]

He often took part in youth events in other churches and was fully
involved in a movement that flourished in the late 1950s and the 1960s,
which had a profound influence on the Baptist denomination: the Baptist
Youth Rallies. These took place in different areas of Scotland. The
Glasgow rallies were held monthly from October to April in Adelaide
Place Baptist Church. There was an annual summer outing and the young
people took part in missions.

The first all-Scotland Youth Conference and Rally was held in Stirling
Baptist Church in 1959, when Stuart Arnold and Lindsay Glegg were the
speakers. The church was so crowded that the last arrivals had to be seated
in the baptistry! The following year they secured the use of the North
Parish Church (Church of Scotland) next door. One of the features of the
Conference in May 1963 was a 'discussion' (actually a scripted dialogue)
between Peter Barber and James Taylor. It was entitled 'Two Men Open
the Bible: A Re-examination of Baptist Principles'. James Taylor asked
the questions (forty-six of them!) and Peter gave the answers. A study
outline for those attending and for further discussion in local groups
emphasized the following Baptist principles:

> We become Christians only by conversion.
> Church membership is only for believers.
> Church government is only by members.
> The Bible is our only authority.
> Baptism is only for believers.

The presentation, with the usual admixture of serious theological points
and natural humour, was very well received by the young people.[14]

Summer Schools were arranged by the Baptist Youth Rallies
committee. Peter was a joint leader with Donald McCallum[15] of one in
Holland (1961)[16] and one at 'Greenhills', Worthing (1962);[17] he was joint

[11] *Focus* (October 1970), 8; (April 1973) Prayer Focus insert: Tuesday 4th April.
[12] *Record* (April 1960), 3.
[13] *Record* (July 1960), 1.
[14] Peter appears on the platform of the Youth Rally held in the Church of Scotland
Assembly Hall, Edinburgh, in May 1964 in a photograph printed in *SBM* (June 1964), 6.
[15] Donald McCallum served as pastor of Bowmore 1946–50; Granton, Edinburgh,
1950–56; Stirling 1956–70; Adelaide Place, Glasgow, 1970–82.
[16] *Record* (August 1961), 2-3.

leader with Jim and Anne Graham of one in Switzerland (1963).[18] His future wife Isobel attended that Summer School.

In August 1967 Peter and Isobel were given 'leave of absence' from church duties for a fortnight to serve the Baptist Missionary Society as president and hostess of a young people's Summer School in Carberry Tower Youth Centre, near Musselburgh. They were responsible for all the aspects of the holiday conference. Peter gave the lectures for one of the two weeks.[19] They reported in the *Record* that 'many of the young people found help in resolving spiritual problems, some reached a point of further surrender in their lives, while others heard and responded to God's call for full-time service'.[20]

Soon after this exhausting time Peter and Isobel enjoyed a restful holiday for the first fortnight of September in the peace and quiet of Strathpeffer in the Highlands.

Broadcasting

Peter had several opportunities of radio and television work. He took part in a live broadcast of the morning service on the Scottish Home Service on Sunday 26 January 1963. It was a United Service of the Protestant Churches of East Kilbride to mark the end of the Week of Prayer for Christian Unity, held in the Moncrieff Church of Scotland, whose minister, the Rev. Andrew R. Morton, led and preached. Peter composed and read a prayer. Representatives of St Mark's Episcopal Church and the Church of Christ also took part. Later that year, on Sunday 4 August, Peter conducted the BBC Evening Service, broadcast live on the radio at 7.45 p.m..[21]

In September the following year Peter was one of twenty ministers from all the 'mainstream' denominations invited to take a two day training course run by Scottish Television, to teach them the difficulties and techniques of television broadcasting. He found the fellowship with the other ministers enriching and was most impressed by the men and women who directed the religious programmes. He pointed out in the *Record* how much church workers could learn from them. They were dedicated people, sparing no effort to perfect the programme they were presenting. They were adaptable: if any programme was not meeting the need, it was replaced, whatever the effort or cost involved. They were humble, sincerely welcoming *any* criticism that was offered: 'They were

[17] *SBM* (October 1962), 17: group photograph.
[18] *Record* (June 1963), 4.
[19] *Record* (August 1967), 5.
[20] *Record* (September 1967), 3.
[21] *SBM* (July 1963), 2; *Record* (August 1963), 2.

not touchy. All that mattered was the worthy presentation of the faith and not their personal feelings.' Some aspects of the course were painful:

> We were even given the very humiliating experience of doing an abbreviated 'Late Call'. This was recorded on video-tape, and we all saw the results the next day. Now we have every sympathy with the men who have done it in the past. There is nothing more impersonal than an unrelenting camera that records your every gesture and expression.[22]

In fact he must have done well, because he was asked to speak on 'Late Call' a few months later (16-18 and 27-29 May 1965).[23] The following year (21-25 November) he broadcast the five minute programme at 7.55 a.m. on Radio Scotland called 'Start the Day Right'. Each of his talks was based on a 'pop' record, chosen with the help of some of the church young people.[24]

In 1973 Peter and the East Mains Congregation were asked to present a programme in the 'Word for Living' series (which had replaced the morning service) on Radio 4. It was recorded on Sunday 3 June 1973 in the church and broadcast the following week (Whitsunday, 10 June) from 9.50 to 10.25 a.m.. In the same month he presented 'Late Call' on seven evenings (17-23 June) for Scottish Television. They were pre-recorded on Thursday 31 May.[25]

Foreign Travel

Peter enjoyed travelling and took full advantage of opportunities of going abroad. In September 1963 he was assistant leader of a group of twenty-four young people (seventeen to twenty-one years of age) from various parts of the British Isles on a visit to the Soviet Union. They were all members of some youth organization and were going in exchange for a visit to Britain of an equivalent number of young Russians. The leader was a field-officer with the Youth Hostels Association and there were two interpreters.

On Sunday 1 September the group sailed from Tilbury on a voyage that took them to Leningrad with brief visits on the way to Copenhagen, Stockholm and Helsinki. They arrived in Leningrad (today restored to its original name, St. Petersburg) on the evening of the 6th. The next eighteen days were spent in Russia, with a programme that included visits

---

[22] *Record* (August 1964), 2-3.
[23] *Record* (May 1965), 11.
[24] *Record* (November 1966), 9.
[25] *Focus* (April 1973), inside front cover; (May), 8; (June–July), 17. Peter's preaching as President of the Union for the Centenary broadcast in 1969 will be referred to in the next chapter.

to a factory, a collective farm, churches and historical buildings. A lot of free time was allowed for personal exploration of the cities and for meeting the people. They stayed in Moscow and Kiev as well as Leningrad. Peter was able to make contact with many Baptists. The return voyage began from Leningrad at midnight on Tuesday 24 September and ended in Tilbury on Sunday afternoon, 29th.[26]

This was a most significant experience for Peter and he gave full reports on it, illustrated by transparencies and films. He addressed a thousand young people about it at the Assembly Youth Rally on Thursday 24 October. Ronald Armstrong reported:[27]

> After hearing a brief description of the Beirut World Youth Congress from one of our Scottish delegates, we were treated to a gripping account of life in Russia today by Rev. Peter Barber, of East Kilbride, who, earlier this year led an exchange party to that land about which so little is known in the West. We learned that Russia is a Socialist, not a Communist country, with only 10 million out of its total population of 200 million-plus members of the Communist Party. Communist leaders are certain that Russia will be a Communist country within twenty years. When we heard with dismay of how propaganda is directed towards the minds of children from kindergarten age right up to adulthood, few of us doubted the very real possibility of this.
>
> Mr. Barber gave a description of living conditions in Russia where everything seemed drab, competition is eliminated in trading, and freedom is curtailed, which made us all appreciate the benefits of conditions in Scotland today much more. He showed forcibly how difficult it is to be a loyal evangelical Christian in Russia today: the average Baptist is subjected to pressure to conform, to join the Party, to abandon faith in God—and yet in that situation there are some 545,000 Baptists with many more attending Sunday services. As one cannot join a Russian Baptist Church before the age of eighteen, only fifteen per cent are young people. The average member is likely to be middle-aged. The people are zealous and will wait for two hours to get into a service where they will hear three sermons during a three-hour service. This contrasts with our impatience if services last more than an hour, with our readiness to sit through two hours of television.
>
> Despite their limited opportunities for evangelism, there are many conversions and Baptisms. Russian Baptists are critical of our misuse of religious liberty in this country and wonder why we are not more zealous in winning people for Christ. Asking the question 'Will this country go Communist?', Mr Barber left us with the challenge of a zealous Communist who will sacrifice everything to advance his godless creed, and with the challenge of our Russian Baptist brethren who under the most difficult conditions are manifesting a

[26] *Record* (August 1963), 5; (September), 2.
[27] *SBM* (November 1963), 8-9.

loyalty and zeal for Christ and His Kingdom which ought to stir us to deeper devotion and higher standards of Christian discipleship in Scotland today.

In 1964 Peter spent a month's holiday (4 August–1 September) in the United States and Canada. The *Record* indulged in some humour at his expense:

VACATION

We sincerely trust that Mr. Barber is enjoying a well-earned rest with friends in America. He is a much travelled man and we understand that before each trip he learns the language of the country to be visited. There is a strong rumour that he intends taking language lessons this winter—MOONTALK![28]

This was a reference to the American Apollo space programme: it was five years later that Neil Armstrong and Edwin Aldrin made the first landing on the moon (20 July 1969).

Peter himself wrote in the same issue on the serious problem of racial conflict:

At the time of writing the newspapers are full of comment on happenings in that part of the world where I am to spend most of my time—the New York and New Jersey area. It is again the sorry story of man's inhumanity to man, of bitterness and prejudice.

Of course it is easy for us in Britain to pass shallow, ill-informed verdicts on our American cousins when we are not living with the problem. And even if we do make judgements, we should surely do so remembering Notting Hill,[29] doors slammed by landlords in the face of coloured enquirers, and West Indians kept out of work to promote full employment for the whites. Our own hands are not clean, when it comes to this.

But whether we be Americans or Britishers does not matter most if we are Christians. It is not then our nationalistic prejudice, nor our social history, nor our political circumstances that forms our judgements. It is Christ himself by whom our standards are to be set and our judgements formed.

Of His attitude to this burning issue, there can be no shred of doubt. He grew up in a society dissected by prejudice-barriers. Think of just a few. Jew/Gentile—Man/woman—Jew/Samaritan—Jew/Roman—Pharisee/publican. But he would have none of it. He sat on a well talking with a Samaritan woman; He dined with publicans and sinners and pharisees; He healed the servant of a

---

[28] *Record* (August 1964), 4.

[29] Notting Hill, London, was the scene of race riots in late August and early September 1958.

Roman centurion. He was a revolutionary who just refused to be hemmed in by prejudice. He was far too big for men's smallmindedness.

And He has left every one of us an example, that we should follow. How can we refuse education, opportunity, respect and justice to those whom He loves as much as He loves us? If Christ be in black and white, then in Him black and white are one.[30]

Wider Service

Peter Barber's gifts as a communicator were widely used. He preached and taught in many churches and in larger gatherings, and particularly valued opportunities to work among children and young people. The qualities of his voice and style were recognized by those who invited him to broadcast.

He took opportunities of travel in Europe and across the Atlantic. These trips were not simply holidays, but times of exploration and reflection. He was keen to add first-hand experience to his background knowledge and to share his discoveries and conclusions not only with his own church but with the denomination in Scotland as a whole. In his thirteenth year at East Kilbride he was given the opportunity to share for three years in the leadership of the denomination.

[30] *Record* (August 1964), 2.

CHAPTER 8

The Centenary President of the Union

Appointment

Peter Barber was called upon to be President of the Baptist Union of Scotland in its centenary year, 1969–70, when he was thirty-nine. Three years of busy responsibilities lay ahead of the person who accepted the Presidency—as Vice-President, President and Past President.[1]

Normally nominations for the office came from the regional associations, but plans for the centenary led to a special procedure. Peter's nomination was recommended by the Finance and Business Committee to the Council in March 1968.[2] The associations were informed: those who replied supported his name and there were no counter-nominations. He was unanimously accepted as Vice-President at the Assembly in October.[3] Scottish Baptists recognized that he was eminently gifted to be their President and representative in the centenary year.

It was, however, a great surprise to Peter himself. In the *Record* of April 1968, soon after the nomination had been made public, he wrote: 'It came as a complete bombshell to me when my name was first considered by the Finance and Business Meeting.' He thanked the deacons and members for their support and explained that the centenary year would not mean a total leave of absence: he would be free for pastoral duties for most of the week and would probably preach in his own pulpit about once a month. He expressed his very real feelings of inadequacy, but also his conviction that in obeying the divine call he would receive divine strength for his extra tasks:

In all sincerity I assure you that such a responsibility is not something I would desire. I feel so raw and inexperienced. It would be so much easier if the matter had not been raised. The only reason I have allowed my name to go forward is because of your support and (supremely) because of the Lord's undeniable leading. Should He finally call me to this appointment I will go forward in the

---

[1] Much of the detail in this chapter was drawn from memorabilia in Peter's BU Centenary Presidency file.

[2] *SBM* (May 1968), 11.

[3] *SBM* (November 1968), 9.

faith that those whom He calls He equips and in the knowledge that behind me there are the prayers and support of my own family in Christ, the brothers and sisters whom the Lord has laid on my heart.[4]

In his acceptance speech at the 1968 Assembly he explained that his unwillingness at first to accept nomination had been due especially to his lack of years, but he had come to see his young age as symbolic:

> Any movement which faces its centenary has one of two options: either it basks in the glory of its past and indulges in happy reminiscences, or else it takes a long hard look at its great tradition and in the strength of it leaps into an exciting future. If my appointment symbolises the second of these options — as I think it does — then I am glad.[5]

Peter's presidential three years coincided with the three-year programme of 'Simultaneous Evangelism' arranged as part of the centenary celebrations by Andrew MacRae, the Office Bearers and the Evangelistic Committee. Peter became fully involved in the planning and the events of it. It ran from the 1968 Assembly to the 1971 Assembly. The years were named 'the Year of Preparation', 'the Year of Proclamation' and 'the Year of Preservation'. The idea began in Brazil and had been taken up by Baptists in the USA, Spain, Portugal, Germany and Holland. Just over half the churches in Scotland participated, eighty-seven out of 160.

Vice-Presidency

As Vice-President Peter gave the address at the Youth Rally at the 1968 Assembly. According to Derek Murray he 'punched home the message of the evening with characteristic vigour and power'.[6] Giving a full report of the meeting Alan Stoddart wrote:

> Taking words from EZEKIEL...'he shall not return by the way of the gate whereby he came in...' Mr Barber said we cannot come into the house of God and meet with Him and go out the same way. Recalling Jesus' story of the two who went into the temple to pray, He indicated that the Pharisee went out the same door by which he entered but the publican entering by confession went out the door of Pardon. This thought was brought into practical terms and the young were challenged with the old. God challenged many, if not all, and only

---

[4] *Record* (April 1968), 10-11.

[5] Peter's notes in his BU Centenary Presidency file: 'Acknowledgement: Acceptance of Vice Presidency, Oct. 1968'.

[6] *SBM* (November 1968), 8.

the years will tell of the number for whom this was a night of decision. Overall impression: — This was not a good night — it was a God night.[7]

One of the vice-presidential occasions he enjoyed was a part of the weekend of celebration for the seventy-fifth anniversary of the Thomas Coats Memorial Baptist Church, Paisley. On the Monday (12 May 1969) they had an evening of song with the title 'A Thousand Tongues of Praise', including choral and congregational singing. This was to celebrate the Union's centenary as well as their own anniversary. Peter gave the address: he 'spoke of the value of singing in the experience of Christians and in the life of the Church, developing his theme with cogent thought and apt quotation, thus matching the mood of a praise service and also giving much food for serious thought'.[8]

As Vice-President he attended the Congregational Union Assembly in Glasgow and the United Free Church Assembly in Edinburgh. He was impressed by his sense of oneness with his brothers and sisters in Christ and by the fact that both the Congregational President and the United Free Church Moderator spoke of the local church as the most effective witness for Christ if it was obvious by the quality of its life that the Holy Spirit was working through it.[9]

In his profile of the Centenary President in the *Scottish Baptist Magazine*, Peter Blackwood commended his friend and former minister to the denomination:

> Peter Barber is a good student, a good planner, is never short of ideas to strengthen the spiritual life of the Church, he is a gifted preacher and teacher and an excellent pastor as many can testify. His home is open to all, his telephone seems constantly to be ringing, but if he ever complains it can only be to his wife! Fortunately he can relax when the opportunity occurs — he enjoys music, dabbles in watercolours occasionally, is a bit of a motor mechanic, is fond of animals, plays golf now and again — but not very well, I think!!!

> At 39 years of age Peter Barber is one of the youngest to become President but he is an experienced member of the Council and has served on many committees including Finance and Business, Inter-Church Relations and a number of 'ad hocs'. He is a past President of the Lanarkshire Baptist Association, a past Chairman of the West of Scotland Youth Rallies, has been on holidays with Scottish Baptist Young People in England and Europe. He has also travelled and met Baptists in Russia, U.S.A. and Canada. His

---

[7] *SBM* (November 1968), 14.
[8] *SBM* (July 1969), 8.
[9] *Record* (June–July 1969), 2.

dedication and gifts of preaching and leadership will serve the Union well in this Centenary year.[10]

Centenary Broadcast Service

It was usual for Radio 4 Scotland to broadcast a Baptist service on the Sunday morning before an Assembly, featuring the new President. On the Sunday morning before the centenary assembly (19 October 1969) a special service was broadcast live from the East Mains church to listeners in Scotland and Northern Ireland. It was a joint service with the Allers (Calderwood) and Westwood Congregations. Andrew MacRae, General Secretary of the Union, was the leader. Bible readings, a solo and a testimony were given by members of the church.[11] Peter preached on 'Christ lives in me', ending with an appeal:

> Who, then, will reign in you? Ego or Christ? Self or Jesus? The decision is yours. May God help you to say, 'No longer I...but Christ!' Then you will enter into the secret of the mystery of the Christian life, and you will shout with adoring wonder, 'CHRIST LIVES IN ME. THANKS BE TO GOD!'

A booklet was offered to any listeners who wished to follow up what he had said. That same afternoon Peter received a phone call asking for the booklet and a woman visited the manse for counselling. There were twenty-five letters requesting booklets: each person received a copy of *Becoming a Christian* by John Stott together with a Good News Version of John's Gospel and a letter. Further, Peter received fourteen letters of appreciation, four requests for the sermon script and one request for a tape recording of the service.[12]

One of the letters was from a member of Charlotte Chapel:

> Your matter and delivery was very clear and informative, in fact it was just like Rev. Joseph Kemp whom I had the privilege of hearing for 7 years—much before you were thought of... Some of us at Charlotte Chapel are looking forward to the DAY when we will again be in the Baptist Union? Keep praying.

Joseph Kemp was minister of Charlotte Chapel from 1902–15. The membership of the church rose from 108 in 1902 to 830 in 1914. The numbers were so great that a new building was needed: it was opened in 1912. Charlotte Chapel withdrew from the Union in 1957 because of the Union's ecumenical involvement. The decision of the 1956 Assembly

---

[10] *SBM* (October 1969), 9-10.

[11] *Focus* (October 1969), 7.

[12] *Focus* (November 1969), 1.

had been to withdraw from the World Council of Churches but to remain in the British Council of Churches and the Scottish Churches' Ecumenical Committee (the predecessor of the Scottish Churches' Council).[13]

Centenary Assembly 1969

The Assembly met in Edinburgh from Monday 20 to Thursday 23 October. Most of the major meetings took place in the Church of Scotland Assembly Hall. It was planned, particularly by Andrew MacRae and Peter Barber, to be an extra-special occasion and the delegates were not disappointed. Well-known Baptists came to the Assembly from other countries. The honoured guest of the Union and the principal speaker was Dr W.R. Tolbert, President of the Baptist World Alliance. He was also the Vice-President of Liberia and on the Friday evening after the Assembly Peter and Isobel, together with the other Office Bearers of the Union and their wives, attended a splendid private State Banquet given in Dr Tolbert's honour in Edinburgh Castle. Ten years later, on 12 April 1980 Dr Tolbert was brutally assassinated in Monrovia during a coup led by an unknown army sergeant.[14]

Peter was welcomed as President at the Monday evening rally; in his reply he described himself as 'an unrepentant Evangelical' and re-affirmed his faith:

I believe in the authority and Inspiration of the Scriptures as the Word of God. I believe in Jesus Christ, the Son of God, born of the virgin Mary, crucified for our sins on Calvary, and raised bodily from the dead on the third day. I believe in the complete sufficiency of Christ's atoning work on the cross, and in the Holy Spirit as the sole Giver of new life. I believe in the judgment to come, the personal return of Christ, and in the Gospel as man's only hope.[15]

His moving statement was loudly acclaimed by the congregation.[16]

A major innovation was the postponement of the President's address from its usual place on the Monday evening to the Thursday in the Thanksgiving and Commissioning Rally, which was the climax of the Assembly. Peter's address was entitled 'Jesus Christ, The Only Hope', which was the theme of the Simultaneous Evangelism programme. He first painted a dark picture of moral decay and general despair in society and then proclaimed that salvation was to be found only in Christ,

[13] Derek B. Murray: *The First Hundred Years* (Glasgow: Baptist Union of Scotland, 1969), 117.
[14] *SBM* (May 1980), 4.
[15] Peter's notes in his BU Centenary Presidency file: 'Presidency: Reply'.
[16] *SBM* (November 1969), 2.

upholding this exclusive claim by giving the evidence for the bodily resurrection. He declared that believers' baptism by immersion was 'a witness to the present resurrection-work of Christ' and the church should live out its identity as 'the Community of the Resurrection':

> Brethren, the time has come for all of us to repent, for by our lives we have not only denied the gospel we profess, we have grieved the Lord whom we say we love.

> God's word to us now might well be, 'Loose Him and let Him go. Let my Son not only rise from the dead, but let Him LIVE in you and in your Church. Loose Him and let Him go. He can do no mighty work because of your unbelief'.

> What tremendous things would happen in our Churches if we really let Christ loose! Worship would be spontaneous and heart-warming. In our Business Meetings we would be directed by a wiser than Solomon. Self-perpetuating auxiliaries would die, and cells of compassionate caring take their place. The proud would be humbled, the broken healed, and the lost found. In other words, Christ would continue from where He left off in Galilee and do His same gracious work, unhindered, in our midst and in our town.[17]

Amid the exhilaration of the celebrations, however, there were tensions in the business sessions. The report of the Treasurer, Jack Carr, on Tuesday morning was disappointing. A large deficit had been drawn from reserves. Reluctantly the Assembly agreed that the allocation to church extension should be cut back if necessary. The Treasurer was given powers to increase the minimum stipend in June 1970, but only if resources were available.[18]

As often the most contentious issue was the Union's relationship with other denominations. The question debated on Tuesday afternoon was whether the Union should remain in the Scottish Churches' Council (SCC) in view of the presence of Roman Catholic observers at their meetings. The Union had opposed the invitation to the Roman Catholics to send observers, but the motion put to the Assembly from the Council did not consider their presence a sufficient reason for withdrawing.

In the September issue of *Focus* Peter had commented on the recently renewed troubles in Northern Ireland and drawn out lessons to be learned: 'the folly of irresponsible talk', 'the mistake of living in the past', 'the sheer folly of being driven by prejudice and fear'. He commented: 'Right now the Roman Catholic Church is being rocked by internal revolution and self-criticism. Protestantism, as such, is no longer

---

[17] The address, *Jesus Christ the Only Hope*, was published by the Union in 1969. The above extracts are from p.10.
[18] *SBM* (November 1969), 8.

the faithful guardian of the Reformed Tradition. I wonder how many realise this?' He went on to refer to the forthcoming Assembly debate:

> The rights and wrongs of the case it is not for me to argue. One thing I would pray, that we will learn the lesson of this past month...

> One Church has already threatened to leave the Baptist Union over the issue unless the Union withdraws from the Council; action that can only be interpreted as a form of moral blackmail.

> This is not the time for rash speech or hasty action. In the face of our opportunities for evangelism during the Centenary it would be altogether tragic if the picture we present to Scotland is that of a wrangling divided denomination, censorious and uncharitable.[19]

In an address to the East Mains people after the Assembly Broadcast Peter commented: 'People are afraid of the Ecumenical Movement. Yet we must take our place in the National Church scene.' And about this and other changes taking place he went on: 'My concern is that those of us given responsibility in leadership should not go so fast as to alienate sympathies, yet neither so slow as to play into the hands of those who are negative and fearful.'[20]

At the end of the debate by a ballot vote the Assembly decided to remain affiliated to the SCC by 320 votes to 153. A further amendment was put forward that the Union should withdraw in the event of Roman Catholics being admitted as members to the Council. The result of the ballot vote was much closer: 211 for maintaining the previous decision, and 197 against.

The *Magazine* reported: 'The question...was debated in a most dignified and controlled manner, each one who participated accepting the direction of the Chairman, as regards the time allocated to speeches. The whole debate was well directed by Rev. P.H. Barber, who had appealed for restraint, relevance, respect and resolve.'[21]

Peter himself commented in *Focus*: 'During the Conference and Business Sessions we were so conscious of the Lord's leading as we grappled with some of the great contemporary issues of our day. The loving restraint and deep seriousness with which each person contributed to the discussions befitted the occasion and spoke of a maturity that was (in the light of former Assemblies) heartening to behold.'[22]

---

[19] *Focus* (September 1969), 1-2.
[20] Peter's notes in his BU Centenary Presidency file: 'Address to E. Mains Church at close of Broadcast'.
[21] *SBM* (November 1969), 8.
[22] *Focus* (November 1969), 2.

There had, however, been strong feelings expressed and one incident was particularly distressing. At the conclusion of the debate, the Rev. Jack Seaton announced that the Inverness church was withdrawing from the Union, in accordance with a decision it had made. He had, previous to the Assembly, circulated a special issue of the Inverness church magazine (*The Wicket Gate*, October 1969) crusading against the Council motion and expressing his own personal grievance that the Ministerial Recognition Committee had not granted him ministerial standing. In fact the Committee had deferred a decision to its next meeting. The withdrawal of the Inverness church caused great pain to Peter, particularly because of his family connections with the church. He expressed to the Assembly his hope that in the not too distant future the church would reconsider its decision. It was a great joy to him that this hope was fulfilled thirteen years later, when he was General Secretary of the Union.

On the Wednesday morning in the discussion of the Ministerial Recognition Committee report a question was raised about the deferment of Mr Seaton's application for recognition. Mr Seaton himself wished to speak. According to press reports the President told Mr Seaton that technically he was no longer a member and could not be allowed to speak, with the result that he left the meeting. This does an injustice to Peter's handling of the situation. According to the minutes he first referred the point to the Secretary (Andrew MacRae), who ruled that as the Inverness church had withdrawn from the Union Mr Seaton was no longer a member of the Assembly and had no right to address it. Although he agreed, Peter 'nevertheless proposed that the Assembly delegates could make an exception in this case and allow Mr Seaton to speak'. The Assembly voted by 'an obvious majority' to close the discussion.[23] At this point Mr Seaton left.

Later in the Assembly Peter found it necessary to spell out exactly the implications of the decision on the membership of the SCC:

> The decision we have made is clear, but because it is open to misunderstanding and could be open to misrepresentation, I feel constrained (as your President) to say something by way of explanation. As an Assembly we have NOT said that we approve of the presence of Roman Catholic observers in the Scottish Council of Churches, nor have we said that we would stay in should Roman Catholics become full members. While we HAVE decided that the presence of Roman Catholics as OBSERVERS is not of sufficient magnitude to force our complete withdrawal, we have simply refused to PREJUDGE any future developments within the Scottish Council of Churches.
>
> What we HAVE affirmed (and affirmed strongly) is that we WOULD be forced to withdraw from this Council [he quotes from the motion] 'were our influence

---

[23] *SBYB*, 1970, 62.

or our distinctive doctrinal emphases to be clearly rejected.' And this, we recognise, could happen as clearly in ANY OTHER ISSUE, as in the question of Roman Catholic representation.

THAT is why we have refused to prejudge the issue. And let me remind you that we have publicly committed ourselves as a Union [he quotes from the motion] 'to maintain clearly our Baptist Evangelical Witness' within the Scottish Churches' Council.[24]

The only other church to withdraw from the Union over the decision was Hermon, Glasgow, though several other churches dissociated themselves from the decision.[25] Peter described the withdrawal of the two churches as the keenest disappointment of his presidency.

Various delegates were asked to say something for the *Magazine* about the things that impressed them at the centenary assembly, and one wrote:

I felt I had made a thrilling discovery during the week, and it was something that I scarcely expected. It was that God had raised up a spiritual leader who matched the hour. We have had many fine men as our Presidents in the past, but Peter Barber, it seemed to me, displayed qualities of true leadership. His handling of Assembly business and his chairing of meetings was superbly done, and he has the vitality as well as the vision to bring inspiration to all our churches in this Centenary year. We should be praying that this may indeed happen. And let's not forget that unassuming and so gracious lady, the President's wife—thrust into the limelight after only a few years of marriage. Let's pray for her and their two little children as the President travels throughout Scotland visiting practically every Baptist Church.[26]

In the same issue Peter gave his own impressions of the Assembly. He highlighted its international feel: 'We FELT (possibly for the first time) that our Union was part of an Alliance of some 30 million Baptists in 124 different countries.' He called it 'an Assembly of abandoned giving'—the choirs had given themselves to their music, speakers had given their best, more than £1,300 had been given in the offerings in addition to £52,000 already given to the Centenary Fund and more than £10,000 given to the Union by the Women's Auxiliary.

There were so many other impressions...of hastily snatched meals between meetings: of a warm sense of brotherhood in the jostling crowd: of gales of laughter during bursts of spontaneous humour: of a hush of holy reverence at the impressively large communion service: of lively discussion during conference sessions and thoughtful debate during business sessions. But above

---

[24] *SBM* (November 1969), 10.
[25] Harper Memorial, Glasgow, had already withdrawn from the Union over the ecumenical issue in 1966.
[26] *SBM* (November 1969), 15.

all else one's impression was of Christ, the living Christ, the Lord Christ, mighty to save and able to lead His people into promising future. HE was in the midst, and HE was glorified.[27]

In *Focus* he wrote:

Speaker after speaker called us to the urgent task of Christ-centred evangelism, the most dynamic of them all being Avelino Ferreira, a Brazilian Baptist Bombshell. The choirs sang inspiringly; there was a deep sense of oneness in Christ; there were moments of sheer joy. We met to celebrate the Centenary of a Union; we ended by exulting in the Saviour—'Jesus Christ, the only Hope'. No wonder we sang our closing hymn with such gusto. It had been an unforgettable week and the Lord had been in our midst and had been gracious. And so we sang, 'Thine be the glory, risen, conquering Son'.[28]

Grand Tour of Scotland

A punishing programme of engagements lay ahead. He served his own church for one Sunday a month, but apart from holidays he devoted the other Sundays to the service of the Union. It was his aim to visit all the churches in what he called his 'Grand Tour of Scotland' and this could be done only by preaching in different churches morning and evening and asking churches to arrange joint meetings on Saturdays or Sundays. His schedule from 9 November to 14 December was given in *Focus* under the ironical heading 'Keeping up with Mr Barber'—as if anyone could! Twenty-five different churches are mentioned, including a Saturday rally and one Sunday's services at East Kilbride.[29]

Peter gave some early 'presidential Impressions' in the January 1970 *Focus*. He thanked the East Kilbride congregations for their prayerfulness: his first two months of presidential service had been most encouraging, but the 'one major snag' was his 'enforced absence from East Kilbride'. To remedy this he decided to have a 'vestry hour' one night a week at the East Mains church and to try to get round all the homes of the membership in the next few months.[30] This proved impossible, but in the months after his presidential year he carried out systematic visitation of all the members area by area.[31]

The centenary year was the central one of the three-year programme of Simultaneous Evangelism ('the Year of Proclamation'). Throughout the winter of 1969–70 visitation was carried out, followed in March and

---

[27] *SBM* (November 1969), 7.

[28] *Focus* (November 1969), 2.

[29] *Focus* (November 1969), 8.

[30] *Focus* (January 1970), 1-2.

[31] *Focus* (October 1971), 1.

April by campaigns. Most of the evangelists were ministers and laymen from the denomination, numbering around sixty. Peter said that one of the highlights of his presidential year was the conference held for the evangelists in Gean House, Alloa, in November 1969. He himself undertook two of the campaigns: in Granton Baptist Church, Edinburgh, (14-22 March 1970) and Downfield, later renamed St Kilda Road, Dundee (27 March–5 April).

The climax of this phase of the programme was the largest ever gathering of Baptists in Scotland: the All Scotland Rally at the Ice Rink in Paisley on Saturday 25 April 1970. Over 4,000 attended. Two prominent Christians who addressed the rally were Mr Edward (Teddy) Taylor, at that time MP for Cathcart, and Dr Edwin Kerr, Principal of the Paisley College of Technology. The main speaker was Andrew MacRae. In his President's remarks Peter affirmed: 'This massive demonstration of our togetherness is in itself a witness and a thanksgiving to God for His blessing on our hundred years of united service.' A souvenir edition of the Glasgow *Evening Citizen* was issued for the occasion, with a front page devoted to it, with the banner headline 'CENTURY OF DEVOTION'. Peter contributed an evangelistic piece and is described as 'the driving force behind the Simultaneous Evangelism Campaign', though no doubt he would have wanted to give full credit to the Office Bearers and the Evangelistic Committee.

In April he spoke at the Scottish Baptist Ministers' Fellowship Annual Conference at 'Piersland', Troon, and represented the Union at the BUGBI Assembly in London. In May he was a delegate at the Denominational Conference of the BUGBI at Swanwick and attended the Church of Scotland Assembly in Edinburgh, including the Garden Party in the Palace of Holyroodhouse.

At the East Kilbride church anniversary social reception on Monday 1 June he was presented with an academic robe and hood, a gift from the whole church. He admitted that this was one of the rare occasions when he was speechless! He had previously borrowed a robe and hood for his special engagements and thanked the fellowship as he was now able to return them to the 'kind lender'.[32] At the end of June he attended the BMS General Committee, which met in Dundee for the first time.

In September Carluke Baptist Church moved to a building that had belonged to the original Secession Church and Peter officiated at its opening for Baptist worship on 12 September. A few days later the EBF Council met in Glasgow, as Andrew MacRae was taking up the Presidency of the Federation at this time.[33] Peter was able to take part in the reception—he gave the address of welcome—before embarking the next

[32] *Focus* (June–July 1970), 7; (August), 6.
[33] 18-21 September 1970. This was the first EBF Council to be held in Scotland.

day on an eight day tour of the north, visiting Orkney, Shetland, Caithness and the Moray coast.

The presidential year came to an end at the Assembly in Adelaide Place, Glasgow, in October. In *Focus* James Murdoch reported:

> Mr Barber was warmly thanked for his splendid leadership during the Centenary Year, a tribute justly made, for surely his service to his own church as well as to the denomination is an outstanding example of sacrificial stewardship.

He then quoted the text that was exemplified in all Peter's ministry: 'If anyone will come after Me, let him deny himself and take up his cross daily and follow me' (Luke 9:23).[34]

Past President

Two events Peter took part in as Past President had more significance for him than anyone realized at the time. First was the opening of Church House (known later as Baptist House, and at present as Resource House). The offices of the Union were transferred from West Regent Street in the centre of Glasgow to 14 Aytoun Road, a villa in a spacious area of Pollokshields, two miles from the centre on the south side. Andrew MacRae had suggested this move. John D. Arton, the Building Advisory Convener, and Robert Rankin, the Union's Architect, had done sacrificial work on the project. At an opening service for this 'New Church House' in Pollokshields and Titwood Parish Church on Saturday 9 January 1971 Peter led in prayer and when afterwards a large crowd gathered at the door of the House the new President, James Webster, led in prayer and Peter 'turned the key', having received it from Robert Rankin. He was to turn the key many more times as General Secretary!

The second was an all-day conference of the Office Bearers of the Baptist Unions of Great Britain, Scotland and Wales, and the BMS held in London in September 1971. This was a forerunner of the Fellowship of British Baptists, which Peter as General Secretary helped to create. It came into being shortly after his death.

In *Focus* Peter thanked the people of the East Kilbride congregations, Isobel, Fiona and Susan for their patience and support during his three years of office. He was left with very mixed feelings:

> I feel a sense of gratitude to God. It has been a very great privilege, so early in life, to share in the leadership and planning of our Union's work, to visit the Churches throughout Scotland and to see God's hand at work.

---

[34] *Focus* (November 1970), 1.

I also feel tremendously relieved. The number of hours spent on Baptist Union Committees and Baptist Union business has been almost unbelievable. As you can imagine, there have been few hours to spare once the work of our own Church and town and Association, plus interdenominational tasks have been fitted in. You can understand how I felt when I received a form from the Baptist Union the other day asking me to state on which TWO committees of the Union I now wished to serve. TWO committees. Bliss![35]

Positive Leadership

The choice of Peter at the young age of thirty-nine to be President in the Union's centenary year brought him to prominence in the denomination in a way that prepared for his later appointment as General Secretary. The East Kilbride church was not at all resentful of the time he spent for three years on Union work. He became known in all parts of the constituency because of his determination to make contact with every church. Only a few people would have had the stamina to fulfil the punishing schedule he took upon himself.

The aim to cover the whole denomination was special to the centenary, but even in normal years a great deal was expected of the President. Peter thoroughly enjoyed the busyness and the opportunities of his presidential years and was convinced that those who took the task on received the strength to perform it. However, in later years decisions were made to lighten the load and in the restructuring of the Union accepted at the October 2003 Assembly the post of President was abolished.[36]

Peter's personality and approach were such that most people admired and appreciated the gifts God had given him, but in his role as President he was confronted with opposition. The declaration of his personal faith at the start of the 1969 Assembly was his reply to strong but unfounded charges of heresy against him. The ecumenical controversy he faced in the business session was a foretaste of the long-running ecumenical question he had to face later during his General Secretaryship. He did not retaliate when falsely accused. He rose above controversy, though he felt it keenly. He rejoiced in the experience of fellowship in the corporate life of the churches and the Union and set out to give at all times positive leadership.

---

[35] *Focus* (October 1971), 1.

[36] The last President was Dr J. Brooks of Queen's Park Church, Glasgow (2002–03).

CHAPTER 9

Continuing Innovation at East Kilbride

New ideas were constantly being introduced at East Mains right to the end of Peter's time there. There was no danger of settling into a rut. Pastor and congregation were always on the lookout for fresh approaches. Rigorous and honest appraisals were made of experiments, lessons were learnt and modifications made.

A fresh look at the work and direction of East Mains was the purpose of a Congregational Conference for members and adherents entitled 'At the Cross-Roads' on Saturday 9 October 1971, when the subjects to be examined were their worship, evangelism, stewardship and fellowship. Peter reported in *Focus* that the attendance was most encouraging and those present had tackled the topics with vigour and imagination. 'It was a memorable day of fellowship and discovery and the results of it will be long with us.'[1]

Worship

A major re-structuring of the Sunday morning programme had already been introduced earlier in 1971 on the first Sunday of February. The Family Sunday School had no longer been catering for the education of the whole congregation as only a minority of adults had been attending classes. The arrangement of Sunday School at 10.15, followed by the service at 11.30, made for too long a morning and the attempt to compress the service into one hour made for rushed worship. And so the service was brought forward to 11.00; infants and toddlers were cared for in the nursery; children aged three to twelve left during the service for classes, but the young teens (twelve to fifteen), the Boys' Brigade Bible Class and the adults met at 10.00.[2] The March *Focus* reported that nearly every group had increased in number, but the adult group had been

---

[1] *SBM* (November 1971), 14.
[2] *Focus* (January 1971), pink centre pages.

much depleted.[3] The May *Focus* reported that the group was down to seven.[4] The days of the flourishing all-age Sunday School were past.

The East Mains quarterly business meeting in December 1971 decided that 'A Communion Service occupying the whole of morning service time would be tried on two Sundays as an experiment'.[5] It was a successful experiment: the full integrated communion service fulfilled a need and was continued.[6]

The last Sunday of 1971 was Boxing Day and the evening service was an informal one in the church hall. Peter Barber and Jim Hamilton experimented with a 'new form of communicating the Christian message'. Instead of a sermon they discussed together John 1:1-18 and by question and answer brought out the meaning of the passage.[7]

Evangelism

On three Sunday evenings in December 1971 all three of the congregations held an evangelistic rally in the Ballerup Hall in place of their evening services. The title for the series was 'Meet Christ at the Centre' (the Hall being part of the Civic Centre). Special choirs took part. Peter preached at the first rally; 'The Heralds', a widely travelled rhythm group (including Ian Leitch) from Edinburgh, took the second; at the third the chalk artist Robert Robertson portrayed the Christmas message in a series of lightning sketches and Andrew MacRae preached.

The Evangelistic Committee made its evaluation: 'Criticisms...were that they were too varied, too long, too few outsiders came, publicity was too sparse and they were worth a better build-up. The hall acoustics were very poor. But a great sense of fellowship and unity was felt in this all-church venture and they are worth repeating'.[8]

A further experiment was a drive-in cinema. This was first tried at the close of one series of drive-in services in the Olympia car park, but it was too noisy and brightly lit. Moreover the sun had not set by the starting time! In October 1971 films were shown on two Sundays after the evening service at 8.30 p.m. in the quieter and darker Glenburn Way car park.[9]

Peter gave a frank report: the weather had been so bad on the first evening that the drive-in cinema had been cancelled and the film was shown in the hall. 'It was providential that this was the case, the sound

---

[3] *Focus* (March 1971), 3.

[4] *Focus* (May 1971), 14.

[5] *Focus* (December 1971), 8.

[6] *Focus* (August 1972), 4.

[7] *Focus* (December 1971), 12.

[8] *Focus* (March 1972), 5.

[9] *Focus* (September 1971), 14.

quality of the film proving to be very poor.' On the second evening the technical quality of the presentation was excellent but the films had limited appeal (one appealing to the old and one to the young), the weather was unpleasant and only twenty-five cars turned up.[10] However, another attempt was made in September the following year when the Cliff Richard and Cliff Barrows film *His Land* was shown at 9.30 p.m. in the Glenburn Way car park.[11]

Youth Work

When the Glasgow Youth Rallies closed the 1967–68 series the East Kilbride young people were left in a vacuum and Peter planned to fill it. He got together with Church of Scotland colleagues, David Maclagan and G.A. Sawyers, to arrange a new series of rallies in the Moncrieff church. They were called 'Seven Twenty Seven Rallies' because they were planned to start at 7.27 p.m..[12] More than 400 young people attended the first one on Saturday 4 January 1969 and twenty-four walked to the front of the church to indicate their desire to follow Christ.[13] These rallies continued for two years.

In 1970 Peter got together the students in the East Mains Congregation for a day at the manse, talking about living the Christian life at university. At their request this was repeated in December 1971, the invitation being widened to all students and former students from the three congregations, the venue being Church House (the 'Grotto'), Maxwell Drive.

In 1972 Peter introduced a preparation course for those contemplating marriage. There were five sessions over a five-week period. This was much appreciated.[14] The following year it became a one whole day course, which was attended by nine couples and a girl whose fiancée was with the army in Germany.[15]

Farewell to East Kilbride

In April 1973 Peter accepted the call to Upton Vale, Torquay, and had to break the news to the folk at East Kilbride. In *Focus* he expressed his conviction that he was following a divine mandate:

---

[10] *Focus* (November 1971), centre page 4.
[11] *Focus* (August 1972), 8.
[12] *Record* (December 1968), 5.
[13] *Record* (January 1969), 9.
[14] *Focus* (March 1972), 12; (August), 4.
[15] *Focus* (December 1972), 11.

'I being in the way, the Lord led me.'

With these words Abraham's servant described, with a sense of wonder, his experience of the guidance of God. In each detail he had seen the hand of God at work in his quest for a wife for Isaac.

Such has been our own experience in the matter of the call that has come to us to go to the Upton Vale Baptist Church in Torquay, Devon.

These eighteen years in East Kilbride have been memorable and happy years. As a family we have rejoiced in the warm friendliness and appreciation of the Church. We have been constantly filled with thanksgiving at the way the Lord has blessed and prospered the work far beyond our deserving or imagining. It certainly will not be easy to leave.[16]

Jim Murdoch found it hard to believe that Mr Barber would not be involved in the twentieth birthday celebrations of the church the following year and summed up his ministry:

To come straight from college to be the first permanent minister of a new church and give 18 years inspired and dedicated leadership is remarkable by any standard. To see the small group to which he came in 1955 grow and blossom out into three congregations by 1973 is something not given to many. But then probably few men would have had such faith and vision as to send out part of his 'flock' to 'pastures new' on two separate occasions.[17]

On his last Sunday morning (26 August) Peter showed the children a model aeroplane and pointed out that it was like a non-Christian: it did not know where it was going, it had no power and no-one in control. He flew the plane into the congregation and the boy who caught it was able to keep it. In his sermon on 'The Fellowship of the Holy Spirit' he referred to the story of Elijah at Mount Carmel: it was not enough to lay the sticks on the altar—to organize. The fire must fall. 'The Spirit says: "Come to Christ. Come into partnership with me".'

In the evening he testified to the reality of the Lord's Prayer in his life: it was a touchstone for the Christian way—and for all prayer. He spoke on 'Hallowed be Thy Name; Thy Kingdom come; Thy will be done.'[18]

About 400 people attended the farewell social the following day in the Ballerup Hall, which was chaired by Peter Blackwood, who gave a witty but full history of the church, its minister and his wife. Andrew MacRae (as General Secretary of the Union) inspired the gathering with a sermon

---

[16] *Focus* (May 1973), 1.
[17] *Focus* (June–July 1973), 1.
[18] *Focus* (September 1973), 3.

on 'I thank my God whenever I think of you' (Philippians 1:3, New English Bible).

The *Focus* report says, 'All present were aware of the power of the Holy Spirit among us and far from being a sorrowful occasion, it was an extremely happy evening.'[19] Peter and Isobel were grateful for that. In his final *Focus* letter Peter wrote:

> It had been our hope and prayer that our Farewell Gathering would not be a mournful, backward-looking occasion—and it did not turn out to be so. Seldom have we laughed more, as so many humorous asides were woven into the evening. We were glad this was so, for above all else our years in East Kilbride have been very happy years, full of fun, and it was right that they should end thus. Indeed it was just because the evening together had been so happy and natural that Isobel and I were able to do what at first we thought might have been impossible—namely, to meet you individually at the door of the Hall and bid you farewell.[20]

On Tuesday night Peter took the dog for a walk and wandered into and out of the church grounds in the darkness, giving thanks for the privilege of ministering there for so long.[21] On Wednesday afternoon the Barber family set out for the South, completing their journey the next day.

[19] *Focus* (September 1973), 5.
[20] *Focus* (September 1973), 1.
[21] *Focus* (September 1973), 2.

CHAPTER 10

Contrast at Upton Vale

Following the Call

And so Peter Barber's pioneering work at East Kilbride finally came to an end after eighteen and a half years. It was followed by nearly seven years of ministry in a large, well-known and well established church on the south coast of England.

There had been previous attempts by churches both in Scotland and in England to prise him away and he and Isobel knew the day would come to leave East Kilbride. The folk at Upton Vale, Torquay, convinced him — at their second attempt — that he was the man of God's choice for them.

Not long after the Rev. Dr Raymond Brown had left Upton Vale in the summer of 1971 to become a tutor at Spurgeon's College, Peter was invited to meet the deacons. They knew of his reputation through the *Baptist Times* and other reports. One of the deacons, Don Crocker, and his wife Vera took the opportunity of a holiday in Scotland to go and hear him at East Mains: they came back with a good report. As a result of the interview the deacons asked him to preach with a view to the pastorate, but he felt it was not right to leave East Kilbride at a time when the third congregation at Calderwood had recently been formed and the two ministers at Calderwood and Westwood needed his further support.

However, he was booked to speak at the 141st church anniversary meetings in March 1973. It is quite usual for Upton Vale to look two years ahead in the planning of church anniversaries. The time approached and the church had not been able to agree on another man to be their pastor. The conviction that Peter Barber was the man was re-affirmed by the deacons and he was now prepared to consider the possibility.

He met the deacons again. It was a daunting interview, with Jack Harmer, church secretary and headmaster of Torquay Boys' Grammar School, in the chair. Jack was a disciplinarian, typical of headmasters of his time, and the candidate must have felt like a schoolboy again! But all the deacons were so impressed by his sincerity and humility that they had no doubt in recommending his name to the church.[1] Their unanimous resolution was voted upon by the church meeting on Tuesday 10 April 1973. There were 200 in favour, seven against and ten abstentions.

His letter of acceptance reveals that Peter's motivation in making the move was faithful obedience to the conviction that this was the call of God. Part of it reads:

Never have my wife and I been surer of anything being God's will than that we should come to Torquay to serve you.

We are glad that this is so in the light of the immense challenge the pastorate poses. We are very conscious of the great tradition of the Church and the outstanding ability of the men who have formerly served you. The prospect of following in such a succession appals us. We feel like saying, 'Who is sufficient for these things?'

We can only answer, 'Our sufficiency is of God.' Because He has called we feel sure He can equip, provided we walk humbly with Him.[2]

It was an enormous wrench for the whole family to leave East Kilbride and go so far away. His mother felt it very keenly. Her sister Jessie in Kyle of Lochalsh had a phone call from her one morning. It was most unusual for her to phone at that time of day, so Jessie asked instantly: 'What's wrong?' 'Peter's leaving, going down to Torquay', Nellie said.[3]

Peter described the situation of the Upton Vale church for the East Kilbride folk:

In terms of size it has just over 500 members and the building can seat 800. Many of the members are retired people, and many of them young people, with a fair number of very able middle-aged people in between. In terms of evangelistic opportunity, it is placed right in the centre of the town (the population of Torquay is 65,000) and is a favourite place of worship for holiday visitors. I understand that it is packed out during the holiday season. Part of the church's evangelism is a Dial-a-Message Ministry in which the minister records a two-minute telephone message for people to ring up and hear. Another feature of the church's evangelism is its 'sail-in' services (shared with the other two Baptist Churches in the town) in which a service is conducted from a boat in the harbour while holidaymakers listen on the quay-side! As a church it has been blessed with able ministers in the past; the last minister was Dr. Raymond Brown (who left in August 1971) and before him the minister was the Rev. Stanley Voke. Both these men (and those before them) exercised a teaching ministry both on the Sundays and on the Tuesdays,

---

[1] Information on Peter's call from Ken Cutts, Reg Sage, Reg Vigurs and Michael Quantick.
[2] Letter to the church secretary, Mr Jack Harmer, 15 April 1973.
[3] Information from Jessie Sutherland.

with a fair number coming from nominal churches on the Tuesday evenings. It
is also a very busy church with many organisations catering for all ages. To
help share the load an assistant minister will be appointed. It also gives every
impression of being a very happy church, with a real sense of fellowship in it
despite its size; certainly in all our dealings with the church we have found
them to be helpful and friendly.[4]

Reflecting on his two pastorates to a ministers' fraternal soon after he
returned to Scotland in 1980 Peter listed the notable contrasts between
them. He had gone from a young church in an industrial New Town in
Scotland to a church 141 years old in a well-established holiday resort in
England; from a church with many young families, no traditions and no
predecessors to a church with many retired people, many traditions and
illustrious predecessors; from what he described as a 'people-centred'
church to a 'pulpit-centred' church. There were bound to be tensions.

Over 500 people, including seventy from East Kilbride, attended the
induction on Saturday 8 September 1973. After a welcome tea in the
Torquay Assembly Hall, the service was held in the church in the evening.
The Area Superintendent, the Rev. Ralph Darvill, led the induction and
the Rev. Jim Graham[5] preached on Joshua 1:1-9, commending to the
congregation in a time of change the words of challenge, comfort and
caution contained in those verses.[6]

Settling Down

Peter gained the confidence of the people from the beginning. They saw
him as a man with authority. The fact that he wanted something done
carried weight and they were glad to comply. His first pastoral letter to
the fellowship in the church magazine, *Vision*, displays his usual facility
for letter-writing. He gets alongside his people, shows himself aware of
the culture differences from East Kilbride, admits he is likely to make
mistakes. He is aware of the traditions of Upton Vale, feels unworthy, but
is convinced of the call. He then expounds 'We make it our aim to please
Him' (2 Corinthians 5:9) with brilliant simplicity:

> This is an aim great enough and demanding enough to occupy a lifetime, yet at
> the same time down-to-earth enough to fit any and every situation. It is also an
> aim which, as I contemplate it, seems to run counter to the two other
> tendencies which spell death to effective Christian service.

---

[4] *Focus* (May 1973), 1-2.
[5] Jim Graham had been the student pastor at East Kilbride before Peter's pastorate
there. At this time he was minister of Gold Hill Baptist Church, Buckinghamshire.
[6] *Vision* (November–December 1973), 4.

The first is to please ourselves—to make our own comfort, reputation and interests come first in the choices we make. The second is to please others—to seek the praises of men rather than the approval of God.

Like every other servant of God I am subject to these temptations. Yet in this first letter to you as a congregation I want to make this my stated objective. As I come among you I make it my aim to please HIM. It is not an objective I will always reach; it is an objective for which, with the help of God, I will always strive.[7]

In the same issue there was a letter from the church secretary, Jack Harmer. He recognized that a new man had come with new ideas, but knew that he and others would not find change easy:

As we look forward to the future let us remember that the risen Lord said *'Behold I make all things new'* (Rev. 21v.5), and this will surely be the case in future. The coming of Mr. Barber means a new beginning for Upton Vale, not just a repetition of the past under new direction. The Gospel of Christ is ever the same, but times change, ideas change, people change, and this often calls for changed methods, though we must not lightly throw over what the Lord has used in the past. Our great need, then, is first to know the Lord's will and then fearlessly and in faith to put it into practice.[8]

Reflecting on his experience after four and a half years in Torquay Peter wrote:

When I first came to Devon I was told that the Devonian was conservative by nature and slow in action so that prospects of change would be limited. This I have discovered to be true only to a measure, and that given time for reflection and prayer believers in Devon are willing to be blown by the wind of change provided they are sure the wind is the wind of the Spirit.[9]

The church people were glad to welcome Peter, Isobel and the girls. Fiona was seven and Susan four when they went to Torquay. However, they all found the settling-in period difficult. In some personal remarks on the fifth anniversary of his induction Peter admitted that at first it had been 'a massive adjustment'.[10] Around the same time he wrote in *Forum*:

For ourselves as a family we did find our first eighteen months in Torquay very demanding partly because of homesickness, partly because of the enervating climate that swamped us with constant drowsiness and partly because of the

---

[7] *Vision* (September–October 1973), 3.
[8] *Vision* (September–October 1973), 4.
[9] *Forum: The Magazine of the Friends, Students and Former Students of the Baptist Theological College of Scotland* (June [1978]), [7].
[10] *Vision* (September–October 1978), 7.

adjustments we had to make in such a different situation from that which obtained in East Kilbride.[11]

Peter's accent caused problems to some of the older folk. He was happy to joke against himself, particularly about his Scottishness. When he apparently announced that his text was from the 'Book of Sam's' people thought he had discovered a new book of the Bible, but it was just his pronunciation of 'Psalms'! People were bemused by references to his 'pinkie' until he explained he meant his little finger! He found he had to refer to 'the notices' rather than 'the intimations' and remember to 'ask after' people rather than 'ask for' them.[12]

The Scottish motif was constantly used, particularly on social occasions. Peter and Isobel arranged Scottish evenings for the Baptist Women's League, and other general fellowship events had a Scottish flavour.

Well known names from Scotland appeared in the church's programme: Andrew MacRae spoke at the church anniversary in 1975. Bruce Milne (then a tutor at Spurgeon's College) and some of his students conducted a 'Meet Jesus' mission later that year. George Young (formerly a missionary in China and then minister of Adelaide Place Baptist Church, Glasgow) paid two visits to the church. Bill Freel (then minister of Duke Street Baptist Church, Richmond)[13] was the guest speaker at the 1980 church anniversary and the Scottish Baptist Youth Choir sang on Sunday 13 July that year.

Isobel took two years to settle and feel at home. She was highly valued for her caring approach and people found her to be as approachable as Peter. She was a great encourager and took part in all three women's groups: the Baptist Women's League (BWL), the BWL Young Wives and the Women's Meeting. She also worked hard for the Girls' Brigade company and was appreciated for the guidance she gave to the officers and helpers. Peter and Isobel had a very close partnership in ministry, although Isobel preferred to have a low profile. In Torquay they were seen as a team and tremendously loved.

Peter was fully convinced that his going to Upton Vale was the call of God, though the pain of the transition and their distance from relatives was inevitable for the whole family. Peter himself soon threw his energies into the busyness of ministry and faced the new challenge with confidence. He brought much from his past in Edinburgh and East Kilbride, but adapted to a very different situation and was open to learn from it.

---

[11] *Forum* (June [1978]), [7].

[12] *Forum* (June [1978]), [6-7].

[13] Bill Freel had previously been minister of Rattray Street, Dundee, and Viewfield, Dunfermline. Later he was minister of Castle Street, Inverness (1984–95).

CHAPTER 11

Leader and Innovator

It is more appropriate to describe Peter's years at Upton Vale under the various aspects of his ministry than to give a chronological account. Reflecting on Peter's understanding of his ministerial role is tantamount to taking a course in pastoral theology! In this chapter we shall consider his approach as a leader, his building on the previous foundations and the ideas he introduced from his previous experience and elsewhere. In chapter 12 we shall explore the many ways in which he fulfilled the basic tasks of a pastor–teacher.

Assistant Pastors

Peter had been at Upton Vale for nearly eleven months when he was joined by an assistant minister, David Hewitt, who had just finished his course of training at Spurgeon's College. He came from Purley (an outer London suburb, previously in Surrey), and was married to Katheryn Foster at Newhaven, Sussex, on 13 July 1974. Three weeks later he was ordained and inducted at Upton Vale on Saturday 3 August by Dr Bruce Milne, who also gave the address.[1]

At first it was not at all easy for David and Katheryn to adjust to marriage and all the demands of ministry at the same time, but Peter and Isobel were a great help to them and the two men did work happily together. They met every week on Tuesday mornings, when they bounced ideas off each other and discussed what they were going to preach. The system they used for ministerial visitation was suggested by David: Peter was very happy to accept it. Peter had Mondays off, David had Wednesdays off. David had a particular remit with the youth, but not exclusively.

David remembers Peter's remarkable energy: he worked from seven in the morning to midnight; he would do pastoral calls after evening meetings. David tried to keep up with him at first, but soon realized his mistake! He never got the impression that Peter was hard on himself: he just woke up in the morning with such enthusiasm for the day and wanted

---

[1] *Vision* (July–August 1974), 8, 12; (September–October), 12-13.

to get on with it. His enthusiasm was apparent in everything he did. He once showed David round Edinburgh and gave so much information with so much verve that he could easily have got a job with the Scottish Tourist Board!

After three and a half years David, Katheryn and their young son Timothy moved on to Counterslip Baptist Church, Bristol. The time had come for him to develop his own ministry. A farewell service was held on 11 March 1978 in the church hall. Seventy people from Upton Vale attended the induction in Bristol on Saturday 1 April, when Peter gave an address on 'Partnership: in the Gospel, in Grace, in the Spirit, in Affliction'.[2] The Hewitts had been deeply appreciated by the Upton Vale church. David left Bristol in 1990 and served as Churches Secretary of the Evangelical Alliance before moving to Andover Baptist Church, Hampshire, in 1992, where he is still serving.

Peter became sole pastor again for nearly sixteen months before Nicholas (Nick) Mercer was inducted as assistant minister on Saturday 30 June 1979. He too came straight from Spurgeon's College, where he had been chairman of the student body. When his Principal, Dr Raymond Brown, had first suggested Upton Vale to him he was reluctant, but after a visit to see Peter in the autumn of 1978 he knew that he wanted to work with and learn from him. In January 1979 the church unanimously issued a call to him for a term of about three years. Peter wrote: 'The final heartening news that Nick Mercer felt the Lord was leading him to accept the call raised a Doxology in many hearts—not least my own!'[3]

Nick was born and brought up in Shoreham-by-Sea, Sussex, and became a Christian through the ministry of the Baptist church there. He studied science at Cambridge for four years and taught at Lancing College, an independent school in West Sussex, for two years before embarking on four years at Spurgeon's. He was ordained by his Principal in Shoreham Baptist Church on Sunday 3 June. The act of induction on 30 June was led by the Rev. John R. Blanshard, Secretary of the Devon and Cornwall Baptist Association, and the preacher was the Rev. Peter D. Manson, tutor at Spurgeon's College. A greeting from the students was given at the tea afterwards by Steve Gaukroger, who said that Nick had had a great influence in the College and had led the students in spirituality and growth in Christian things.[4]

What no-one was to know at the induction was that the partnership between Peter and Nick was to last only eleven months before Peter's return to Scotland, but Nick has described that time as 'formative and

---

[2] *Vision* (May–June 1978), 6-7.
[3] *Vision* (March–April 1979), 4.
[4] *Vision* (May–June 1979), 6; (September–October 1979), 4-5. The Rev. Stephen Gaukroger was President of the BUGB in 1994 and is currently senior pastor of Gold Hill Baptist Church, Buckinghamshire.

memorable. His kind humour and his fatherly encouragement stand out vividly in my mind.'[5] In a letter to Isobel he wrote, 'I count myself so privileged to have had such a mentor at the start of my ministry... He was wise and godly and I cannot think of anything I found difficult or annoying. In every way he was the pattern for me of Christian ministry... It is difficult to express in words all I feel and owe to Peter, but I hope that through my ministry I can pay tribute to him and honour Christ whom he served so faithfully.'[6]

Nick continued to serve at Upton Vale with Peter's successor, David Coffey, until 1983, when he left to pursue research at London Bible College. He later joined the teaching staff and served as Assistant Principal. On leaving the College he became an Anglican priest.

Church Secretaries

Just over a year into Peter's pastorate Jack Harmer stepped down as church secretary, a post he had held for fifteen years, and became a life deacon. Peter wrote, 'In all my dealings with God's servant I have found him courteous, considerate and competent. He did all he could to make my settling into a new pastorate as easy a transition as possible. In all his busyness he never lost sight of spiritual priorities and always sought his utmost for God's highest.'[7]

Ken Cutts, who had been Jack Harmer's assistant, succeeded him. He is the son of the Rev. Abraham Cutts, who served as pastor of Upton Vale from 1934–41. Ken is a most gracious man who worked in happy partnership with Peter, fully appreciating his spiritual influence and giving him his complete support, sometimes in situations of great difficulty.

The Deacons

The composition of the diaconate was static and it took time for younger men to be elected to it. Women were not eligible in Peter's time at Upton Vale. The meetings were formal occasions, with the men sitting round in a big circle in the vestry. Peter chaired them all. Ken Cutts admired his chairmanship: 'Peter had a quick grasp of situations and of the main points of a discussion. He was an excellent summarizer. He could sum up a two hour discussion in four sentences!'

The deacons examined all aspects of the church's life and stewardship carefully. They considered the roles of the various organizations and

---

[5] From a letter to the author, 1 May 1997.
[6] From a letter to Isobel Barber, 23 August 1995.
[7] *Vision* (January–February 1975), 5.

asked whether any should be trimmed. They used to go through the membership list, discuss problems and offer financial help to those in special need. There was no eldership, but deacons gifted in certain areas were able to help with particular pastoral problems. Sometimes during the deacons' meetings Peter would introduce a time of prayer.

One idea that Peter soon brought in from his practice at East Kilbride was the 'Deacons' Day Conference'. The first was in March 1974 at Charter House, Teignmouth.[8] He used it to discuss strategy:

> One thing which troubled me on settling into Upton Vale, this 'preaching-centre' of the South West (as many have called it), was the feeling that while the church was well-geared to serve the evangelical holiday-maker, it seemed unrelated, largely speaking, to the pressing needs of the community. But how were things to change, if change they should?
>
> It was this issue I shared with my deacons when we held our first ever day-retreat. Each aspect of the church's life was explored that day—its worship, fellowship, stewardship and outreach—and the findings were carefully listed then shared with the church. These findings became a kind of 'blueprint' for much we have developed together (not without a few 'growing-pains') as we have sought to change the church from a passive audience of Sunday listeners to an active fellowship of caring witnesses.[9]

The Deacons' Conference became an annual event. They included a lot of fun, but the programme was always balanced and uplifting. The morning would be spent in a teaching or devotional session and the afternoon was taken up with thinking about the future. It was not used for simply catching up with routine business.

The deacons discussed whether to introduce elders. In the end there was unanimous agreement on a compromise: from April 1978 the deacons were divided into two groups: 'Pastoral and Fellowship', 'Fabric and Finance'. There were two deacons' meetings a month: the first began with a brief combined session but then divided. The two groups reported back to the second meeting.

Pastoral work was also carried out by a 'caring team'. This went back to Stanley Voke's time and Peter encouraged it. The members of the team were gifted visitors, who each had a small group of people to visit.

Controversies

Peter's ministry is remembered as one without major controversy, but there were problem people and difficult issues that exercised him and the

[8] *Vision* (March–April 1974), 4.
[9] *Forum: the Magazine of the Friends, Students and Former Students of the Baptist Theological College of Scotland* (June [1978]), [7].

deacons. Sometimes he felt frustrated when he was up against theological intransigence.

Church unity caused some heated arguments in deacons' and church meetings. There were stormy church meetings over the World Council of Churches' policy on arms. In November 1976 the annual church meeting discussed the Churches' Unity Commission propositions: it accepted five of them with qualifications and rejected five. The majority agreed 'that sympathetic concern be expressed in our official reply, but that theological and doctrinal issues cannot be compromised'.[10]

Peter tackled the issue of Roman Catholics head-on in the church magazine at a time when much publicity was being given to the visits of Pope John Paul II to Southern Ireland and the United States. Peter was complimentary to the Pope himself:

> Fair is fair. Let tribute be paid where tribute is due. Pope John Paul II has given a new face to the papacy; he has brought it from the musty depths of the Vatican out to the people of the Church. He is a very gracious man who exudes warmth and love to people of all classes. His speeches have been eloquent, passionate, relevant and courageous. Indeed, in the heat of the moment, many of us even dared to hope that his appeal might be heeded by the IRA and might mark the beginning of the end of violence in Ireland.

But he went on to point out that in recent pronouncements on Mary and on the Mass the Pope had been re-iterating the traditional doctrines of Roman Catholicism:

> and to what he says we must answer—he is wrong, he has departed from the faith of the apostles and the teaching of the Scriptures and is misleading the people. Salvation is by FAITH in Christ ALONE, the ONLY Head of the Church.

> Let us be in no doubt about it. It is our duty, as Christians, to voice such a protest if we are to 'guard the faith'; and no amount of religious euphoria or goodwill must prevent us from doing so. By all means let us seek friendly relationships with Roman Catholics, and by all means let us take every opportunity to discuss the Faith with them; and by all means let us be willing to co-operate with them where it does not compromise the truth of the Gospel. But let us not be deluded into thinking that the Roman Catholic Church in its official pronouncements is so very different theologically from what it was in Luther's day. And let us not be unfaithful to Christ, to our Roman Catholic friends or to others, by failing to spell out the Biblical Gospel as God has entrusted it to us.[11]

---

[10] Minutes of the meeting; cf. *Vision* (January–February 1977), 3. See The Churches Unity Commission, *Ten Propositions* (London: British Council of Churches, 1976).

[11] *Vision* (November–December 1979), 1-2.

The question of divorce caused a lot of heart-searching for the deacons. Guidelines were drawn up regarding divorce and re-marriage. In certain circumstances re-marriage of divorced persons was allowed, but each case was considered by the deacons. The subject of divorce and office was discussed at the Deacons' Conference in 1977, when two deacons presented the issues. The recommendation that divorced men should not be eligible to become deacons was accepted by a large majority at the church meeting. Peter presented a paper on the issues of divorce and re-marriage for the local fraternal, which many ministers found very helpful.

The charismatic movement had some effect on Upton Vale in these years. Peter was cautious about it and met the challenge of charismatic doctrine head-on by producing Bible study notes on 1 Corinthians. In 1978 there was a small group holding a regular charismatic meeting. Peter, with his church secretary and another deacon, met with them and reported to the deacons, who felt that 'whilst certain needs were worthy of consideration and certain expression of warmth and openness in worship and prayer was worthy of encouragement, the need for firm and clear pastoral leadership and control was vital'.[12]

In his book *The Power of Love*, David Hewitt recalls that Peter loved Wesley's hymns but on one occasion expressed disagreement with one of the lines in 'Lord from whom all blessings flow'. The third verse begins: 'Sweetly may we all agree, touched with softest sympathy'. Peter's suggested alternative was: 'Sweetly may we disagree'! He knew that differences of opinion were inevitable, but they could be handled with love and acceptance.[13]

Ken Cutts describes Peter as 'a diplomat, a healer rather than a stirrer-upper. He was absolutely sincere, but without doing despite to his own convictions he was able to bring an accord to most situations. He had a very sensitive heart but a harder skin.' Nick Mercer paid this tribute to Peter's skill:

He taught me so much, without patronising me, and I still find myself at times in difficult personality/management problems thinking of how Peter would have handled it. And I know he would have been firm & uncompromising, yet patient and willing to be thought of as 'weak'; because he was so strong and had a great inner composure & trust in the Lord. He displayed the meekness of Christ.[14]

---

[12] Minutes of deacons' meeting, 3 May 1978.
[13] David Hewitt, *The Power of Love* (Basingstoke: Marshall Pickering, 1987), 35.
[14] From a letter to Isobel Barber, 23 August 1995.

Fellowship

Peter was keen to encourage arrangements for effective pastoral care of the congregation and means by which members could get to know each other better. At the beginning of 1975 the Fellowship Steward Scheme was re-organized: appointed stewards were responsible for welcoming and getting to know and care for those who usually sat in particular areas of the church. Further, the Torquay district was divided into twelve areas with a deacon and his wife responsible for each area, and another married couple who were members assigned to each area. Regular visitation was carried out on this basis. Then, in the early months of that year six receptions, called 'At Homes', were held in the church hall for members in the various areas. The aim was to have relaxed fellowship and an opportunity to learn more about Upton Vale. The programme was the same for each one and included a Sankey sing-along, slides and a quiz. Peter wrote: 'In a congregation of our size it is so vital that we should work at getting to know each other that we may really be one large Family in Jesus Christ.'[15] Similar receptions were held for groups of new members, and a later series of 'At Homes' was organized on an alphabetical basis.

Peter also started house groups. There were about twelve, with between eight and twelve people in each. They met once a month on Thursdays. On Saturday mornings Peter gathered the leaders together at the manse for a prayer and study session. He would go through the questions that might arise in the discussions and the leaders found this very valuable. Every three months several housegroups got together for a social evening with games—and the wearing of tartan!

Organizations

The church had many organizations and activities for different groups of people and Peter related to each of them in various ways. He fully encouraged David Hewitt and the young people. The Young People's Fellowship was very active. It arranged house parties at Haldon Hall, Exmouth, and promoted youth missions. A 'cottage' adjacent to the church had been used as the caretaker's residence, but it badly needed renovation. When another house was purchased for the caretaker, the 'cottage' was left free, so on Peter's initiative it was converted into a young people's fellowship centre. A coffee bar for contacting teenagers was constructed in it for Mission '77.

---

[15] *Vision* (January–February 1975), 5.

The Girls' Brigade and Boys' Brigade were strong. The BB celebrated its jubilee in 1974[16] and the GB in 1979.[17] Peter paid visits to BB camps and took part in spot inspections.

One new activity that Peter introduced was the 'Friendship Centre', better described as 'the Monday Luncheon Club'. It began in September 1975 and continues to this day. The plan was to offer a maximum of fifty meals each Monday to elderly and lonely folk. Half of the places were offered to the Torbay Council for Voluntary Services so that the church would be serving the community as well as the congregation. Mrs Anne Warren became the leader of it. The cost of the lunch was 25p to membership card holders. The first meal merited a story and picture in both the *Torquay Times* and the *Herald Express*. The project arose from Peter's concern for the practical aspects of fellowship and community care, but there were some members at the time who did not see this as the church's work.

The church carried out a community survey to help it cater better for people in the area. Later, as General Secretary in Scotland, Peter used his experience in Torquay to commend the idea:

> We discovered that 33% of the residents of the town were retired and that 33% of the congregation were also pensioners. Yet we did not have one aspect of ministry or evangelism in our Church's programme geared for retired people. When this was changed I tell you we began to see several breakthroughs for Christ in Torquay we never dreamed possible.

> It was the same in terms of ministry to families. Being a downtown Church we assumed that other than shops and businesses the remaining houses in the area were almost entirely occupied by elderly people, many of them widows or widowers. A community survey of our immediate neighbourhood undertaken in house-to-house visitation soon exploded the fallacy.

> To our surprise we discovered that house after house had been bought by young couples as their first home because they could not afford the more expensive houses in the suburbs. We were surrounded by mums and toddlers yet we had no play group facilities and a Sunday Church programme not at all geared to suit young families.

> When, after discussion and prayerful planning, this was changed we began to make inroads into the community where formerly there had only been cul-de-sacs.[18]

---

[16] *Vision* (November–December 1974), 4-5.

[17] *Vision* (January–February 1979), 6.

[18] *SBM* (October 1983), 10.

Stewardship

Peter had been at Upton Vale for a year when he advocated a stewardship campaign to the deacons and put BUGBI literature on the subject into their hands. In a 'From the Manse' letter in the church magazine he explained the need to see stewardship as applying to the whole of life and the whole of a church. In particular it applied to church property, entrusted to them by the Lord to be used in ways the Lord appointed. 'Might it be that our doors need to be much more open to the community? And what about Hotel Adyar, which becomes ours in the autumn of 1976?' This hotel adjoined the church building and when its lease ran out it reverted to the ownership of the church.

He went on to claim: 'The love the Holy Spirit has put into our hearts is also part of our stewardship' and then directly put the challenge of the financial situation:

> to maintain our Church property to the proper standard and to make necessary improvements we will require an additional £6,000 per annum for the next seven years (and this is at present-day prices!). This means nothing less than a doubling of our present income in our regular Sunday giving. I know this sounds impossible, especially when it is remembered that not a few in the congregation are either retired or on fixed incomes, and many are giving already to the limit. I can only assume, however, that if the Lord has presented this challenge to us as a congregation, then the resources must be within the congregation to meet it—but only if those of us who can do so re-assess our stewardship in giving to Upton Vale and are prepared for some further sacrifice.

He then pointed out that another vital part of stewardship was the gospel itself and gave details of the evangelistic work planned for the next few months. The conclusion of his letter takes us to the basis of his appeal and to the heart of his own motivation:

> But where does all true stewardship begin? Not within a Church Hall, or through a Church programme, or before a Financial Statement, or with an Evangelistic Campaign. It starts at the Cross with the realisation of the incalculable debt we owe to the suffering Son of God. Seeing His 'love so amazing, so divine' we cannot but first give ourselves to the Lord; and, having given ourselves, all else follows. At that Cross and there alone is true Christian stewardship initiated, and only there is it endlessly inspired.

May God bring us all close to that Cross day by day till nothing the Lord ever asks of us even begins to feel like a sacrifice.

Yours in the bonds of Calvary,

Peter H. Barber.[19]

He took up the theme again later in the year under the ingenious heading 'LET'S TURN ON THE TAP', TAP being an acrostic for 'Time, Abilities, Possessions'. On the possessions of the affluent West he quoted the dictum of Jesus: 'To whom much is given of him will much be required.'[20]

> But what is required of us now, many are asking, in the light of our possessions? Are we meant simply to give them all up and live like paupers, or can we selfishly enjoy them? The answer, in Bible terms, lies in neither extreme. What we are to do is to recognise that they are not ours first and foremost, but the Lord's and that they are only ours on trust, entrusted to us that we might care for them and make use of them as our Lord directs in the service of our fellows and ourselves.[21]

There was some resistance among the deacons to certain aspects of normal stewardship campaigns and modifications were made. The grand meal by outside caterers in a non-church setting was scaled down to become a Stewardship Fellowship Evening in November 1975 in the church hall, with 'a pleasant buffet supper' arranged by the catering committee. All members were invited. The stewardship response forms were given out to those who attended, and handed or sent to the other members. They were available to adherents on request. They were to be placed in prepared boxes at the church within two weeks.

The form suggested twenty-three specific offers of service and twelve specific requests that might be made. It had a space for any suggestion that would improve church life and made an appeal to members to ask themselves how faithful they were in daily devotions and church attendance. The deacons had resolved that finance should be mentioned on the list 'in terms of responsibility to the Lord, but not to be pursued in terms of written commitment to the Church'.[22] The form encouraged regular and sacrificial giving and suggested: 'You might find it helpful to write down an exact amount on a piece of paper which you can keep somewhere private as a reminder.'

---

[19] *Vision* (May–June 1975), 3-4.
[20] Luke 12:48.
[21] *Vision* (September–October), 3-4.
[22] Minutes of deacons' meeting, 11 August 1975.

1. Vacation work in a road gang, July 1951.
Peter Barber is third on the left

2. The student evangelist

3. Andrew MacRae,
Ronnie Scott and
Peter Barber as
young men

Joe, Jean, Wilf,
Peter, Ronnie
and Helen early
in the 1980s

5. *An early deacons' court, at East Kilbride. Peter Blackwood is on Peter Barber's right*

6. *Deacons' court at East Mains, 1973. Alex Calder is on Peter's left*

Wedding day: Friday 13 August 1965   *8. Preaching from the East Mains pulpit*

Peter and Isobel with Fiona and Susan shortly before leaving East Kilbride in 1973

10. *Evangelist at Downfield (St Kilda Road), Dundee, during the simultaneous evangelism of 1970. Those seated: Lord Provost, Rev. Douglas Hutcheon (minister), Rev Jim Powrie (Church of Scotland)*

11. *Ordination and Induction of Jim Hamilton at Calderwood, 7 August 1971. Principal R.E.O. White, Rev. Alex Hardie, Mr James McDonald (secretary), Peter Barber, Pauline and Jim Hamilton, Rev. Jim Murdoch*

12. With the deacons of Upton Vale, Torquay, 1973. Ken Cutts is in front of the window

13. In the pulpit of Upton Vale, Torquay, with members of the team from the Movement for World Evangelisation, 1977

14. Peter and Isobel at the EBF Congress in Budapest, July 1989, when he became President of the Federation

15. In Glasgow's George Square with an Argentinian couple who were delegates to the BWA Youth Conference, July 1988

16. With Mrs Irmgard Claas at the Brandenburg Gate, Berlin, Sunday 13 April 1991

7. The leaders of the Foreign Mission Board and the EBF meeting in Hamburg, Germany, September 1992. The result was the 'Hamburg Agreement' on the Rüschlikon Seminary

8. Karl Heinz Walter (standing, extreme left) and his wife Traute (seated, third from left) with the leaders of the Baptist Union of Scotland and their wives in the Barbers' home, summer 1990

19. With his son Colin
(about 14) and a dog
called Peg on the hill
above Kiloran Bay on
the Island of Colonsay,
around 1990

20. Portrait taken by Stephen
Younger at the first
ministers' prayer day at Perth,
1 September 1993

21. With granddaughter
Zoe at Kiloran Bay on
the Island of Colonsay,
July 1994

Peter was delighted at the level of response: 233 forms were handed in.[23] The treasurer was able to report the following March that total giving over the year was up by 32%.[24]

Evangelism

Peter encouraged the church to engage in a busy programme of evangelistic activity. Door-to-door visitation had been introduced in Raymond Brown's ministry and this was extended. Peter enthused people to participate in visitation and literature distribution, which were carried out systematically. There was a regular pattern of door-to-door work through the year. At Christmas groups went carol singing in the areas that had been visited and gave out invitations to Christmas services.

Before the visitation week in September 1979 Peter appealed in the church magazine for more support by using a recently reported incident. An eleven-year-old boy was being swept out to sea on an airbed at St Ives in Cornwall. Because holiday-makers were occupying the part of the beach that should have been kept clear and refused at first to move, the life-boat launch that should have taken less than two minutes took ten. Fortunately the crew were in time to save the boy.

> Soon it will be September 24th, 25th, 26th and 27th. Each evening another rescue mission will be launched and another crew will go out to reach those in peril. It will not be to boys on airbeds at sea but to families inland in their homes. We will call it a mission of visitation but in ultimate terms it will be a rescue mission as we carry the Good News of Jesus to those who are lost.[25]

In the next issue he expressed his pleasure at the response:

> I am happy to report that no less than 57 of our congregation undertook visitation and 30 helped with administration. We were able to make 507 new visits and 132 follow-up visits. Of those contacted 4 have asked for ministers' visits and 101 showed a definite interest and should be worth a later visit. I think you will all agree that it was a worthwhile effort. So thank you to all who took part, notably Mike and Sue Quantick who carried the weight of the administrative load.[26]

During Peter's years there were various special missions to children and young people. During the summer the church took part with other churches in a mission to overseas students studying English in Torquay,

---

[23] Minutes of Church meeting, 13 January 1976.

[24] *Vision* (May–June 1976), 5.

[25] *Vision* (September–October 1979), inside cover-1.

[26] *Vision* (November–December 1979), 4. Mike Quantick has served the BMS as an administrator at Didcot since 1989.

with some meetings held on the church premises. The early campaigns were led by Dr Keith Stokes of the Universities and Colleges Christian Fellowship (UCCF) and Christian Union students from elsewhere took part.

A mission to young people arranged by the churches in the Torbay Evangelical Fellowship was held at Upton Vale 6–14 September 1975. Bruce Milne led a team of students from Spurgeon's College. The slogan chosen was 'Meet Jesus' and it appeared all over Torquay. Peter reported: 'Without exception the 9 team members (8 brawny young men and one beautiful young lady) worked hard and harmoniously. Their work in the secondary schools has been widely praised both by staff and pupils, while their evening meetings were always marked by freshness and sincerity.' He gave full credit to David Hewitt 'for the formidable amount of thought, time and energy he put into steering the Mission through from start to finish'.[27]

The most extensive evangelistic effort for the whole church was Mission '77, which Peter masterminded. It centred on a fortnight at Easter 1977 (26 March–10 April), but the congregation had been in preparation for it for over a year and the deacons had been considering it for two years before that. Afterwards there were follow-up visits by members of the team, which came from the Movement for World Evangelisation, led by John Blanchard.

For the first part of the fortnight there were various kinds of meetings in the community, including coffee-mornings, evening house-meetings, visits to schools to address the senior pupils and visits to secular organizations. Towards the end of the fortnight, from the Wednesday of Holy Week to Easter Sunday, there were public rallies.

A year before Peter had summoned his folk to instant action:

> I wonder, are you prepared to 'get involved' right now? I am sure it will be a mistake if we think we should wait until Easter 1977 to start thrusting out in evangelism. The openings the team get then for sharing the Gospel in their own expert way will entirely depend on the degree to which we have prepared the way by making contacts and praying for the work of the Spirit in people's lives. NOW is the time to start inviting friends and neighbours into our homes, so that they will readily come to the coffee mornings and evenings in 1977; NOW is the time to start interesting colleagues and workmates in the Christian faith so that they are ready for the fuller presentation of the Gospel: NOW is the time to start praying for an opening in your place of employment, your secular club, or your neighbourhood for a special evangelistic meeting.[28]

---

[27] *Vision* (November–December 1975), 5-6.
[28] *Vision* (March–April 1976), 1-2.

Later in the year he appealed for loving unity in the church, quoting David Watson's view that 'the most crucial factor of all' in evangelistic missions is 'the depth of unity within the body of Christians'.

Does that sound an exaggeration to you? If so, perhaps you would care to reflect on two facts.

One is (from the man-ward angle) that only a loving united church is a true witness to the transforming and reconciling power of the Gospel. Where there is disunity or discord cynics can be forgiven for doubting the claim that we are 'new creatures' in Christ Jesus.

The other is (from the God-ward point of view) that it is only in a loving united church that the Holy Spirit, who is love, is free to work as He wills. Where there are conflicts and hostilities He is grieved and His freedom to work restricted.

Might I therefore suggest that we begin to prepare for the Mission now by continuing where we began on January 1st. We adopted then a church motto whose message is plain and whose challenge is inescapable—'Let us love one another for love is of God'.[29]

Peter wrote his pastoral letter for the magazine of May–June 1977 on the day the Mission started. These paragraphs were among his general reflections:

I think the Mission has also served to demonstrate the fact that, large though our membership may be, we can undertake ventures such as these together. It would be easy for us, as a Church, to think that our numbers militate against any united effort. But this is not so. We need not think of our Church as simply a large audience at Sunday services. Given imagination, organisation, and enterprise there is no reason why we should not explore at greater depths the possibilities of closer fellowship, wider service and more effective outreach. We can (and indeed we must) discover what it really means to be the Body of Christ, however large the body may be.

This further reflection I share with you, even before MISSION '77 begins...and that is that Mission as such must never stop. MISSION '77 must become MISSION '78, '79, and so on. For Mission is not, of course, meant to be the occasional effort by a specialised few on the part of a Church. Mission is meant to be the continuing effort of every member of the whole Church. Mission is presenting the whole Gospel to the whole man the whole time throughout the whole world.

MISSION '77 has, I think, rightly highlighted the task of Mission among us...and I believe this to be right, just as I see the wisdom in a shop that sells

---

[29] *Vision* (September–October 1976), inside cover, 1.

all year round having a special annual sale. There are men specially gifted for evangelism it is right for the Church to use to help intensify the effort of Mission. But this cannot, and must not, replace the untiring efforts of the whole membership to go on making known the Good News of Jesus Christ by every means at our disposal.[30]

There were disappointments in the Mission, particularly the low attendances at the public rallies, but there were lasting conversions and many contacts that were followed up. The young people had been busily involved and it proved to be a great stimulus to their varied church and evangelistic activities.

Open-air Services

There were two kinds of opportunity for open-air witness that were well established. Peter enjoyed taking part in both[31] and they continued throughout his time in Torquay. One was an open-air service on Torre Abbey Meadow, situated just across the road from the sea front. The Free Church Council had been given permission to hold the services and the Upton Vale church was responsible for the programme on three or four occasions during the summer season.

The other was the boat service, which was organized by the three Baptist churches of the town (Upton Vale, Barton and Hele). They chose weekends with high tides. The boat, with the choir, service leaders and other members, came round from the harbour to Torre Abbey sands. The steadily increasing sound of the singing was very effective and aroused interest. Tracts were given out during the service. Afterwards the boat toured the bay and circled any naval vessels that were anchored there.

Despite the major emphasis on evangelism the number of church members remained static. The figure was reviewed frequently. Shortly after Peter arrived it was 504 and just before he left it was 501, having reached a peak of 522 before going down at one point to 491. This needs to be seen against the background of the decline in the response to the gospel in Britain and Europe generally during the twentieth century. One factor militating against growth was the need of the younger people who had committed themselves to Christ and the church to move away from the area to find work.

Support for Missionaries

Upton Vale had always been a missionary-minded church and this had been one of the special emphases of Stanley Voke's ministry. Peter was

---

[30] *Vision* (May–June 1977), 2-3.
[31] *Vision* (July–August 1974), 7.

pleased to discover that 10% of the Sunday offerings was given to the support of the members who were missionaries. In his first year the church held its eighteenth Worldwide Missionary Convention, which had begun in Stanley Voke's time. These were usually held in June, over four days, and featured the work of a wide variety of missions, including contributions from the church's own missionaries. Peter was delighted that over £2,000 was given to the various societies during the convention, as it was a sign that the church was alive to its missionary responsibilities.[32]

He encouraged the members to increase their knowledge of the work and become full partners with the missionaries in the gospel. He urged them to be up-to-date in their approach to missionary service and to be aware of the actual situations missionaries were working in. He gave regular news of the church's missionaries. He himself wrote to them regularly and was deeply concerned for their needs and problems, giving love and understanding to those who had to return to Britain early when unforeseen difficulties in their situations or health problems intervened.

He was able to commend the members for their increasing interest and their practical support. In particular he commended Terry Browse, one of the tape-recording team, for a new initiative: the Overseas Christian Cassette Tapes Service.[33] Terry had discovered how many missionaries longed for Bible teaching and offered tapes of the Upton Vale church services and Bible School addresses to missionaries free of charge. The service was also available to other Christians working overseas. Encouraging comments came from all over the world and there were requests for tapes to cover children's work, ministry on special subjects, Christian music and personal messages to individuals. As the work progressed Terry had to build a sound-proof studio adjoining the bedroom in which the work started.[34]

Peter stimulated the missionary council to more imaginative approaches to the Missionary Convention. In 1976 he announced:

The exhibition stalls are to be given an overdue face-lift and the presentation promises to be different. On the Friday evening (when we are to have four 'workshops' on overseas mission) we are to have a special Zairian chicken dish and banana bread for our buffet supper and this will be followed by an amazing missionary film demonstrating the power of the Gospel in an apparently hopeless situation. On the Thursday evening the introductory meeting is also

---

[32] *Vision* (September–October 1974), 3.
[33] *Vision* (July–August 1976), 5.
[34] *Vision* (November–December 1977), 3.

to have a wholly new approach and will really give us an opportunity to meet our missionary guests.[35]

In 1977 there were events for different age groups: Friday was Young People's Day; on Saturday there were children's meetings, a tea for the elderly, films and workshops, a Nepalese meal. Peter announced details of the 1978 Convention with a typical pun:

A JAPANESE HONDA: No, I am not advertising a motorcycle or car—just introducing one of our guests at the forthcoming Missionary Convention (8th to 11th June). Rev. K. Honda, who has been called the 'Billy Graham of Japan', will be preaching through an interpreter on the Sunday morning and interviewed on the Saturday afternoon. Partly in his honour, our meal on the Saturday evening will not be Zairian, nor Bangladesian, but Japanese.[36]

Two 'geisha girls' served the food. During the weekend Mr Honda made a public apology for the cruelty of the Japanese in the Second World War.

Wider Relationships

Peter was a committed Baptist. He was committed to his local Baptist Fraternal (Torbay District) and had good relations with the ministers of the nearby Barton and Hele churches in Torquay. Bob Davey was at Barton and Geoffrey Larcombe at Hele, followed by John Harris, with whom Peter played golf.

Upton Vale was one of seventy-eight churches in the Devon and Cornwall Association, with a total membership of around 5,300. Within the Association it was in the local grouping of fourteen churches known as the Torquay District. Peter served a term as President of the District and was held in high esteem as a wise elder statesman by the folk in the churches there. He had an influence his church members were not aware of. He kept them informed of news of District and Association matters and of the individual churches, but did not broadcast his own role. He was delighted when the three churches at Bovey Tracey, Lustleigh and Moretonhampstead were in the process of uniting to become three congregations in the one East Dartmoor Baptist Church, as the arrangement was similar to that at East Kilbride.[37] Chudleigh and Christow have since become member congregations of the church.

Upton Vale was not a member of the Torquay Christian Council but did participate in the Free Church Council. Peter himself was not anti-

---

[35] *Vision* (May–June 1976), 4.
[36] *Vision* (May–June 1978), 9.
[37] *Vision* (May–June 1976), 4.

ecumenical and was open to other denominations as far as he could be. He did not attend the ecumenical fraternal, but was committed to co-operation among evangelicals on an Evangelical Alliance (EA) basis. He was the first Secretary of the Torquay Evangelical Fellowship, which was later renamed the Torbay Evangelical Fellowship (Torbay includes Paignton and Brixham as well as Torquay). Its first convention took place in November 1976, when the Rev. George B. Duncan of Glasgow was the speaker.[38] It was at Peter's instigation that the Fellowship held a series of fortnightly talks on all aspects of marriage for engaged and courting couples.

Peter represented Upton Vale and the Torquay Evangelical Fellowship at Evangelical Alliance Assemblies and gave the Bible Studies at the EA Ministers' Conference at Swanwick in February 1979.[39] In asking his people to pray for the preparation and delivery of those studies Peter confessed: 'I make no secret of the fact that my supreme aversion in life is ministering to ministers. I suppose it mainly reflects on my own sense of inadequacy for such a task and my own unworthiness of such a privilege.'[40]

He enjoyed a happy relationship with evangelical Anglican churches and clergy, particularly Upton Parish Church and Holy Trinity, which has since closed. He took part in pre-Easter series of events in Holy Week, arranged by the central churches.

Social Issues

The church sometimes felt it right to make protests on social issues. In September 1976 the deacons resolved that Peter should write to the local MP stating in the strongest terms their opposition to the production of a pornographic film about Christ and that David Hewitt should write to the local newspaper objecting to the proposed use of a Torquay beach for nude bathing.[41] Peter reported this in the church magazine and commented: 'For myself, I would ask all of us as Christians to be alert to the decadent trends in our society, and to write to those involved or with influence in the situation. Your one letter may seem little, but you can be assured it does carry weight, especially when it arrives as one of many such personal protests.'[42]

In June 1979 Peter shared in a church protest in the local licensing court against the application of the Coral Leisure Group to open a casino in the Coral Island Leisure Complex. With him were Alex Gibson,

---

[38] *Vision* (November–December 1976), 4.
[39] *Vision* (September/October 1978), 8.
[40] *Vision* (January–February 1979), 4.
[41] Minutes of deacons' meeting, 13 September 1976.
[42] *Vision* (November–December 1976), 4-5.

representing the Free Church Council, and the Rev. John Harris, representing the Torquay Evangelical Fellowship. He shared what he had learned from the experience in the church magazine. He was sure that such protests were worthwhile, but only if Christians were convinced of the grounds on which they protested. He and the other representatives had been tremendously impressed by the courtesy with which they had been received at the court. They had learned the vital importance of being there in person. They were the only three 'lay-people' from Torquay at the hearing who voiced a protest. The local casino owners, the Ratepayers' Association and the Gaming Board were represented by lawyers.

> And I dare to think that the very fact we were there may have had something to do with helping the three magistrates to sense the local feeling that the proposed opening of the casino had aroused.

> In the event, not least because of the prayers of many of you in the Church, the application was firmly turned down. As a result many families (150,000 people went to Coral Island last summer) will have been spared a serious threat. I believe it is up to us as the Lord's people to continue keeping something of a watching brief on our society's life, not simply as negative 'kill-joys' but with a view to opposing those things which are truly damaging to our community. Above all, however, let us pursue those things that make for the enhancement of the society in which we live. Let our light shine before men.[43]

Summary of Peter's Leadership

Peter Barber's leadership style at Upton Vale was exemplary. He earned the respect of his people, coaxed and persuaded them. He earned the moral authority to lead, but was not an autocrat. This is seen in his relationships with his assistants and church secretaries: he always considered their judgements and took ideas from them. Just as at East Kilbride, there was a sharing of responsibilities and mutual support.

There were times when he was frustrated by the entrenched positions upheld at deacons' meetings, but he worked patiently for as much agreement as possible on contentious issues. As previously, and later again in Scotland, he faced the ecumenical issue fairly and squarely. He was balanced, but direct and firm in his view of Roman Catholics. He was keen to foster co-operation with other churches as far as possible.

In a large congregation, where many simply came to hear the preacher, he took the lead in making arrangements to enhance the experience of fellowship: people were given the means to get to know each other. He

[43] *Vision* (July–August 1979), 1-2.

promoted new activities that showed the community around that the church cared, particularly for the older people and the young married couples. He introduced the stewardship campaign, as he had at East Kilbride, and although it was modified in the Upton Vale situation, it was gratifyingly successful. It is no surprise that he built on previous foundations of evangelistic activity. The stimulus and teaching he gave for Mission '77 is notable for careful advanced planning and theological undergirding.

The horizons of the church were further stretched by a programme of missionary support in which all ages became involved and by a social conscience that made its protests on a carefully considered basis. Peter was the first to give due credit to his fellow workers in all of this, but they would respond that there was much that would not have been done without the encouragement and stimulus of his loving, clear, strong leadership.

CHAPTER 12

Pastor and Teacher

Preaching

Peter amply fulfilled the role that was expected of him in the pulpit at Upton Vale. People came to the church from a wide area locally and in the summer the holiday-makers swelled the congregation to 800. Some people took their holidays in Torquay especially to attend the church and hear his preaching. Some came from struggling churches and were spiritually re-invigorated.

His preaching was 'straight from the shoulder', revealing that he had the heart of a pastor and the heart of an evangelist. He preached for conversions. He studied hard and his sermons were always 'meaty', though spiced with natural humour, often with reference to Scotland. He used notes but found a full script inhibiting, though sometimes he wrote one out and memorized it. He never waffled and never wasted words. His sermons usually lasted up to forty minutes but the time seemed much shorter.

He moved his congregation with truth rather than sentiment, preaching deep messages explained simply. Nick Mercer found Peter's passion for preaching to be an inspiration and remembers 'his Scottish lilt, mannerisms, with those big thick hands, dry humour and wonderful use of language'.[1]

One aspiring preacher on whom he made a deep impression was Rob Shaw, who writes:

> His preaching? To be quite honest I didn't realise how good Peter was until I began to preach myself. As an apprentice lay preacher I'd present my efforts in some country chapel on a Sunday morning. Then in the evening I'd go to Upton Vale and hear Peter. That's when I began to see how extraordinary he was. Exegesis, exposition, application, illustration, delivery...he seemed to master them all. Stephen Madden, a previous pastor at Upton Vale, told me he would listen to Peter and think 'Why didn't I see that?' Absolutely. In fact the sheer quality of his mind and his ability to think deeply about a text have meant his sermons are just as telling and apposite today. And then there were his illustrations. I loved them. I was often on the edge of my seat because no

---

[1] Letter to Isobel Barber, 23 August 1995.

one told a story like Peter. I once asked David Hewitt if he was going to visit Filey or the Keswick Convention. And he said in effect, 'Why should I bother? Peter's preaching is as good as anything you'll get there.' Peter was a joy to listen to. He spoiled you for anyone else.[2]

Worship

In his address to the Scottish Baptist Ministers' Conference in March 1994 Peter reflected on the contrast in worship with that of the East Kilbride church:

> It was very different in Upton Vale with its 500-member congregation, its robed choir, its magnificent organ and its well-established routines. There I discovered the witnessing power of congregational singing when the hymns are sung with sensitivity and understanding. I also discovered the benefits of shared leadership as I planned and shared worship with assistants. But I also saw very clearly the dangers of pulpit-dominated worship when so much is made to depend on the minister.

Peter encouraged contributions from other members of the fellowship in the Sunday services. There was a traditional choir of a high standard, which practised the hymns on Friday night. It sang cantatas such as *Night of Miracles* and *Love Transcending* at Christmas and special music on Good Friday: one year with other choirs it sang *The Messiah*, a favourite of Peter's. It took part in the open-air boat services and in special missions, and took programmes to the country churches. The choir leader was Mrs Joyce Taylor, who celebrated twenty-five years of service in 1979.[3] Peter valued the choir's contribution to the worship and service of the church. His epilogues at choir concerts were always apt and incisive.

He also encouraged youth singing groups and incorporated them in Sunday worship. Controversy about styles of worship was beginning in Peter's years at Upton Vale, though it came to a head later. When David Hewitt first played the guitar in a church service he had anonymous letters of complaint.

Children

Peter loved children and was always looking out for material for his interesting children's talks. His daughters were used to some of their possessions appearing in the pulpit! The previous owners of the manse in Furzehill Road, where the Barbers lived, were church members who had sold the property to the church. Raymond Brown, Peter's predecessor,

---

[2] Letter to the author, 30 October 1996.
[3] *Vision* (July–August 1979), inside front cover.

had been the first pastor to live there. One of the objects the Barbers found in the house was a Duke of Wellington doorstop. Peter used it as an object lesson for a children's address. The previous owners of the manse were in the congregation—and claimed the doorstop back after the service!

Peter grew potatoes and showed his two daughters how to put a potato in the ground to produce more potatoes. Fiona put one in and watered it regularly. When the potatoes were harvested Peter's were nothing special, but Fiona's produced half a basket full of huge potatoes! Another children's talk!

Aubrey Cutts had an oak tree that had been gradually choked by ivy. He had just felled it and cut it into logs when Peter called. He asked to take a section of the tree away with him to use for another memorable children's talk!

One Christmas Peter was persuaded to dress up as Father Christmas at the Sunday school party. One child was terrified to go near him. Peter was distressed and said: 'I will never ever do that again.' He had seen the fear in the child's face and never wanted to be the cause of such fear again.

Sunday school anniversaries on the second Sunday of May were great occasions in the traditional style. Flowers were worn in button holes. The girls wore long dresses. All the Sunday school processed into the church. They sang special pieces rehearsed for weeks before. It was sometimes called 'the day of rush and madness' (as a parody of the first line of the hymn 'O day of rest and gladness'). The pastor was expected to give the address every other year. Peter's first year was 1975 and he wrote appreciatively of it:

> As you know I had never attended such an occasion south of the border before, and having heard such enthusiastic comments on it, I hoped it would live up to its reputation. Well, it did! The singing was of a high standard, the conduct of the children exemplary, their appearance most fetching, and the support from parents and members of the congregation thrilling. My one regret is that I have to wait two years before I can see it again.[4]

For their part the congregation appreciated the easy way Peter fitted into the spirit of the occasion and the imaginative illustrated addresses he gave.

Another great occasion in the church's life was the Harvest Festival. Peter's daughter Susan has vivid memories of the amazing displays: from the ground to the high pulpit across the whole front there was a bank of flowers, vegetables and beautifully baked and shaped bread.

---

[4] *Vision* (July–August 1975), 5.

Tape Ministry

Recordings of all the church services were made available. Once a month a cassette tape of a service was produced for visitors to take round to the 'shut-ins'. As some of the elderly folk found the whole service too long, a ten-minute summary of the sermon was produced. On one side of the tape was the service with the summary sermon, and on the other side the full sermon. The church had five play-back 'Slimline' machines that visitors took round. The summary of the sermon was recorded separately and Edwin Taylor, who was in charge of the recording, greatly admired the skill with which Peter reduced his forty-minute sermons to ten minutes. When Family Worship at 11 a.m. replaced the traditional separate Sunday school sessions at 10 a.m. and 3 p.m.,[5] tapes of the morning service were provided for Sunday school teachers.

Bible School

The weekly Tuesday evening Bible School had been established in the ministry of Stephen Madden (1942–54). Stanley Voke (1954–63) continued it and introduced duplicated notes. It continued to grow under Raymond Brown (1964–71). Peter and his assistants followed the tradition. About 200 people gathered in the hall to hear in-depth Bible study each week. Usually a book of the Bible was expounded chapter by chapter, but some of the series were on biblical themes. The addresses were recorded and the notes were sent to around eighty people in various parts of the world.

Vision Magazine

Peter made a large contribution to the writing of the *Vision* magazine, which was issued every two months. Not only was there a pastoral letter of more than a page, entitled 'From the Manse' (though he alternated with his assistant in writing this), but a further couple of pages of 'From the Pastor's Desk', in which he gave information on a wide range of subjects. These were so varied and far-ranging that there was no excuse for *Vision* readers to be ignorant of what was going on in their church or in the wider world.

He often used 'From the Manse' for exhortation and correction. He encouraged his people to fulfil their duties as church members: to pray, to be involved in evangelism and to be good stewards. Several pastoral letters are on the subject of church growth. At the end of 1975 he expressed appreciation for the church's work:

---

[5] This was on 2 October 1977. *Vision* (November–December 1977), 8.

With you, I thank God for all that Upton Vale has been in the past with its widely-respected reputation for Evangelical fidelity and heart-warming worship. I thank God too for that which only those of us in membership can know, namely, the depth of its concern for those in trouble and the generosity of its response to those in need.

But he wondered what were the ways the church could go forward in 1976 and drew upon an article that had come recently in his post. It shared the fruit of research on seventeen very different churches in three continents. All were growing and there were ten things they had in common that might account for their growth: prayer, witnessing, conversions, joy, scripture, preaching, outreach, family life, leadership and love. These challenged him personally and he commended them to the fellowship.[6]

Early in 1977 he expressed his hesitation about over-precise aims in church growth:

It's a good thing to have an aim in life. People who are aim-less are usually aimless; people who aim at nothing usually succeed in hitting it. It is therefore appropriate that, as our motto-text for 1977 we should have a clearly defined aim—'We make it our aim to please Him' (2 Cor. 5:9).

While our aim is clearly defined, you will notice that it is not over-precise. At the present time there is a move among prominent Evangelicals in this country to prescribe percentages of church growth over a fixed period (e.g. Guildford Baptist Church has set itself the target of a 200% growth over the next five years, and has increased its full-time staff from 3 to 6 to achieve this); but I do wonder if this does not verge on programming the Holy Spirit. Our own aim set out in the motto-text is not as precise as this, but it is no less demanding, since it covers so many areas of life.[7]

Early in 1979 he referred to church growth as a fashionable topic and mentioned a weekend teach-in under the auspices of the Evangelical Fellowship to be held in April, but he commented:

There is that inner, hidden growth for which mere additions to membership cannot compensate. I mean that growth in love as members are drawn closer to each other in Christ, that growth in knowledge as we get to know HIM in whom we believe, and that growth in maturity as we manifest these Christlike qualities in which the Lord delights. This growth matters too—indeed, without it there is little point in adding to our numbers if those we add are not knit to the Body of Christ, enriched in faith and matured in discipleship.

---

[6] *Vision* (November–December 1975), 3-4.
[7] *Vision* (January–February 1977), 1-2.

The church motto for the year was to be Ephesians 4:15: 'Grow up in every way into Christ.'[8]

Evangelist

Peter showed by his example the importance of personal witnessing. When the church roof was being replaced he went on to the scaffolding and up on to the ridge—a frightening experience for most people—to chat with the men. He had a winsome way of telling the gospel. All the workers on the roof were presented with a Bible.

Through Peter's ministry Harry King was led to faith in Christ and his wife Catherine was led back to the Jesus she knew as a young girl in Wales.[9] Harry had previously felt that his views about creation and other matters were not compatible with his becoming a Christian, but Peter was able to discuss these things so openly and helpfully that Harry came to see there could be no real conflict between science and faith, and the Christian faith had nothing to be afraid of in science. Peter had the ability to hold things in tension academically and to encourage minds to be open to truth.[10]

He was concerned for the strengthening of those who were new in the faith. Early in his ministry he reported that Ken Cutts (assistant secretary at the time) was leading a discipleship class of very promising young people, that he himself was taking a series of five classes for those preparing for baptism and church membership and that a partnership scheme entitled 'Forward with Christ' had been introduced for adults who had made a recent commitment. This was a twelve-week scheme in which the new convert was teamed up with an older Christian. They would meet for an hour each week and share a lesson on such topics as prayer, witness and Bible study.[11] The 'New Membership Pack' started in Peter's time included a personal letter to each member.

Pastoral Work

Those who were in the Upton Vale church in Peter's time have paid eloquent tributes to the quality of pastoral care they received from him. People warmed to his approach and found him totally genuine. They felt he was a friend as well as a pastor, so that there was no distance between them and him. He was utterly discreet and never broke a confidence. He was a tireless pastor and gave so much of himself.

---

[8] *Vision* (January–February 1979), 1-2.
[9] They are the parents of the Rev. Keith King.
[10] Information from Keith King.
[11] *Vision* (January–February 1974), 5.

Time meant nothing to him and he was always on the spot when he was needed. When Reg Sage's mother died Peter was away from the town, but he was informed of her death and visited the family at 11 p.m. on his way home. When Aubrey Cutts' mother had a stroke Peter visited once or even twice a day—more than the doctor. At first he prayed for healing, but when it became clear that she would not regain her powers he said: 'We must release her to the Lord.'

He visited all the church members on a regular basis. The visits had to be kept short, but his reasoning was that people were more likely to unburden themselves of problems in their own homes than at the church. He introduced a vestry hour, as he had at East Kilbride, making careful arrangements for it: a deacon or deacon's wife was in an adjoining room and could be alerted immediately by a bell. He also spent time with people on the fringe of the church and outside it.

He used letters pastorally. For the first three wedding anniversaries a letter went out to every couple and for the first three anniversaries of baptisms a letter went out to each person who had been baptized. He encouraged church members to write to missionaries, ministerial students and prisoners.

There were situations in which Peter exercised discipline. He had the moral authority to take a firm line to deal with unwise or wrong conduct or to pre-empt trouble. There are those who are deeply grateful that he guided them through stormy waters. Sometimes he had to deal with tragedies, such as the suicide of a young lad. He was able to tackle some difficult marital situations directly with skill and wisdom, and provide on-going help: he saved some marriages. Later he said that he went to Upton Vale as an ordinary pastor but left as an experienced counsellor, because this was the time when family and marriage problems began to multiply, inside the church as well as outside.[12] He started preparation classes for engaged couples and classes for married couples.

A young member of Upton Vale who was already training for ministry before Peter arrived was Keith King. The Barbers already knew him well because he was taking a course at the Bible Training Institute in Glasgow. When he heard that they were moving to Torquay he was very helpful in allaying some of Isobel's fears about the cultural differences she was to encounter. He pays tribute to the encouragement he received from Peter at various stages of his training and especially in the crisis that came when his son Simon was born. Keith had just finished his course at the Bible Training Institute and was about to start at Spurgeon's College when his wife Lynne gave birth to their first child, Simon, on Thursday 11 September 1975. The midwife was Kath McBride, a member of Upton Vale. Having been trained at a Salvation Army school and Mildmay

---

[12] Information from Ken Cutts.

Christian Hospital, she always prayed a silent prayer with a new-born child. When Simon was born she knew at once that he had Down's Syndrome, but was not allowed to say anything to the parents. She prayed with them a special prayer, the significance of which they saw later with gratitude.

It was twenty-four hours after the birth that the consultant paediatrician gave Lynne and Keith the news, which had been confirmed. They were devastated. The next day Lynne's sister Carol was to be married and that night there was a rehearsal. Saying nothing to the family, Keith disappeared from the rehearsal early and went to see Peter at the manse. He felt a kind of shame that his son would not be like other sons, and was asking himself what he had done wrong. He felt hurt for Lynne and wondered how they would cope with the problems in the future.

Peter was obviously busy but immediately welcomed him to his study, where they knelt together in prayer and wept together. Peter read Psalm 34 and verse 5 stood out: 'Look to him, and be radiant, so your faces shall never be ashamed.' God gave Keith a clear sense that everything was all right and he felt a new man. He was worried about seeing Lynne in hospital the next day, but by the time he saw her Peter had already visited her and she had had the same experience. Peter had prayed that she would receive 'the peace that passes understanding' and she was given that peace.

When other people came to know about Simon, some said, 'We'll pray that God will heal him', but Keith and Lynne felt that to pray for Simon's healing would be like not accepting him as he was—God's very special gift. They also believed that God was going to use their special little baby to heal so many others, and that is exactly what he did do, until on 1 July 2001, aged twenty-five, he went to be with the Lord.

In the churches where Keith has ministered[13] Simon had a ministry in bringing people together. He created a following and people loved him. The experience of bringing him up had its effect on Keith's ministry: he now has a full understanding of mental handicap and he and Lynne conducted seminars on the subject at Spring Harvest. The experience of communicating with Simon helped Keith to reduce complicated jargon to more manageable 'bite sizes'.

Peter described one of the adjustments that he had to make in moving to Upton Vale as 'a death—the death of my idyllic image of Torquay, Devon'. This was because of the serious social problems that he met in his pastoral work. Involvement in the occult was well above average. As a member of a counselling team Peter discovered that around sixty percent

---

[13] Keith King served in Leigh-on-Sea (Leigh Road), Luton (Central) and Torquay (Hele Road). He is now one of the ministry team of Gold Hill Baptist Church, Buckinghamshire.

of the cases they dealt with had an occult reference. There were large witches' covens in the area that were aggressively active. The rate of marital breakdown was overwhelming. In one primary school in Torquay half of the children came from broken homes. With regard to drug-taking Torquay was the worst affected area per capita outside London. Suicide in Torbay was three times the national average and many who had retired to the area and lost their life-partner had no friends around them.

> As you can imagine those who jokingly spoke to me of my Torquay ministry as preaching to big holiday crowds in the summer and lazing on the beach in the winter could not have got it more wrong. Pastoral work here has proved much more complex and demanding than anything I had experienced before.[14]

Telephone Ministry

Peter continued the Dial-a-Message ministry that Raymond Brown had begun. It was described in advertisements: 'A 24-hour Christian Telephone Ministry. Just listen for 2 minutes. A new message is given each day.'[15] Later the duration was lengthened to three minutes. A week of messages was recorded at a time in a home cellar. Peter soon enlisted the help of two of his members, Mr John Lipscombe and Dr Richard Dobson, in this work and when David Hewitt came he and others joined the rota. Mike Quantick administered this service and Terry Browse was the recording engineer.

In 1974 Peter encouraged prayer for the telephone ministry and reported: 'Quite recently I heard from one blind lady who finds it a daily source of comfort and strength. Another man phoned from Exeter to say that through the daily message and a subsequent contact he had been fully restored to Christ.' In October 1977 a week's messages took the form of interviews with Cliff Richard by David Hewitt.

The showing of the controversial film *The Exorcist* in local cinemas in 1974 led to a further development in the telephone ministry. Ivor Gane remembers how Peter emphasized the need for personal faith to be relevant in the community and in society: 'When *The Exorcist* was shown in Torquay, he described it as being "spiritual pornography" and put his name and phone number on a leaflet, with other ministers' details. The leaflets were given out as folk came out of a local cinema and those who were distressed could phone at any time for counsel. Peter was outside the cinema each evening, leading the "troops". This was wonderful pastoral

---

[14] *Forum: The Magazine of the Friends, Students and Former Students of the Baptist Theological College of Scotland* (June [1978]), [6-7].
[15] *Vision* (March–April 1973), 12.

leadership.' Peter reported that as a result of the leaflets several men and women were contacted who were in urgent need of pastoral counselling.[16]

A similar initiative was taken in Plymouth by Gordon Wright. He was the leader of a group of Christians who gave cards to those who had seen the film, with two phone numbers on: the Samaritans' and his own. This led to the foundation of the general Christian counselling service 'Crossline' in Plymouth, operated by the Highway Trust under Gordon Wright's leadership.

In 1978 a local version of Crossline was set up in the Torquay area as the 'Lifeline Christian Counselling Service', with Peter as chairman. There were differences between the two schemes. In Plymouth the service was a twenty-four hour telephone ministry, but in Torbay other means of contact were also used. A team of volunteers set up a counselling room in the 'Open Scroll' Christian Bookshop in Paignton.[17]

Other Activities

Just as at East Kilbride, Peter was in demand for wider ministry. He and his assistants took a Pontins Holiday Camp service at 9.30 on Sunday mornings during the season. He was guest speaker at church anniversaries, conventions, Christian Unions, youth conferences and fraternals in various parts of Britain.

He led parties on fifteen-day visits to the Holy Land at Easter 1975[18] and in October 1977.[19] On the second of these trips a romance blossomed between Joyce Shuttleworth and Ambrose Dallyn that led to their marriage the following September. This trip (when he was leading a party of thirty-seven people) formed the first half of a 'sabbatical month'! The other two weeks were spent in study.[20]

In October 1979 Peter was joint-leader of thirty-eight people who travelled 'in the steps of St Paul' to Greece, the Greek Islands, the coast of Turkey and Rome.[21] This was also treated as sabbatical leave.[22]

---

[16] *Vision* (September–October 1974), 8-9.

[17] Some information in this and the previous paragraph is from the Rev. Graham White.

[18] *Vision* (July–August 1975), 3.

[19] *Vision* (March–April 1976), 3.

[20] Minutes of the church meeting, 18 January 1977; minutes of deacons' meetings, 17 March and 7 November 1977.

[21] *Vision* (January–February 1979), 4-5.

[22] Minutes of deacons' meeting, 15 January 1979.

Practical Skills

Peter had many practical skills and was not too proud to use them alongside his church members and under their direction. Aubrey Cutts volunteered to widen the entrance to the manse and build up the wall. There was a vast amount of earth to be moved to the back of the house, where it formed the base of a lawn. Whenever Peter arrived home he helped with the wheelbarrow.

Then there was the time when the church decided to lower the ceiling in the missionary room by three or four feet. To save money it was agreed that church members would do the work. Aubrey Cutts agreed to be overseer. The response was poor: on the first evening only two men turned up. Peter presented himself the next night in his overalls with his box of tools. 'I've come to help', he said to Aubrey, 'you're the boss and I'm the workman.' He reported for work on the remaining evenings of the week.

He was quick to offer practical help on his pastoral visits. Reg Vigurs recalls a visit he and his wife Irene made to two ladies in their eighties, the Misses Leeson. It was a Saturday in winter. They were upset because no water was coming through their taps, as something was wrong in the attic. Reg and Irene returned home so that Reg could get his equipment. He went back to the Leesons' house only to find that in the mean time Peter had visited them, returned to the manse to get his beautiful set of tools, sorted out the problem and already left!

Mrs Stacey, the mother of Vivienne Stacey (the missionary) lived alone. She had once confronted a burglar, a masked man: the experience haunted her and she was never the same again. Peter went to her flat one tea-time to see how she was. Somebody had brought her some fish, but she was at a loss what to do with them. Peter took off his coat and cooked her evening meal. He was known to be a good cook, especially of clootie dumplings, which are a traditional Scottish treat consisting of a rich dark fruitcake boiled or steamed in a cloot (cloth).

Isobel too is a good cook. On one occasion their daughters' school held a coffee morning. Isobel baked some delicious cakes, packed them in boxes and sent them with the girls. When Susan came home she said, 'O mum, they were pleased to see me coming. They were very short of cake boxes!'

Humour

Peter had a great sense of humour, which some people appreciated more than others! His puns surfaced as headlines of items in *Vision*. 'Upton Vale Revokes' introduced an announcement of Stanley Voke's return for a church anniversary. 'What's Cook(e)ing?' advertised Frank Cooke as the church anniversary speaker. 'Overhalled' headed a note of thanks to those who had renovated the rear hall. A notice of forthcoming ordinations was entitled 'Revving Up'. When Mr Harold Peters and Mr Will Wicks were made life deacons Peter remarked to the church meeting that there would always be light in the deacons' court as 'Wicks' never 'Peter' out!

He had a great sense of fun on appropriate occasions. The wedding reception of Reg Sage's daughter Beverley was held at the Hansom Cab Restaurant on the afternoon of Hogmanay. Naturally Peter and Isobel introduced a Scottish element into the celebrations and Peter wore a glengarry cap. The restaurant proprietor took a fancy to it and tried it on. Generous as ever Peter let him keep it.

Early in his ministry one of the young men of the church, David Voyce, gave a testimony from the pulpit. After it Peter commented to the congregation, 'My! That guy would look good in a kilt!' He kept promising David and his wife that he would prove his point and the day came when he phoned them and asked them to come to the manse, where David was photographed in a kilt. He did look good in it too!

Fellowship Evenings were enlivened by Peter's creative use of fun. On one such occasion Peter mentioned that David Hewitt had recently made a trip to Scotland and added, 'I'm sure it hasn't changed him at all.' At once David appeared complete with kilt and ginger beard!

At the end of one year Peter arranged a fun evening called 'Finally, Brethren'. In one sketch he sat in a rocking chair, mimicking the Irish singer Val Doonican on television, and sang 'I'm dreaming of a white Christmas'. In the closing bars white flour was poured all over him!

His propensity for practical jokes came to the fore in his famous rivalry over growing tomatoes with Reg Vigurs. Peter set out to grow tomatoes from seed. While most people are content to get gardening tips from friends, he as always was determined to do the job properly and so he bought a book on the subject. Reg Vigurs was well known for his excellent tomatoes, but Peter wanted to outdo him and boasted in a children's talk that he would 'grow better tomatoes than Reg Vigurs'. A few weeks later he was telling people he had succeeded. Reg was not convinced. He crept to the manse with a torch and saw that Peter had stuck two large plastic tomatoes on to his plants and put them in the porch where visitors could see them!

Family Life

In 1976 Isobel and Katheryn were expecting babies around the same time. Peter let the church know in typical style:

GREAT EXPECTATIONS: Just in case the grapevine has failed to do its work in your case let me keep you up with the Manse news by letting you know that a little bundle of joy is expected in the Furzehill Road Manse in early

August, and another in the Shiphay Park Road Manse in late August. Both ladies of the Manse are keeping reasonably well—and both the men of the Manse are deliriously delighted! Talk about ministerial teamwork![23]

A few months later he reported:

In August a member of Upton Vale, speaking to a visitor: 'Did you know that our ministers' two wives are both having babies?' (Shades of Mormon! To think it all depends on an inverted comma!)[24]

The Hewitt arrival came earlier than expected: Timothy John was born to Katheryn and David on 3 August. Colin George was born to Isobel and Peter on 9 August. Peter pointed out that the date of birth was 9-8-76![25]

Kath McBride (a midwife and member of the church) had just gone on duty when she heard that Isobel had been admitted to the ward and asked to look after her. This was a time when the husband was expected to be present, so Peter was there for the birth. As soon as Colin was born Peter said, 'Let's pray!', but Kath had to ask him to be patient while she attended to the mother and the baby, carrying out vital duties. Then both she and Peter prayed.

Despite his active nature and hard work Peter did not find it hard to relax. He enjoyed taking the family out on the moors. On his day off (Monday) Dr Richard Dobson, a member of the church, made sure Peter played golf with him.

Fiona and Susan remember the great generosity to the family of Ray and Jimps Wyatt. They lived on a farm with a swimming pool and every Wednesday afternoon (after school in term time) all through the summer and early autumn the family had access to the pool and the farm. Jimps let Fiona ride a retired race-horse, which started her continuing obsession with horses. She was also able to stay at the farm at weekends. She took after Peter with his love of animals.

He was particularly fond of his collie dog 'Darroch' and the attraction was mutual. One Sunday afternoon the family had hospitality at a house in the country. Peter left by himself to go to the evening service. Darroch heard the sound of the car and jumped out of an upstairs window to try and go with him! He did himself an injury, but fortunately recovered!

In one of his sermons Peter revealed that at one time he felt he was being called to the mission field abroad. He wrestled with God concerning the sacrifices he would have to make. He came to the point when he was willing to give away the dog in order to go abroad, and God said to him, 'I was just wondering whether you were willing'.

---

[23] *Vision* (March–April 1976), 3.
[24] *Vision* (September–October 1976), 6.
[25] *Vision* (September–October 1976), 2 and 4.

By all accounts Darroch was the only one who liked Peter's driving. The car he had for most of his years in Torquay was a J-registration beige Volkswagen 'Beetle', which he had bought while at East Kilbride. It was nicknamed 'Midge' from the registration letters MYJ. He was a fierce driver, noted for doing U turns in the rather narrow St Marychurch Road. He once arrived late for a young people's house party at Haldon Hall, Exmouth, and had to confess he had been booked by the police. He had overtaken a car on double white lines—and then noticed that it was a police car.

When the family went back to Scotland for holidays they set off at 9 o'clock after the Sunday evening service and all four of them (five after Colin arrived) plus Darroch squeezed into 'Midge', with Peter and Isobel alternating the driving every 100 miles.

In 1979 a car fund was launched by the church and Peter expressed appreciation:

> OUR ESTATE: My wife Isobel and I both want to say a warm 'thank you' to all of you who contributed so generously to the Car Fund. So magnificent was the response that, far from having to buy a 3 year old car (as we anticipated), we have been able to purchase a year-old Cortina Estate Car. Just the thing for a growing family and for northern treks. Many many thanks![26]

Unfortunately the gift of the car led Peter into a tax-trap, but he was eventually rescued from it!

Leaving Upton Vale

In August 1979 Andrew MacRae tendered his resignation as Secretary and Superintendent of the Baptist Union of Scotland (as from 1 July 1980) in order to take up an appointment at Acadia Divinity College, Nova Scotia, as Professor of Evangelism. When Ken Cutts read this news in the *Baptist Times* he had an instant conviction that Peter would be called to fill the post. Everyone in Scotland felt the same.

The letter of invitation from the Rev. George Hossack on behalf of the unanimous Nominations Committee arrived while Peter was in Israel. Isobel had opened it and when she met Peter they went for a meal together. Isobel then revealed to him that at the time they were leaving East Kilbride she had received a conviction through an Old Testament text that they would return to Scotland after seven years and Peter would be Andrew MacRae's successor.

Peter expressed his certainty of the call to go back north but his regret at having to leave Upton Vale at this time:

[26] *Vision* (July–August 1979), 5.

MARCHING ORDERS

It was with great reluctance and a heavy heart that I entered the pulpit on the morning of Sunday, 13th January. I knew by the end of the sermon I would have to tell you all of my acceptance of the call to be Secretary of the Baptist Union of Scotland.

Even as I looked round the congregation during worship I could feel the strong bonds of affection that bound me to you and I kept telling myself that I should forget the whole thing and stay. And yet, I knew that simply could not be since the call had been so clearly confirmed as God's call and could not be dismissed without stepping out of the centre of God's will. So whether I liked it or not, and whether you liked it or not, it simply had to be and the news had to be broken. With you, I had to say (in the words of our text) 'The will of the Lord be done.'[27]

Peter's last Sunday at Upton Vale was 1 June, which was the twenty-fifth anniversary of his ordination. To mark this at the morning service Jack Harmer presented him with a complete set of the three volumes of the *New International Dictionary of New Testament Theology*, edited by Colin Brown.[28] This was a gift from East Kilbride and Upton Vale.

The farewell gathering on Monday 2 June was a blend of sadness and happy fellowship with the usual humorous, in fact hilarious touches. The large church hall was 'packed to suffocation'. There were musical items by the 'Meet Jesus' group and the church choir. Slides, with a taped commentary, entitled 'This is Your Life' showed facets of Peter's bachelor days, his courtship, marriage, family life and church fellowship. A sketch by the young people, announced as 'A Country story of Simple Folk' made the audience aware of the difficulties the pastor had suffered in (a) playing golf and (b) preparing his Sunday sermons![29]

Tributes to Peter's Ministry

The Upton Vale folk remember Peter as a complete, all-round pastor. He was a good mixture of visionary and realist; an enthuser who used to catch people up in his own enthusiasm. He had colossal energy and total commitment. He wore himself out, packing fourteen years' work into less than seven. He was thorough and systematic in all he did, but was good at delegating: he was happy to let others do things. He had the ability to see when people were taking on too much: he was an encourager, not a driver. He always had his finger on the pulse and was involved in everything. People respected him but did not need to stand on ceremony

---

[27] *Vision* (March–April 1980), 1.
[28] Exeter: Paternoster Press, 1976.
[29] *Vision* (July–August 1980), 6-7.

before him. They felt at ease with him: they found he saw them as individuals, not just part of a crowd. Peter and Isobel were always available: the manse was an open house twenty-four hours, day and night. He had a contagious sense of fun but people also sensed a deep holiness in him.

He came to Upton Vale respecting its traditions. He took them and enhanced them, making his own contributions to them. He also came with his own ideas and was sometimes frustrated when he met with entrenched conservatism. He found it difficult to live with the complacency of a large church that was set in its ways. Upton Vale had been successful in its traditional form. Many members did not want the patterns of church life changed. But change was needed. Peter's successor, David Coffey, was grateful that Peter had prepared the way for him.

Peter had great insight into the direction the church needed to take. It had a widespread reputation as a preaching centre, but he introduced more emphasis on pastoral care and team ministry. In his penultimate article for *Vision* he could not resist expressing his hopes for the future of the church. He hoped it would continue to be a FAMILY CHURCH and develop its ministry to whole families; a COMMUNITY CHURCH, showing practical concern for the many retired, lonely and needy people in Torquay; a SHARING CHURCH, being more committed to activities such as house groups, where believers could meet in smaller numbers to talk about their faith; a CARING CHURCH: a framework of more effective pastoral care had been established, but was this enough?[30]

Ken Cutts wrote the final tribute:

Our Lord makes no mistakes—though sometimes, in our weakness of faith, we're tempted to think we could do better!—and, as He certainly made no mistake in bringing Peter and Isobel Barber to us, what comfort to realise that He's making no mistake in taking them from us. When it's the Lord's doing, all must be well!

Not that the grief of parting is any the less painful, nor a certain sense of emptiness any the less real: one just realises all that this family meant; all that this pastor did; and all that the Lord of the Church used him to be:— Administrator-skilled; brother-beloved; counsellor-sensitive; friend-faithful; pastor-totally caring; preacher-challenging and inspiring; of himself totally unwith-holding; to others, always available.

---

[30] *Vision* (May–June 1980), 1-2.

How—and why was he all these? Because he was Christ's man; from start to finish; from inside to outside. He truly could share Paul's glorious assurance and assertion 'to me to live is Christ.'[31]

---

[31] *Vision* (July–August 1980), 3.

CHAPTER 13

Leader of Scottish Baptists

Called Back Again

It was no surprise to anyone when Peter was appointed General Secretary of the Baptist Union of Scotland. The skills, interests and experience required had been apparent for a long time. The wise judgement, meticulous organization, pastoral ability and powers of effective communication were all gifts that had been obvious at an early age. He had diligently developed them with a dedication to which he felt utterly obligated by the love of God in Christ.

Peter Blackwood had the pleasure of moving the acceptance of Peter's nomination at the Council. He commented that Andrew MacRae would not be easy to follow: Peter's leadership would be different, but no less inspirational or effective. The office would be challenging 'at a time when the Union has set new goals for much increased giving and church growth'. The Nominations Committee felt sure that Peter's experience of ministering in England would add another dimension to his work.

Peter worked alongside Andrew MacRae during June 1980 and took over full responsibility at the beginning of July. There was a Service of Thanksgiving and Recognition on Saturday 7 June at Adelaide Place Baptist Church, Glasgow, at which Andrew and Jean MacRae were farewelled and Peter was inducted. As old friends and sparring partners Andrew and Peter insulted each other in love with typical sharp humour. In more serious vein Peter said that at this stage he had no new programme in mind and he would need time to become more acclimatised to the situation in Scotland, but he hinted that he would seek to build a closer relationship with fellow-Baptists in the South.

Peter and his family moved into the house owned by the Union and previously occupied by the MacRaes, situated in the Mansewood area on the south side of Glasgow. He and Isobel became members of Queen's Park Baptist Church and made a full contribution to its life. They knew its minister, Edwin Gunn, very well from their East Kilbride days.[1] He had settled at Queens' Park the previous year. In his address to the Scottish

---

[1] Peter had baptized him on the same occasion as Isobel and four others. Edwin had been President of the Youth Fellowship when Isobel was the Secretary.

Baptist Ministers' Conference in 1994 Peter commented that in his membership of fourteen years at Queen's Park he had 'lived through the transition of a church from traditional to charismatic renewal worship. I have recognised the greater sense of congregational involvement in worship singing; the sense of openness to the supernatural in the context of worship; the struggle to hold in balance unhelpful spontaneity and good order; the ultimate centrality of good Biblical preaching.'

Family Life

The family were glad to be back in Scotland and nearer their relatives, but they had adjustments to make. Colin, though born in England, soon picked up a Scottish accent when he went to school. Fiona and Susan, though born in Scotland, had English accents to embarrass them at their new school!

The children found themselves in a different situation, as their father now was not in a local pastorate, though they still felt they were in a 'goldfish bowl'. They could seldom go for a walk with their father without someone recognizing him and wanting to talk. They got to know Baptist churches all over Scotland and felt privileged to have so many people to meals and to stay. Their political awareness was enhanced because the visitors came from so many backgrounds and countries.

Their guests were often surprised by Peter's practical jokes, though they realized that the intention was never unkind. There was the mustard jar, from which a snake popped out; the coffee percolator placed under a chair that would suddenly start to bubble; the 'After Eight' mint that proved to be made of rubber! Peter loved comedy. On television he enjoyed the comedians Morecambe and Wise, and the practical jokes of *Candid Camera*. After he broke his sternum in a car accident he had to leave the room when *Candid Camera* was on, because it hurt him to laugh so much. However, the children knew that it was serious work that he did in the study and they should not disturb him. He always wore shoes there and never slippers—because he was at work.

When with his increasing responsibilities Peter was away from home more often, he missed the family very much. The children got used to his absences and realized that he was on very important business. He relied on his home base: it was a different world for him to come back to and Isobel sought to be an enabler there. He talked with her a lot and when he wanted to unburden himself about confidential matters they would get a child minder and go out for a drive so as to talk. There were, however, times when Peter did not confide in Isobel because he knew she would be more hurt for him than he was for himself.

The children were sure of their parents' love. They knew there was not much money to spare, but never felt the lack of it. They do not remember their parents raising their voices to each other: they discussed things, but not in anger, and never criticized each other in public.

They appreciated their parents' open and accepting attitude to people and their various views. Because there was no prejudice at home they were at first unaware of the depth of religious prejudice in Scottish society. They never felt brainwashed in any way.

Peter always made a tremendous effort to be at home for all the birthdays and join in the fun, however full his diary was. Susan remembers that on one of her birthdays he arrived later in the evening and was upset that he had not been home in time for tea.

He delighted in children. He loved playing with his granddaughter Zoe. He loved the wide-eyed wonderment that children have when experiencing something for the first time. He liked parks and Sunday afternoon walks. He took the family to Strathaven Park where they enjoyed rides on the miniature railway. He walked with Isobel in Pollok Park when the rhododendrons were in flower.

He wrote in a letter to Isobel before his first operation for cancer (23 April 1993): 'Your love has been such a mainstay over the years. I have never doubted it, only been amazed at its sheer constancy and generosity. Your love has shown me more about the love of God than all the books I have read about it.' Colin remembers the love he received in his rebellious teenage years: 'As a family there was love everywhere, which gave you a lot of freedom to do what you wanted to do and come back to the fold.' It was a home where the love of Christ was shown.

Decisive Leadership

As with the Upton Vale period, it is more helpful to look in turn at the various aspects of Peter's General Secretaryship rather than follow it chronologically. This chapter concentrates on his style of leadership, particularly as it was expressed in his relationships with colleagues and in his ministry to the denomination at Assembly level and in the local churches. Chapter 14 describes the development of his leadership in his major emphasis, the stimulating of the denomination to mission. Chapter 15 reviews the ways he approached the controversies that inevitably came.

Peter exercised his leadership as one who had been appointed to lead from the front. This inevitably led to occasions when he suffered deep hurt, for he was more sensitive than most people realized. Leaders of denominations are inevitably shot at from all directions. They have to accept criticisms, knowing that they are based on limited knowledge of the facts, for confidentiality cannot be broken.

Peter always had his finger on the pulse of the denomination's life.[2] From January 1982 he wrote an article every month in the *Scottish Baptist Magazine* under the title 'Scene Around' (changed to 'By the Way...' in May 1991), in which he gave constant direction and encouragement. At meetings of the Executive, Council and other committees he was always well prepared, ready to consult and to receive ideas, but also able to summarize clearly the discussion and indicate the right direction to take. He handled 'difficult situations with a fine mixture of grace and strength'.[3] As Jim Taylor wrote:

> The burden of responsibilities, and wider contacts, often causes a Christian leader to draw back into a strange isolation or superiority, but not so with Peter. He was essentially loyal and that we all appreciated. Amidst all the demands made on his attention, he had obviously thought deeply on the subject under discussion and his views were both wise and penetrating.[4]

Colleagues in Service

In a stimulating address at his first Assembly in 1980 Peter made it clear that his leadership style would be as leader of a team, in full co-operation with his colleagues: 'I fly better in formation than solo.'[5] His colleagues at Church House found him to be a leader who led by example and welded the team together. He was good at delegating. Office Bearers' meetings were times of rich fellowship.

The situation that he inherited was full of expectancy and Peter sought to build upon the foundations laid under his predecessor. In January 1979 a new departmental structure had been introduced in anticipation of significant church growth. Ron Scott, who had already served since 1975 as Assistant Secretary, was re-appointed and given responsibility for the Department of Mission as well; Robert Armstrong was brought in from the pastorate of Thomas Coats Memorial Baptist Church, Paisley, to lead the Department of Publications; Willie Wright was persuaded with some reluctance to leave the pastorate at Kirkintilloch to lead the Department of Church Life.

The office that Peter inherited ('General Secretary and Superintendent of the Baptist Union of Scotland') combined the roles of administrator and pastor. As Superintendent he related to the General Superintendents who had pastoral oversight of the 'areas' in England and Wales, and attended their meetings. However, there was already a strong feeling that

---

[2] Eric Watson, *SBN* (October 1994), 1.
[3] The late Fred Wilson in a private letter to Isobel.
[4] *SBN* (October 1994), 1.
[5] Report by R. King, *SBM* (December 1980), 6.

the office should be divided and a separate Superintendent appointed, who would be able to give pastoral care to ministers and their families.

The Nominations Committee made it clear to Peter that there was a momentum towards separating the General Secretaryship and the Superintendency. Peter accepted this—he had experienced Superintendency in the South—but he asked for a delay of a couple of years while he made his own evaluation of the system. He soon came to appreciate the impossibility of fulfilling both responsibilities adequately and turned to Eric Watson for advice. They had known each other when Eric was at Dennistoun and Peter at East Kilbride. Peter asked Eric to jot down the strengths and weaknesses of the Superintendency as he had experienced it in England and they worked together on a job description, developing a more caring role and including the administration of the pension fund. The Superintendent was to do everything concerning ministers and their relation to the churches; the General Secretary was to be concerned for church growth, church planting, representing the denomination, etc., though there would inevitably be overlap. The General Secretary would continue to have overall responsibility, but Peter was insistent that the leadership should be seen as one, which was characteristic of his generosity and humility.

The plan was to appoint a Superintendent in December 1983, when Ron Scott's term of office was due to be completed. However, this was brought forward when after a short illness Ron tragically died of cancer in May 1982, just over a month short of his fiftieth birthday. In his tribute at the funeral Peter said: 'His knowledge of practical matters was encyclopaedic and the skill of his hands legendary. Like his Master before him "he went about doing good".'[6]

The denomination mourned for two Rons that year. Ron Swanson, the pioneer minister of the Bourtreehill congregation in Irvine, had died of cancer in February, also just short of his fiftieth birthday. Peter confessed his perplexity:

Like the Psalmist before us, we wonder why worthless rogues should live to full years while good men, who are scarce enough, should be taken when they have so much left to give.

We can only dare to believe that one day, when we see the full picture, 'We'll bless the hand that guided, and bless the heart that planned.' Meantime we can only leave such ultimate issues to God and instead claim what is immediately needed, namely strength to cope with new demands and grace to respond to the inevitable challenge that the passing of men so young must bring.[7]

---

[6] *SBM* (June 1982), 14.
[7] *SBM* (June 1982), 10.

The October 1982 Assembly welcomed the appointment of a separate Superintendent. As suggestions were made to the Search Committee, one name kept coming up: Eric Watson. When they had been working out the job description neither Peter nor Eric had had any idea that Eric (an Englishman!) would be appointed: their idea had been to find a Scot to do it.[8]

Peter commended Eric to the denomination as 'a man diligent in study, wide in sympathy, faithful in preaching, devoted in pastoral care and wise in leadership'.[9] He was inducted as Superintendent on 10 March 1983 and had a happy working relationship with Peter. They supported each other and often prayed together, particularly when crises arose, but always maintained the confidentiality that their separate roles demanded. Wounds received in the course of their duties were healed through prayer and the grace of God. Peter found that the appointment of a Superintendent took the loneliness out of his job. When Eric retired in March 1993 Peter wrote a fulsome tribute, stressing from his own experience the onerous, exhausting nature of the task of Superintendent: 'He has fulfilled his role with dignity, discretion, sensitivity and at great personal sacrifice. He has somehow blended self-discipline with personal care and, in every sense, magnified his office.'[10]

At the service in Stirling where Eric was farewelled on 2 April 1993, Douglas Hutcheon was inducted as his successor. He too had a very happy relationship with Peter, though sadly for a much shorter period. He regarded Peter as his friend and mentor.

When Willie Wright went back to the pastorate in 1981 he was succeeded as leader of the Department of Church Life by Mrs Muriel McNair. She was followed in 1985 by Ian Mundie, who came from the pastorate of Whyte's Causeway Baptist Church, Kirkcaldy. Peter was keen to support work among young people and instrumental in the appointment of a full-time National Youth Worker. The Youth Weekend in October 1984 had requested this.[11] Derek Clark was appointed at the age of twenty-nine in 1987. At the time he was a member of the Dumfries church and a teacher of physics at Lockerbie Academy. He had obvious skills in communicating with young people and set about his tasks with much enthusiasm.[12]

Peter also had a hand in the appointment of David Neil as Mission Field Worker from May 1988. He was a Scot with earlier connections with the Shettleston church, Glasgow, but all of his previous ministry had been in the north of England. Since 1983 he had been Northern Association

[8] The above information about the Superintendency was provided by Eric Watson.
[9] *SBM* (February 1983), 10.
[10] *SBM* (March 1993), 3.
[11] *SBM* (December 1984), 8.
[12] *SBM* (October 1987), 5.

Minister and Secretary. He served in Scotland until his retirement in 1994.[13]

There was a long review of the structures of the Union in the late 1980s. Some of the 'core groups' (committees) were ineffective, some were not even meeting. Specialists who had attended core group meetings did not see the point of attending departmental meetings as well. A first report from the review group was considered to be too radical. A second report, not quite so radical, was accepted by the Council in April 1991. There was to be a change from the departmental structure to a team, which would comprise the General Secretary and three Assistant Secretaries responsible for Mission, Youth and Church Development, supported by an Administrator. The Council was to be reduced from 130 to seventy-eight members. The Executive was to be reduced to twenty members and have a more initiatory role. The Union's Bookshop in 12 Aytoun Road was to be closed. The Council Room at 14 Aytoun Road was to be used as an office and the Council was to meet elsewhere. The role of the Administrator would be to relieve the General Secretary of detailed administration.

The Assembly in Motherwell in October gave the proposals overwhelming support, but during the next few months they had to be drastically changed because the Union was overtaken by a financial crisis. The new team structure went ahead, in place of the departmental one, and Ian Mundie was re-appointed as Assistant Secretary to Peter, but the Council decided not to proceed with the appointments of the Youth Co-ordinator, the Administrator or the Church Development Officer. The Publications Department Secretary's post was in any case being discontinued. Robert Armstrong had served in that capacity since 1979. The Council also agreed on a more stringent policy for grants. Peter was deeply disappointed about these inevitable cuts. He admitted to the Council that he was concerned about having to write letters to churches reducing their grant aid.[14]

There were howls of protest about the axing of the Youth Co-ordinator's post. Derek Clark had held it for five years. Ron Armstrong was due to retire as Scottish Representative of the BMS in June that year and Derek was appointed his successor. Robert Armstrong commented in the editorial of the *Magazine*: 'The energy, drive and vision which Derek brought to his work among the young people of our denomination will be an asset to the Society, which seeks to use the Bi-Centenary as a launch pad for the future.'[15]

---

[13] His title changed in 1993 to Mission Co-ordinator.
[14] *SBM* (June 1992), 8.
[15] *SBM* (June 1992), 1.

Peter had to explain and defend the decision in the *Magazine*.[16] He pointed out that as well as not proceeding for the time being with the Youth Co-ordinator they were also not appointing an Administrator or a Church Development Officer as originally hoped in the re-structuring. The reserves would have been used up in two years had they gone ahead with those plans. He emphasized that as soon as giving to the Scottish Baptist Fund increased sufficiently a Youth Co-ordinator would be appointed.

The matter was discussed at the Assembly. One church felt so strongly that it had offered to pay a substantial sum annually towards the cost of the post. However, most people felt that it was unwise to establish Union posts on the basis of general appeals and that the real answer was for churches to increase their giving to the Scottish Baptist Fund. An overwhelming majority decided not to appoint a Youth Co-ordinator, but to make such an appointment a priority as soon as finances were available through the Fund.[17]

In the office at 14 Aytoun Road Peter's first Personal Assistant was Eleanor Bernard. When she left for another appointment in 1985 she had served the Union for over twenty-six years. Morag Gunn succeeded her for over six years, having already served the Union for six. In May 1992 Christine Mitchell succeeded Morag.

Peter expected efficient work in the Union offices. He said that he found it very difficult to be a manager, because he had not trained to be a manager. So a management team was set up, which met monthly. But his sense of humour was all-pervasive and those who worked with him have many memories of his lighter side: the jokes both verbal and practical!

The Union extended its office space in 1981 by purchasing the house next door (12 Aytoun Road) on a fifty-fifty basis with the Baptist Theological College of Scotland, which was re-named the Scottish Baptist College at this time. The College continued to use these premises until they were sold and it moved to the main campus of Paisley University in 2001. There were great advantages for the College and the Union in being side by side in Aytoun Road. Peter had a very happy and fruitful relationship with the College Principal, the Rev. Dr Gordon W. Martin (in office 1979–88), whom he had known since they were BD students together in Edinburgh. The happy partnership continued under Dr Ivor Oakley's Principalship (1988–94).

---

[16] *SBM* (July 1992), 10-11.

[17] In fact it was not until August 1997 that Gary Smith was appointed as National Youth Worker. At first this was a part-time appointment, but he became full-time in August 2000 as the 'National Youth Development Officer', renamed in 2004 'Young People's Advisor'.

Denominational Gatherings

Peter's command of his roles at the Annual Assembly was greatly admired. He prepared for it meticulously and exercised firm leadership. He used his humour to great effect, at least in the opinion of most people: there were some who thought humour to be out of place in such gatherings. He used Assemblies to review past progress and failures as well as to challenge the delegates to greater commitment and to set before them future aims and goals.

Over his fourteen years the format of the Assembly changed considerably. Less time was spent on business sessions and more on inspirational and educational activities. The evening 'rallies' became 'celebrations', more professionally produced, with less formality, more visual aids and more contemporary styles of worship. As the years went by he was happy to take a less prominent place at the evening meetings.

Well-known Baptist speakers came to the Assemblies: in 1983, for example, Dr David Russell (General Secretary of the BUGBI) and the Rev. Tom Houston (Communications Director of the British and Foreign Bible Society); in 1984 Dr Gerhard Claas (General Secretary of the Baptist World Alliance); in 1985 Dr Isam Ballenger (Director of the Southern Baptist work in Europe and the Middle East); in 1992 Theo Angelov (President of the Baptist Union of Bulgaria); in 1993 Dr Karl Heinz Walter (Secretary of the European Baptist Federation). There was controversy about Dr Tony Campolo in 1991: some objected to his style and approach. Peter commented: 'It confirmed what has been said in the past about Tony Campolo: you will love him or you will hate him, but you cannot ignore him and you will not forget him.'[18]

The Frustration of Finance

The Honorary Treasurer of the Union (in office 1971–96) was Mr Ian M. Bremner, CA. He presented the accounts at Assemblies with cheerful humour, but finance caused him and Peter great anxiety. Peter's term of office began after a surge of optimism in which the development of the Union was expected to prepare for immediate growth in the churches. The Council had agreed to launch a million pound fund. The appeal for the cost of 12 Aytoun Road in 1981 was then regarded as the first instalment of that fund, but the giving to that cause was slow and the million pound fund never got off the ground. In many years the Scottish Baptist Fund was in deficit.

For Peter the answer was good teaching on stewardship. He spoke and wrote persuasively on the subject. In his report for the 1981 Assembly he listed thirty-eight causes and churches supported by grant aid from the

---

[18] *SBM* (December 1991), 12.

Scottish Baptist Fund and wrote: 'In giving to the Baptist Union we are
not so much giving TO a disembodied thing called a "Union" as giving
THROUGH the Union to churches and to ministries.'[19] Sadly the results
of his endeavours were not as successful as they had been in the
stewardship campaigns at East Kilbride and Torquay.

At the Assembly in October 1984 the budget for 1984–85 had to be
substantially reduced because of a failure to meet it. The Church
Extension allocation was removed. Peter wrote a 'diary' for his *Magazine*
piece in November. For the day of the Council Meeting when this had
been agreed (11 September) he wrote wistfully: 'The treasurer had to
announce a deficit in the Scottish Baptist Fund. Wouldn't it be lovely if
we didn't have to plead for money, just decide what to do with our
surplus?!'[20]

He expressed further frustration after the 1985 Assembly:

[The delegates] could see from the treasurer's presentation that with more than
50 per cent of the Scottish Baptist Fund going directly to grants for ministry a
large part of the Fund was the Home equivalent of our Overseas giving to the
BMS. They also recognised that much of the remainder of the Fund is not so
much paying for a top heavy administration as making available nationwide
ministries and services to further the advancement of the denomination in
Scotland.

The frustration the delegates felt—and which I constantly feel—was how to
communicate this to each congregation so that the Scottish Baptist Fund
became a priority item on the local church budget.

It really is a thought that for only 5p per day or 35p per week from each
Scottish Baptist we can do all the work to which the Lord has called us. If
every church put that figure in its annual budget and met it we would have no
more talk of deficits. Blessed thought![21]

In 1992, when so much of the planned re-structuring had to be
abandoned, Peter noted that lack of giving was a general malaise among
Christians, affecting many Christian organizations. He identified the root
of the problem as 'a diminishing commitment to Christian stewardship on
the part of many believers. In part the reason may be a lack of teaching
on the subject...; on the other hand it may be that the spirit of the
consumer society is getting a hold on many of God's people and we are
losing sight of the romance and privilege of Christian giving.'[22]

---

[19] *SBYB*, 1982, 29; *SBM* (December 1981), 5.
[20] *SBM* (November 1984), 10.
[21] *SBM* (December 1985), 7.
[22] *SBM* (April 1992), 10.

Encouraging Partnership

Peter was keen to lead the churches into effective partnerships. In his *Magazine* article for August 1982 he encouraged 'partnership in the gospel' and gave several examples from across Scotland to show the effective results of co-operative planning and activity. He knew there were barriers of suspicion and apathy to break down:

> I know that as Baptists—and as Scottish Baptists at that!—we pride ourselves in our independence. Knowing how easily such independence can degenerate into isolationism, I praise God for so many of our churches that are discovering and demonstrating the enrichment of inter-dependence.

He gave examples of co-operation in the east side of Glasgow and in Aberdeen and commented:

> This really is partnership in the Gospel! It seems to me that it takes the churches in such a city meeting and praying and planning together to get the vision of reaching a whole city for Christ. Otherwise we may spend our time paddling in the puddle of parochialism.[23]

Much of what Peter recorded on his *Magazine* page sheds light on his own itinerant ministry as he travelled extensively in Scotland, bringing encouragement himself and being encouraged in such a way that he had to pass the encouragement on to the denomination as a whole. The ways in which he had contacts with particular churches and groups were numerous: they included ordinations, inductions, special anniversaries and other preaching and teaching engagements. He regularly attended the men's, women's and ministers' conferences at St Andrews.

In the April 1984 *Magazine* he gave a detailed account of his travels and experiences from Shetland to the south-west of Scotland. 'There is no doubt about it,' he concluded, 'February was a month that for me gave meaning to what "the Baptist Union" is all about. I might be excused for calling it "a caring, sharing co-op".' This was a well-known advertising slogan.[24]

He strongly maintained the necessity of interdependence. In 1991 he wrote:

> I do not for a moment question the right and ability of each individual congregation to seek and find the will of God for its life; and I would want to defend the freedom of that church to do God's will in the face of any external authority, be it civil or ecclesiastical. But, as a balance to that, I would want to affirm that if it wants to be a New Testament style of church in the Baptist

---

[23] *SBM* (August 1982), 12.
[24] *SBM* (April 1984), 10.

tradition, it will recognise its connection with, responsibility for, and dependence on, other churches if it is to be all that the Lord intended it to be.[25]

In September 1990 Peter went on a seven-day visit to Caithness, Orkney and Shetland. He found himself 'among a people with a heart-hunger for God and a givenness to prayer'. He became conscious of the blessing of Scottish Baptist fellowship. In Shetland he teased the Office Bearers of the Association by asking them, 'What would you do if the Baptist Union decided to abolish District Associations?' Their response was unanimous: 'We would make an alternative arrangement of our own!'[26]

Peter believed very firmly in the system of associations and regretted that some were weak. A series of consultations with the associations took place in 1993 and he produced a draft paper for the May Council, from which he was absent due to his first operation. It contained a fine definition of an association: 'a constituted grouping of Baptist churches and Baptist fellowships within a defined geographical area which accept the Declaration of Principle of the Baptist Union of Scotland and which are covenanted together to co-operate with one another in the fulfilment of the Aims of the Union'.[27]

Ministry to the Churches

Peter wrote notes for his *Magazine* page for September 1991 on the train from Oban to Glasgow. He had taken part in the Mull Centenary Celebrations, which had caused him to reflect on smaller churches. More than half of Scottish Baptist churches had under seventy members. He wrote about the benefits and drawbacks of small churches:

It is a fallacy to think that all the benefits belong to the big churches. They have their strengths (in abundance of resources, of money and of gifted leaders), but they also have their weaknesses. They produce parasite Christians who live off the church without contributing much to it. They can lack coherence. Instead of being one fellowship sharing together in a common task and with a common sense of purpose they can become a conglomerate of individuals or a coterie of groups each pursuing its own interests.

In the smaller church it is usually otherwise. Each member is known, each matters and the contribution of each is important. It takes the whole fellowship to match up to any of the opportunities. Small can be beautiful.

---

[25] *SBM* (February 1991), 3.

[26] *SBM* (November 1990), 10.

[27] *SBM* (June 1993), 11. A radical new structure was adopted by the Union in 2003, in which the associations were replaced by regions. Part-time Regional Networkers were appointed to stimulate mission in each region.

It can also be ugly, of course. Especially when individuals within a small church fall out, or one individual browbeats the rest, or where a spirit of backward-looking conservatism takes possession of the leadership. Parochialism, petty-mindedness and timidity are diseases to which small churches are more prone than others.

But it need not be so. And if small churches are to change and grow, it must not be so.

He then addressed the problem of financing ministry and saw a danger in opting for part-time or shared ministry, which could become 'ministry on the cheap' simply with a view to maintaining the work.

What I have seen this past weekend in Mull has convinced me again that smaller churches can grow both in numbers and in their impact on the community round them. But it will only happen when vision is shared, the past abandoned, leadership encouraged and the church positively committed to community involvement.[28]

On three occasions Peter was involved in negotiations that led to the combining of two churches into one. His skills were deeply appreciated by all concerned. In 1983 the Gorgie church in suburban Edinburgh had a pastor but no building, while the Stenhouse church had a building but no pastor. In July the two were constituted as the Stenhouse Gorgie Baptist Church, having the pastor from Gorgie (the Rev. Alan Montgomery) and meeting in the Stenhouse building. Peter had guided the whole process of union.[29]

He was chairman of the advisory committee whose work led to the uniting of Rattray Street and Ward Road in Dundee.[30] He led the act of union at the uniting service on Saturday 28 February 1987 and gave the address, in which he recognized that some would have feelings of nostalgia or guilt, but gave the assurance that 'God always leads us on to better things and he wants to surpass all our expectations with a future full of His surprises'.[31]

He also guided the George Street and Victoria Place churches in Paisley as they agreed to become Central Baptist Church (meeting in the Victoria Place premises). He led the act of union on Saturday 14 April 1990 and conducted the first services of worship the next day.[32]

There were disappointments when a few churches left the Union. Two withdrawals were reported to the May Council in 1988: Lunnasting

[28] *SBM* (September 1991), 10-11.
[29] *SBM* (August 1983), 5: the Recognition Service was on Sunday 3 July 1983.
[30] *SBM* (January 1987), 11.
[31] *SBM* (April 1987), 4.
[32] *SBM* (April 1990), 16.

church in Shetland could no longer function as it had only one member, but its building was being used by Methodists. The Christian Centre in Bishopbriggs, which had been in membership since 1974 and had been given financial support by the Union, withdrew because they were now linked with a group called the King's Ministry.[33]

However, it was a great joy to Peter that the Inverness church, which had left the Union in his presidential year, 1969, re-affiliated in 1982. When the Rev. Jim McLean died in 1985, Peter shared the memory of a meeting with him and his deacons to look together at the possible re-affiliation:

> At that moment he exemplified for me the spirit of the true peacemaker. His gentleness, his patience and his unquestionable integrity had formed a bridge of trust and openness that made for a moving and creative meeting.

> To hear the thrill of joy in his voice when he phoned some weeks later with the news that the church had decided to re-affiliate was one of life's unique privileges.[34]

At the Assembly in Dundee (October 1982), when the seven Inverness representatives came forward to be greeted by the President (Dr Charles Anderson) the whole company spontaneously rose to its feet and applauded.[35]

Co-operative Leadership

In this chapter we have seen how Peter Barber was the obvious choice to succeed his close friend Andrew MacRae as General Secretary and Superintendent of the Baptist Union of Scotland. He soon agreed that the office should be divided and worked closely with the first separate Superintendent to be appointed, Eric Watson, and his successor, Douglas Hutcheon. However, Peter's role was by no means mainly administrative. He was appointed not simply as the figurehead of the denomination, but to lead it. This he did with graciousness and wisdom. He worked through the appointed structures of the Union. He was keen to consult, ready to listen and exceptional in his ability to sum up the consensus of a meeting. People trusted his remarkable gifts of judgement, though inevitably there were sometimes sharp differences of opinion. There were some occasions when, with all his persuasive powers, he was not able to convince the denomination of the lead he felt sure he had to give.

---

[33] *SBM* (June 1988), 6.
[34] *SBM* (April 1985), 10.
[35] *SBM* (December 1982), 12.

In his relationship with the denomination as a whole he was admired for his incisive and authoritative direction at denominational gatherings, in particular the annual Assembly, and for his preaching and pastoral role in the local churches, large and small. One of his greatest frustrations was in the area of finance. People in the churches did not catch the vision that he tried to give of the opportunities available for growth through the pooling of resources.

Through his experience with individual churches he reflected both practically and theologically on their situations and their potential for growth. He tried to convince them of the strength that comes from partnership with other nearby churches, in associations and the wider denomination. Interdependence, not independence, was his watchword.

We turn next to the way that Peter stimulated the churches to look beyond themselves and become active in outreach.

CHAPTER 14

Stimulating Mission

Scotreach

Peter always put mission high on his list of priorities. Early in his secretaryship he planned a three-year evangelistic programme, called Scotreach, similar to the Simultaneous Evangelism of 1968–71. The first year (1984) was one of 'Preparation' and included training courses in church growth principles and a denominational conference at Stirling University in June. The second year (1985) was one of 'Mobilisation', in which there were regional and national rallies and the churches engaged in a wide variety of evangelistic activities. The emphasis of the third year (1986) was 'Consolidation', with training seminars on discipleship.

Peter included a challenge to courageous, costly and caring mission in his oral report to the 1982 Assembly.[1] He enlarged upon this on his page in the January 1983 *Magazine*, which was based upon his Advent reflections: what took place at Bethlehem was a co-operative venture between God (Father, Son and Holy Spirit) and Mary, the angels, the shepherds. Mission remains a co-operative venture. It must be outgoing and balanced: the Word should be made flesh. Word and deed went together in Jesus' ministry.

> Each mission will, of course, be costly—costly to our traditions, perhaps, and costly to our complacency. It will involve us in a willingness to take our message and our ministry into the market place where it will not always be appreciated, and may even be rebuffed. But from such a cost we simply must not shrink.[2]

The regional consultations he led as an introduction to Scotreach in April and May 1983 were attended by representatives of around 90% of the churches.

At the Church of Scotland General Assembly in May 1983 'an urgent call to the Kirk' was given by a group of three former Moderators of the General Assembly, including Professor T.F. Torrance, and its Principal

---

[1] *SBM* (November 1982), 7.
[2] *SBM* (January 1983), 10-11.

Clerk. In the face of a steep decline in membership, which was by then well under a million,[3] they called for a repentant return of the Church of Scotland to Christ. They insisted that the truth of Jesus Christ and his gospel, as mediated through the holy scriptures, must be given its rightful place in the preaching and teaching of the Church. Mission and evangelism must be given priority and a controlling place in all worship, life and activity of the Kirk. They called for a stress upon personal faith and commitment, the renewal of prayer life, regular Bible study and the steady rehabilitation of evangelical belief.

Peter welcomed all this and saw possibilities of co-operation in the Scotreach years:

> Given this kind of emphasis I can see increasing potential for co-operation (despite our differences over Church order and baptism) between our own Churches and local Parish Churches.

> In fact I can see that for some of our Churches the evangelism we have planned for the 1985 Scotreach Year of Mobilisation might well be undertaken on a united basis with a neighbouring Church of Scotland (and other sympathetic Churches).

> What is at stake in these days is not just the fate of the Church (the national Church or any other) but the spiritual destiny of the whole nation. That the call to the Kirk recognises that and points so unapologetically to the only answer is in every way welcome.

> Let us pray that the Church of Scotland—and the Church in Scotland—may not turn a deaf ear.[4]

During the second and third years of Scotreach the Union had a full-time 'Evangelist and Field Worker in Mission'. Lewis Misselbrook had served in the Mission Department of the BUGBI for eight years, following his well-known ministries at Leavesden Road, Watford, Rushden, and Chelmesley Wood, Birmingham. He agreed to serve in Scotland for the two years before his retirement, 1985–86. Peter commended him to serve the denomination 'not simply as pulpit supply, but more as an enabler and trainer of others to help them individually and corporately to fulfil their mission'.[5]

Peter was one of the speakers at the Denominational Conference at Stirling University in June 1984. This was a stimulus to evangelism in the middle of the first year of Scotreach. In his address he suggested that those who looked at Scotland from the prophetic perspective would 'feel

---

[3] The population of Scotland was around 5,180,200 in 1981.

[4] *SBM* (July 1983), 10.

[5] *SBM* (February 1984), 10.

for Scotland with God's heartbeat and weep over it with God's compassion'. He described Scotland as 'religiously post-Christian, socially divided and ideologically pessimistic'. It was not enough to say 'Turn to Jesus'. There was a need for Christians to display a model of unity, a ministry of caring and to share a message of hope.[6]

In the July 1984 *Magazine* he emphasized the importance of getting out to where the people were:

> This was how Jesus first meant it to be. To engage in 'mission' is, by definition, to be 'sent'. The Lord's command is to *go* and make disciples, not to sit and wait for customers.

> We simply have to reverse the 'draw them in' syndrome for the 'drive them out' syndrome. We have to get back to the Biblical pattern of a church gathered for worship so that it might be renewed for witness.[7]

In the Summer of 1984 there were two well publicized missions in England: Luis Palau's Mission to London and Billy Graham's Mission England. Before they took place many churchmen expressed their misgivings about mass evangelism and the policies of the evangelists, but Peter came to their defence. He pointed to the remarkable success of both missions, which he regarded as revealing a great spiritual hunger in England. The same was true of Scotland, so that in the Scotreach Year of Mobilization the gospel would find a response when it was faithfully shared.

Part of his defence of the English missions was a reminiscence from an earlier debate:

> I still carry vivid memories of being present at the Church of Scotland Assembly when it was debated whether or not the National Church should give its support to an invitation to Billy Graham to come to Scotland for the 1955 Crusade.

> Many devious arguments were presented about Billy Graham's fundamentalism, the emotionalism of mass evangelism, the threat to the 'Tell Scotland' Mission—and so on. When it looked as if the vote was going to turn against the invitation Professor James Stewart stood up, and in a memorable speech reminded the Assembly that there was once an occasion when Jesus' own disciples had tried to stifle an initiative, saying, 'Master, we saw one casting out devils in thy name, and he followeth not us; and we forbade him, because he followeth not us.' And what was Jesus' response? 'Forbid him not;

---

[6] As reported in the *SBM* (July 1984), 8.
[7] *SBM* (July 1984), 11.

for there is no man that shall do a miracle in my name that can lightly speak evil of me. For he that is not against us is on our part.'[8]

Peter had several opportunities of hearing Billy Graham during his meetings in Scotland in the early part of 1955. Ian Leitch recalls that his first trip to one of the meetings in Kelvin Hall, Glasgow, was led by Peter, who had the group singing hymns and choruses all the way home on the train![9]

In his Annual Report to the 1987 Assembly Peter expressed disappointment that Scotreach had not had a more marked effect in increased membership, but he welcomed a continuing emphasis on mission both in church plans and in denominational thinking.[10] In more recent years it has been claimed that the campaign had more effect on membership statistics than had been appreciated before.

Wider Mission

Peter was a member of the Scottish Co-ordinating Committee for the Billy Graham Satellite Mission in June 1989, when the meetings were relayed to Scotland from Earls Court, London. He was also the Union's representative on the Inviting Committee for Billy Graham's Mission Scotland, which took place in May and June 1991. The venues were Edinburgh, Aberdeen and Glasgow.

At the beginning of that year Peter urged the readers of the *Magazine* (1) to give priority to prayer for the mission; (2) to be alert to take the opportunities for personal witness; (3) to make the churches the kind of fellowships in which new converts would feel at home and in which they would grow in Christ.[11]

After the mission he shared his personal reflections. He felt immense gratitude for the numbers who attended and the thousands who responded and asked what accounted for the response. He acknowledged the technical criticisms of Graham's preaching, though he applauded 'his note of authority, his use of Scripture, his simple clarity and the sheer comprehensiveness of each address... What the preaching lacked in eloquence was more than made up for in sheer faithfulness.' However, the response could not be accounted for by exceptional preaching. The vast amount of prayer was nearer the secret, but much prayer took place in local church work and such results were not seen. He finally admitted

---

[8] *SBM* (August 1984), 10.

[9] Peter's appointments diary has a note of a trip by train to Glasgow with the Charlotte Chapel YPM on Monday 18 April 1955.

[10] *SBM* (December 1987), 13.

[11] *SBM* (January 1991), 10.

that he could not unveil the secret of Mission Scotland. 'It was the Lord's doing, and marvellous in our eyes.'[12]

There were other stimuli to evangelism in 1991. At the January Council Peter advocated the call for Christians of all denominations to make the last decade of the twentieth century the Decade of Evangelism. In particular he advocated the 'Seoul Covenant', the challenge from the Baptists who had gathered for the Baptist World Alliance Congress in Seoul, South Korea, in August 1990. Churches around the world were urged to sign the covenant on Pentecost Sunday (19 May 1991).[13] To emphasize the importance of such an act he made telling reference in the March *Magazine* to the signing of the National Covenant on 28 February 1638, which heralded the start of the 'Scottish Covenanters' movement. He urged every local church to consider 'A Disturbing Agenda'.

> It is an agenda which will help you to look at your church, your budget, your minister, your membership, your organisations, your neighbourhood, your area and your world. It will help you to 'Listen to God' as you face the fundamental question—are we a pastoral centre that cares for the committed or a mission centre that is committed to the outsider?
>
> It is my sincere hope that every one of our churches, whether large or small, will share in this challenge and opportunity. As Scottish Baptists we have the reputation of being evangelistic but those who know us best deny it. They say we are evangelical in theology, but in-turned in practice.[14]

His enthusiasm for evangelism was recognized by the British Council of Churches, which appointed him to the Standing Committee on Evangelism. In his 'diary' of engagements in September–October 1984 he wrote for 17 September:

> In London for a meeting of the Evangelism Committee of the British Council of Churches. A conference for those engaged in Children's Evangelism is planned; we discussed in the afternoon the sharing of the Gospel with those of other faiths. Donald English, an evangelical leader among English Methodists, makes an excellent chairman.[15]

Peter's understanding of Christian mission embraced concern for society and its problems. He was a member of the Church Leaders Forum, which met every two months in St Andrews House, Edinburgh. The Secretary of State for Scotland invited one leader from each of the main denominations to join the Forum. Its purpose was to review any matters

---

[12] *SBM* (August 1991), 10-11.
[13] *SBM* (February 1991), 8.
[14] *SBM* (March 1991), 10-11.
[15] *SBM* (November 1984), 10.

of social or spiritual concern that should be brought to his attention. They covered subjects such as education, the prison service, drug addiction, the steel industry, unemployment, Sunday observance and a teachers' strike. None of the discussions or recommendations was made public, but its work was communicated to the Government through the year and once a year it spent a morning with the Secretary of State going over the matters of deepest concern.[16]

Among the topics that the Union spoke out about under Peter's leadership was a reduction in nuclear weapons and an increase in aid to the poorest countries: at the 1983 Assembly Andrew White introduced a motion on these subjects, referring to remarks made by Peter in his Annual Report, by the President (the Rev. A. Brunton Scott) in his address and by Dr David Russell. There was a lively debate and the motion was approved by 146 to eighty-eight, with fifty-five abstentions.[17]

When he gave his Annual Report to the 1985 Assembly Peter said that representations had been made on behalf of the denomination on the miners' strike, the teachers' dispute, unemployment, the Warnock Report, the American intervention in Nicaragua, the famine in the sub-Saharan region of Africa and the Government's 'Green Paper' on social security benefits.[18]

In January 1986 the Council endorsed the Baptist World Alliance resolution on racism and South Africa, calling on the British Government to press upon the South African Government the need for justice and equity among all their peoples and the total elimination of apartheid. However, it was not in favour of the British Council of Churches' 1985 resolution that called for the use by the British Government of selected sanctions as a peaceful and effective means of bringing pressure.[19]

Church Planting

When Peter took office a movement of church planting was well in progress. In the mid-1970s Andrew MacRae and the Office Bearers persuaded the Council and the Assembly to embark on a new strategy of pioneer ministries. This resulted in the establishment of the following churches between 1978 and 1981: Aberdeen International, Cornton (Stirling), Alness, Bridge of Don (Aberdeen), Dalbeattie and Dedridge (Livingston). The movement continued and Peter took his part in it, giving advice and support. Further churches were founded between 1981

---

[16] *SBM* (August 1986), 10.

[17] *SBM* (December 1983), 2 and 9.

[18] *SBM* (November 1985), 6. For the miners' strike of 1984: *SBM* (November 1984), 1; (December 1984), 12; for the Warnock Report: *SBM* (April 1985), 8-9; for the famine in Ethiopia: *SBM* (December 1984), 12.

[19] *SBM* (February 1986), 8.

and 1990: Wigtown, Collydean (Glenrothes), Newton Mearns, Thurso, Stranraer, Sanquhar, Stonehaven, Ellon, Castlehill (Bearsden), Harestanes (Kirkintilloch), Nairn, and Kinmylies (Inverness).

The Union promoted appeals to raise money towards the cost of buildings for three of these churches: Alness, Dedridge and Bridge of Don. The Livingston church, situated in the Ladywell area, which had been constituted in 1968, began work in the Dedridge area in the south of the town in October 1979.[20] Ladywell and Dedridge became two congregations in the one church. The Dedridge Congregation soon made rapid progress and when the Assembly agreed to promote the appeal for a new building in 1982 it was meeting in a Roman Catholic Primary School and being led with boundless enthusiasm by Alistair Brown (who has served as General Director of BMS World Mission since 1996). The congregation was raising £35,000; the Union appeal was for £60,000. Peter was an ardent apologist for it, especially because of his experience in East Kilbride. He was a strong advocate for building projects:

> To have your own building, while it does add some financial liability, gives a focus to the church's witness, a flexibility in the church's programme and provides facilities for meeting a wide range of needs in the community. I personally have witnessed the undoubted stimulus given to a church's work when it has its own 'home'.

He stressed Dedridge's investment potential: 'To invest in church extension is to give what you can never lose that others may gain what they can never measure.'[21]

Early in 1983 he paid a visit to the Alness church, which had been pioneered by the Rev. Bill Clark from 1975. He was impressed by the love shown by the church to people in need and by the transforming power of the gospel among them. The church's building had been opened in March 1980[22] with Scottish Baptists paying £46,300 out of the total £69,900. 'And what we have done in Alness we will do again in Dedridge. Why? Because mission is at the heart of the Church's business. It is investment in people. It is fulfilling the Lord's command. It is laying up treasure—for eternity.'[23]

During the first year of the Dedridge appeal giving was almost on target, but then there was a lull and Peter used his page in the March 1984 *Magazine* to encourage the denomination to get its second wind and reach the £60,000 total.[24] By the time of the 1984 Assembly (in October)

---

[20] *SBM* (January 1980), 3.

[21] *SBM* (December 1982), 10.

[22] *SBM* (April 1980), 7.

[23] *SBM* (April 1983), 10.

[24] *SBM* (March 1984), 10.

£52,000 of the £60,000 target had been received.[25] The building was opened in November that year.[26]

The next focus of attention was on the new building for the Bridge of Don church. An appeal was launched at the 1984 Assembly for £50,000 over the next two years, towards a total of over £300,000. The response to that appeal was disappointingly slow.[27] The building was opened on Saturday 16 April, 1988. Following the Bridge of Don Appeal the appeal for church extension became more general.

The new fellowship at Newton Mearns was planted by the church of which Peter and Isobel were members, Queen's Park, Glasgow. In March 1983 twenty-four members of the new church were commissioned as the nucleus. Peter saw this as an event reminiscent of the setting apart of Paul and Barnabas in Acts 13. He argued that there was a 'need for displaced persons' and encouraged others to support or begin local fellowships, particularly those travelling miles to attend a large church.

> I am really challenging individual Baptist families in Scotland to get involved in Christ's mission in their own neighbourhood. This in some instances could mean joining the local Baptist Church. It might even mean forming a group of Baptists in the district with a view to establishing a totally new cause. It certainly does mean being willing to begin at our own Jerusalem.
>
> Jesus said: 'You shall be witnesses unto Me.' The question we dare not dodge is—are we such witnesses where he means us to be?[28]

Later in the year he returned to the theme of church planting, describing the different ways the churches at Thurso, Collydean, Newton Mearns and Wigtown had been planted, and commenting:

> We are not out simply to 'save souls', who, once converted, are to live their Christian lives in isolation. Those who believe and are baptized are meant to be 'added' to the Church. The goal of evangelism is nothing less than CHURCH growth. It is within the body of Christ and not detached from it that members of Christ's body are to be nurtured. We ought not therefore to be content until each one who professes faith is fully incorporated into a local congregation.
>
> But if the incorporation of new Christians is the primary objective of evangelism...we ought not to lose sight of the fact that the multiplication of churches is a logical extension of that policy.

---

[25] *SBM* (December 1984), 12.

[26] *SBM* (January 1985), 4.

[27] *SBYB*, 1987, 53.

[28] *SBM* (May 1983), 10-11.

There are so many parts of Scotland where, as yet, there is no effective evangelical witness.[29]

Always an Evangelist

Just as in his churches and with his pastoral experience to inform him, Peter constantly promoted mission as a priority of church life. This meant the sharing of the good news of Christ, caring for needs in the community and having an impact on wider moral and social issues. He encouraged personal witnessing, initiatives by local churches and a special three-year denominational impetus to outreach. He advocated co-operation in mission work with churches of other denominations. He was fully in support of national Billy Graham campaigns. Although well aware of the problems of making Christian witness effective in the late-twentieth century, he never stopped seeking out fresh methods and giving practical advice to churches in their task.

The total membership of Scottish Baptist churches remained more or less the same over the period he was in office, but the number of churches in the Union rose.[30] This was because of the impetus to church planting that began in the mid-1970s and continued. Altogether eighteen new churches were founded between 1978 and 1990. Peter saw this as an important means of growth and believed there were many other areas of Scotland where Baptist churches should be planted.

---

[29] *SBM* (November 1983), 10-11.

[30] When Peter became General Secretary in 1980 there were 159 churches in the Union, with a total of 14,331 members (13,905 from reporting churches, 426 from non-reporting churches). In 1994 there were 170 churches in the Union, with 14,328 members from reporting churches (no figure is given for non-reporting churches). Statistics from *SBYB*, 1981, 31; *SBYB*, 1995, 112.

CHAPTER 15

Confronting Problems

Peter never shied away from controversial topics. Rather, he faced up to them, spoke with directness about them and often made his views clear with great courage. In his management of controversy his experience in England proved valuable to him, for there he had experienced a greater diversity within the Baptist constituency, sometimes within one church. He was able now to accept greater divergence of views and seek to bring different sides together in mutual respect.

Women in the Ministry

Early in the 1980s several women applied to the Union for ministry. The Ministerial Recognition Committee set up a sub-committee and Peter served on it. From his background and experience he was able to appreciate the force of arguments on both sides. The final decision of the Committee, which reported in 1984, was in favour of accepting women on the same terms as men.[1] One of the eight members dissented, advocating a kind of deaconess order. Three members were unreservedly in favour of women ministers. The other four were in favour, but with some reservations about their being in sole pastoral charge of a church. Peter was one of the four.

In the subsequent debates he adopted a neutral stance. The Joint Ministerial Board accepted the report by a good majority, but the Council vote failed to reach a two-thirds majority, so that it was not brought to the Assembly in 1984. However, the Hillhead church, Glasgow, requested that the subject should be debated at Assembly and the January Council agreed that it should be discussed by the churches and brought to the 1985 Assembly. Peter argued that it was important to face the issue in fairness to women who were applying for ministry and to avoid any suggestion that they simply 'slipped into' pastoral office. He believed

---

[1] An edited version of the report was published in the Viewpoint Series: *Women in the Ministry* (Glasgow: Baptist Union of Scotland, 1983).

that the way in which the Assembly discussed this question would be a test of fellowship.[2]

The decision was made that a two-thirds majority should be required, but this caused controversy. At the May Council Peter expressed the feeling of the Executive that 'on a matter of such importance and sensitivity there should be widespread agreement'. He felt that in this way a clear indication would be given of the mind of the Assembly and that those who did not agree with the decision, whatever it turned out to be, would be more ready to accept it if it were given large support than if it were decided on a narrow vote.[3] The question was also raised in the Assembly, which voted that two-thirds was required.

The Hillhead motion was 'That women should be accepted for training for the Baptist ministry and in due course be placed on the accredited list on the same terms as men.' The Stirling church proposed the addendum: 'The Assembly accepts, however, that in terms of our Baptist principles the ultimate final authority for recognizing a call to the teaching and pastoral ministry lies solely with the local church.' This was incorporated into the motion.

The delegates were almost equally divided. The motion just failed to get a simple majority. Of the 466 who voted there were 231 in support of the motion while 235 voted against it.

Before the debate Peter urged the delegates 'to look charitably upon each other, to listen carefully, to speak gently and to accept the decision graciously'.[4] He was not disappointed, as he commented in the *Magazine*:

It was not what we said but how we said it that was most impressive. In speech after speech there was mutual respect, deep conviction, careful argument—and gentleness. It genuinely grieved us that we had to differ and it was obvious that what bound us together was far greater than this issue that divided us.

By the end of the debate I had seen in our Assembly a love and a maturity that moved me deeply.[5]

Divorce and the Ministry

Another thorny issue was divorce, particularly for standards of ministry. Peter had faced up to the question in Torquay and had written a paper on

[2] *SBM* (February 1985), 5.
[3] *SBM* (June 1985), 3.
[4] *SBYB*, 1986, 102 (Assembly Minutes).
[5] *SBM* (December 1985), 7. In 1999 the Assembly voted by a majority of 68.6% that any persons, male or female, called to pastoral ministry may present themselves for recognition, training and accreditation (*SBYB*, 2000, 236-241, 244).

the subject that many colleagues had found helpful. He believed that divorce in certain circumstances was biblical and acceptable. Others disagreed and the Joint Ministerial Board was divided on the subject in various ways. Because of the complexity of the situations involved and the criteria proposed it was extremely difficult to arrive at agreement. The frustration that this caused is brought out by Peter's 'diary entry' on his *Magazine* page in November 1984 for 13 September: 'A very complex discussion today in the sub-committee that keeps under review the issue of Divorce and the Ministry. Nothing is as simple as it seems.'[6]

Guidelines were finally agreed that allowed the acceptance of divorced candidates for ministry in certain very restricted circumstances, but Peter himself would have preferred a wider approach.

The Charismatic Renewal Movement

Controversy over the charismatic renewal movement sometimes arose. One of the 'Viewpoint' booklets produced by the Doctrine and Inter-Church Relations Committee was *Scottish Baptists and the Charismatic Renewal Movement.*[7] Peter wrote most of this. He gave balanced and wise counsel, setting out the strengths and weaknesses of the movement and advice on how to handle it at the local level. In response to a letter to the *Magazine* from a perplexed church member, Peter drew attention to the booklet, which, he said, was intended to offer pastoral guidance, and commented:

Moving among the churches as I do, I find a variety of views on this subject. Some regard the Movement as a Satanic distraction, others as a temporary irrelevance, others as a divisive threat, and others as the supreme answer to the church's contemporary needs.

Because this issue is not of the essence of the faith (such as the Deity of Christ) and one in which equally sincere Bible-loving Christians can legitimately disagree we have not regarded it as a question on which any one 'official' view needed to be propounded.[8]

Freemasonry

The relation of Christianity to Freemasonry was a question on which the Executive was forced to change its mind. In January 1986 it recommended to the Council that Freemasonry should not be made a

---

[6] *SBM* (November 1984), 10.

[7] Published in Glasgow by the Baptist Union of Scotland, [1980s].

[8] *SBM* (February 1987), 2 (the letter); (March 1987) 2 (Peter's reply).

matter of public debate, but should be dealt with by each congregation as
the need arose. Peter explained that it was not causing widespread trouble
in the churches, it was felt to be a matter in which liberty of conscience
should be exercised, and there was sufficient literature available for
individuals or churches to reach an informed opinion for themselves.
However, some members expressed their disquiet, commenting that
declaring it to be a matter for liberty of conscience might encourage
church members to be involved in Freemasonry and that Freemasons
themselves were not fully aware of the spiritual problems arising from the
organisation. There were amendments urging churches to look at the
matter and to invite the Doctrine and Inter-Church Relations (DICR)
Committee to prepare a list of published materials, but they were defeated
and the motion was accepted by a large majority.[9]

This decision caused controversy on the letters page of the *Magazine*
for a few months. A strong letter from the diaconate of the Erskine
church[10] brought a carefully worded reply from Peter, on behalf of the
Executive, saying 'that a denominational stand on any matter is only
called for when we have a widespread denominational issue facing us and
even at that when any pronouncement is made or policy advocated we
would still urge that the adoption of the statement or policy must remain
a matter for the conscience of the individual Baptist or local
congregation'. However, he indicated that the DICR Committee was
surveying literature available on the movement with a view to advising on
the most helpful books.[11]

Feelings remained strong and the Executive brought a recommendation to the September Council to appoint a group to study the
relationship between Freemasonry and Christianity, the findings to be
published in a 'Viewpoint' booklet to provide clear guidance. There was
only a narrow majority in the Executive, but a large one in the Council,
despite the opposition of the Superintendent, the Vice-President and the
Ex-President.[12]

The group, chaired by the Rev. Alfred Peck, was appointed by the
Council in January 1987. It concluded that there was an inherent
incompatibility between Freemasonry and the Christian faith, so that
commitment within the movement was inconsistent with a Christian's
commitment to Jesus Christ as Lord. The report was approved by the
Council on 8 September 1987. Peter himself proposed the acceptance of
the Executive's recommendation that Scottish Baptists should be urged
not to become Freemasons, that those who were already Freemasons
should study the findings of the group, and that young people should be

[9] *SBM* (February 1986), 8.
[10] *SBM* (March 1986), 2-3.
[11] *SBM* (April 1986), 2.
[12] *SBM* (October 1986), 4-5.

aware of the concerns expressed.[13] After some final changes the Assembly in October accepted the report, which was later published as a 'Viewpoint' booklet.[14]

State Control

The issue of state control of churches arose in new legislation in the early 1990s. The Law Reform Act became fully operational in Scotland on 30 September 1992. It was designed to prevent abuses in public charities, but it caused Scottish churches some concern because it gave powers to the state to intrude into and investigate the affairs of charities: if this applied to churches it would raise serious issues about the autonomy of local churches and their independence from state interference. The finances of the larger churches would be open to inspection and ultimately the Secretary of State would have the right to appoint a treasurer.

Peter regarded this as contrary to Baptist principles and a matter for very serious concern. He told the September 1992 Council that the matter was being pursued vigorously and sensitively in co-operation with other churches. The authorities were keeping the churches informed and were willing to reach mutually suitable arrangements.[15] Detailed information on the registration of the churches as charities was given at the Assembly in October.[16]

Peter raised the same matter of principle in the BUGB Council and expected to be strongly supported by the inheritors of the English Nonconformist tradition. He was amazed and saddened to find no resistance from the English body, but rather a reluctance to 'rock the boat'. The matter was talked out by their legal adviser and Peter was isolated.[17] The Act was passed as proposed.

Relations with Other Denominations

By far the greatest source of controversy was the relationship between Baptists and other denominations. This had been so for many years and, as we have seen, was an issue in Peter's presidential Assembly in 1969, but a radically new situation arose in the 1980s.

When Peter took office the Union was in membership of the Scottish Churches' Council (SCC) and of the British Council of Churches (BCC), but not the World Council of Churches (WCC). When the WCC discussion

---

[13] *SBM* (October 1987), 6-7 (Tuesday 8 May is an error for Tuesday 8 September); *SBYB*, 1988, 102.

[14] *Baptists and Freemasonry* (Glasgow: Baptist Union of Scotland, 1987).

[15] *SBM* (October 1992), 13.

[16] *SBM* (December 1992), 7.

[17] Information from Eric Watson.

document *Baptism, Eucharist and Ministry* was published in 1982, Peter drew the attention of the Assembly to it, saying that although the Union was not in membership of the WCC, the document was significant and all Churches were being asked to make a response to it.[18] The Union published its own response in October 1984.[19]

The main concern of those opposed to ecumenical involvement was the Roman Catholic Church. For historical reasons there is a greater antipathy between Protestants and Roman Catholics in Scotland, particularly in the central belt, than in England and Wales.

When Pope Paul II visited Scotland in May–June1982 the Union decided not to be involved with a meeting of church leaders with the Pope or with a Protestant–Roman Catholic consultation on 'the nature of the unity we seek and our expectations of one another' to be held in Dunblane. A letter from Peter as General Secretary expressed unease about focusing on the Pope's visit for ecumenical engagement and made it clear 'that Baptists saw difficulties in uniting in mission with those with whom they were in fundamental disagreement about doctrinal matters not least concerning the nature of the Gospel'.

Peter commented on the papal visit in the July *Magazine*. He acknowledged that it had been a resounding success for the Roman Catholic Church; that Protestants had been surprised by the exuberance of Catholic worship; that evangelicals had been confused to hear them sing choruses that they had assumed to be the exclusive preserve of charismatic believers. He affirmed that the Roman Catholic Church in the British Isles was changing in at least two respects, in its worship style and in the place given to study of the Bible. Yet there was no doubt that beneath the Pope's benign, tolerant exterior he was a man who was inflexible in his adherence to traditional Roman Catholic dogma. He went on to make a plea for the adoption of a positive attitude to the visit and its implications, and listed positive factors that needed to be recognized, but warned against being softheaded or naive in such situations: what was at stake was nothing less than the one and only apostolic gospel: salvation by faith alone 'in what Jesus did for us in the finished work of Calvary'.[20]

Inter-Church Process

At this time the Roman Catholics were not members of the BCC or the SCC, only observers, but proposals were already being considered for 'new ecumenical instruments' within the United Kingdom that were to change the groupings of the churches radically. Many new churches were

---

[18] *SBM* (December 1983), 12.

[19] *Baptism, Eucharist and Ministry: A Scottish Baptist Response to the Lima Document* (Glasgow: Baptist Union of Scotland, 1984).

[20] *SBM* (July 1982), 12.

to be included and the Roman Catholic Church was to be in full membership. The Autumn Assembly of the BCC in London in November 1982 passed a motion: 'The British Council of Churches is ready for change so as better to serve the growth into unity, and invites the Roman Catholic Church to share in the discussion of changes which might hasten the day when it can feel ready to become a member.'[21]

In 1984 the Union received a letter from the Rev. Philip Morgan, General Secretary of the BCC asking it to share in a process of prayer, reflection and debate relating to the nature of the church and its renewal for mission in the context of a possible new instrument of ecumenical activity, and proposals about wider involvement of Christian groups in such a body. The Executive recommended a positive response and this was overwhelmingly supported by the September Council. However, it felt that any participating body should accept a basis of faith; that invitations should extend to evangelical organizations; and that the position of the SCC should be on the agenda.[22]

In a 'diary entry' in the November 1984 *Magazine* Peter wrote for 18 September:

Still in London for a meeting of Church leaders from all over the United Kingdom, under the chairmanship of the Archbishop of York. What is the future for the British Council of Churches? Is another instrument of inter-church co-operation needed? There is a good deal of plain speaking...and no thirst for another conference for its own sake![23]

In the March 1985 *Magazine* he observed that the denomination was being forced to reflect on the new 'ecumenical process' in the United Kingdom. He had recently attended a meeting of church leaders in London when the Rev. Bernard Thorogood, Secretary of the Consultation, had asked searching questions about the relationship between denominations and the church: 'Do we see our church as the whole of the Church, or the essence of the whole, or part of the whole, or a wing of the whole?' Peter then discussed these questions in some depth and gave notice that they were now on the agenda and the denomination needed to face up to them, but he provided no easy answers to them. His concluding paragraph shows how he approached this major new development:

Will you pray that as we give answers to such questions and work our way through these next challenging years we may be given the grace to give

---

[21] *SBM* (January 1983), 14.
[22] *SBM* (October 1984), 4.
[23] *SBM* (November 1984), 10.

answers that are faithful to our inheritance, loyal to Scripture, fair to others and to the ultimate good of Christ and his kingdom?[24]

The May 1985 Council agreed to recommend to the Assembly full participation in the inter-church programme provided that those participating accepted the BCC statement of faith.[25] This was due to concern that one of the groups taking part in the process was the Unitarian Church. This decision was communicated to the organizing committee, but the letter did not arrive until after its meeting. Its next meeting was not until November—after the Union's Assembly—but Peter had indications at an informal level that it was unlikely that the basis on which the process would proceed would be changed at this stage.[26]

In his report to the Assembly Peter re-asserted his own Baptist convictions: he saw the different denominations as meaningful agents for God's work for the foreseeable future. There were distinctive aspects of Baptist denominational life that were attractive. He affirmed his belief in the unity of Christ's people, but said that there were principles that were not negotiable. Among them were those that formed the basis of the Union, dealing with the authority of scripture, believer's baptism and the recognition of the Lordship of Christ: 'As time goes by I feel less and less inclined to apologise for Baptist principles, and as my experience of denominational life grows so does the conviction of its worthwhileness.'[27]

At the Assembly there was a majority of 175 to 133 in favour of sharing in the Inter-Church Process, but only on the understanding that those participating were required to accept the current BCC basis of faith. The debate was complex because of the Unitarian issue. The motion that the Union should participate fully in the Inter-Church Process in Scotland, where Unitarians were not involved, was overwhelmingly agreed.[28] In the *Magazine* Peter commented:

> I appreciate that for some the presence of Roman Catholics in the Process of prayer, reflection and debate, will be a problem. All I would stress is that, in engaging in the Process, we are not constitutionally linked with other Churches, merely committed to meeting and discussing on the understanding that we do so on the basis of a common understanding of the Person of Christ and of God.
>
> If we are to make the contribution to, and gain the insights from the Inter-Church Process that we should as Scottish Baptists, we shall need a great deal

---

[24] *SBM* (March 1985), 10.
[25] *SBM* (October 1985), 5; *SBYB*, 1986, 90.
[26] *SBM* (October 1985), 5.
[27] *SBM* (November 1985), 5.
[28] *SBM* (December 1985), 13-14.

of wisdom, openness, courage and grace. Will you pray that we will not be lacking in any of these as the next three years unfold?[29]

At the January 1986 Council Peter reported that the Process was proceeding for the time being without a basis of faith, though it was a matter which would require to be faced and decided on in any discussions and deliberation. Because of fears about the non-Trinitarian basis and the involvement of Unitarians in the discussions, the Union would take up at this stage only observer status.[30]

In the March *Magazine* Peter urged Baptists to be involved in discussions on the Inter-Church Process at the local level:

To participate in such dialogue is not to say that we agree with other churchmen's views, nor is it to be constitutionally committed to an organisation implying theological agreement. It is to share in a process of prayer, reflection and debate that should deepen our understanding of where we each are. It certainly should serve to remove false misunderstandings and make us think through more clearly why we believe what we do.

Of course there is the risk of theological exposure in such a process but must that not be measured against another risk — that of distancing ourselves from other professing Christians and ascribing to them views that they may no longer hold.

If we cannot walk hand-in-hand with other churchmen, ought we not at least to be walking side by side and on talking terms?[31]

The Inter-Church Conferences

Peter and four other representatives of the Union took part as full members of the Process in Scotland at a Conference in St Andrews early in April 1987. Peter explained the whole situation in the March *Magazine* and commented:

It is desperately easy to view with suspicion and fear any kind of ecumenical endeavour and to fail to be genuinely open to see if perhaps the Lord may be leading his people in a new initiative. At the same time it is possible to be naive and unfaithful to the truth as it is entrusted to us.

The last thing we would want to fall into, I am sure, is blind bigotry.[32]

---

[29] *SBM* (December 1985), 7.
[30] *SBM* (February 1986), 9.
[31] *SBM* (March 1986), 11.
[32] *SBM* (March 1987), 10.

Despite this appeal the very next month there were letters in the *Magazine* from those objecting to the Union's involvement in the Process at all and the correspondence, with views expressed on both sides, continued for several months. A letter from Dr John Drane assured the readers: 'Our own General Secretary (and others) put a Biblical perspective very clearly before the gathering at St Andrews.'[33]

Peter gave his impressions of the St Andrews Conference in the May *Magazine*. Together with the other Baptist representatives he was impressed by the wide range of representation and the seriousness with which the task was tackled.

> In the discussion groups in particular a wide diversity of theological viewpoints came through. We did not all see eye to eye on the church or the sacraments or the nature of mission, though in my own group (which included a Methodist minister, an Orthodox priest, Church of Scotland and Roman Catholic lay-people) I did find a real desire to be faithful to Christ and His Word. It was an arena in which clichés were challenged and we all had to be prepared to justify any claim we made. It was a tough, mind-stretching, heart-warming experience that left us all sharply aware of the differences that do exist between the traditions and they will not be easily resolved.[34]

He found some aspects of the Conference to be immature marks of ecumenical impatience that did more harm than good in inter-church relations, notably the decision to include a Roman Catholic mass and a Church of Scotland communion service in the programme when the delegates included Quakers and Salvationists. He pled for sensitivity to the pace at which change was possible or responsible:

> You simply cannot brush aside 427 years of Scottish Reformation history in 13 months' discussion and a 48-hour conference. There are deep issues that divide Protestant and Catholic theology, many of which touch on the very heart of the Gospel. These issues need to be faced, aired and debated in the interests of truth and the kingdom. To ignore such fundamental differences and rush into any kind of union would be to fail both past and future generations.[35]

At the May Council Peter presented a 'Statement on Unity', which was based on the one prepared for the 1967 Assembly, a balanced statement insisting on spiritual unity prior to organic union, recognizing stumbling blocks, but noting a number of areas where there were prospects for co-operation and fellowship. He also gave the Council a report on the impressions of the delegates at the St Andrews Conference:

---

[33] *SBM* (May 1987), 3.
[34] *SBM* (May 1987), 10.
[35] *SBM* (May 1987), 11.

We were aware of representing a denomination in which many have expressed serious reservations about the ecumenical movement, fearing guilt by association with a Process which includes Roman Catholics. As representatives of the denomination we gave expression to Baptist and evangelical principles which were not always popular but found an echo among other delegates...

Questions are...raised as to how we can justify separating ourselves spiritually from the company of those who trust in Christ and seek to do his will, how we understand Christ's prayer for the unity of his disciples and whether as Scottish Baptists we really want greater Christian unity and how far our Baptist tradition of tolerance and historic concern for religious liberty relates to ecumenical involvement.[36]

The UK Inter-Church Process Conference took place at Swanwick, Derbyshire, in September 1987. The 'Swanwick Declaration' appeared in the October *Magazine* and Peter gave a full report of the conference because it was important for all church members to be aware of the developments. He felt that the conference had made a major contribution to strengthening inter-church fellowship.

The spirit of acceptance and forbearance over a spectrum of churchmanship reaching from Christian Brethren and Salvationists to Anglicans and Roman Catholics was unmistakable. There was a joyful sense of fellow believers discovering each other.

Not that this meant a fudging of very real theological differences. These were voiced and aired, not, however, in a spirit of harsh rancour but rather in a spirit of openness and respect.

The discussions were supported by a large programme of meditation, prayer, and shared worship. A wide range of worship styles was used.

For not a few, a high moment in the conference was to hear delegates sing, under the leadership of a black pastor, 'Spirit of the Living God, fall afresh on me'.

Many at the conference spoke of their sense of the Spirit leading the proceedings especially as the delegates arrived with amazing speed and clarity at statements, suggestions and a declaration that pointed a possible way forward.

He was pleased to report: 'There was a strong feeling that whatever form the new instruments might take they should be on a shared faith basis that was both Trinitarian and Biblical.'[37]

---

[36] *SBM* (June 1987), 9.
[37] *SBM* (October 1987),10.

In commenting on the Process in his report to the Assembly in October Peter said: 'In testing out the Process we will be tested and in any judgments we make we will be judged.' He warned against allowing fear and excitement to blind Scottish Baptists to the real issues or the real facts within the Process. He urged that they should be as fully informed as possible before even beginning to discuss the Process and the Union's response to it.[38]

In reporting to the Assembly on the conferences and discussions Peter said: 'If Baptists had not been there it would have been a dereliction of duty.' The Baptist delegates had found the official report of the St Andrews Conference too euphoric in its tone and too presumptuous in its claims. It had not reflected the intense pressure of the conference or the sluggishness of the ecumenical interest of many Christians. The 'Swanwick Declaration' had caught something of the mood, but had not done justice to the qualifications nor reflected the sum of the proposals for new instruments. The important question for the denomination to answer was whether it wanted Christian unity and whether it wanted Christ's prayer for his people that they should be one, answered.

In the ensuing discussion hesitancies and reservations were expressed as well as support, but on all sides there was appreciation for the way in which Peter had explained the Process.[39]

Coming to a Decision

Early in 1988 Peter sent a letter to the churches with suggestions about how to discuss the Inter-Church Process. The Union's Statement on Unity and the full report on the Swanwick Conference[40] were available. Peter was pleased to report to the January Council that the Scottish proposals were recommending a faith basis for any new ecumenical arrangements, which would be fully Christological, Trinitarian and with an emphasis on evangelism as well as social concern.[41]

The final decisions were made in 1989. In March that year the firm proposals for the new instruments were printed in the *Magazine*. The SCC was to be replaced by Action of Churches Together in Scotland (ACTS). The BCC was to be replaced by the Council of Churches for Britain and Ireland (CCBI) in 1990.[42]

---

[38] *SBM* (December 1987), 13.

[39] *SBM* (December 1987), 15.

[40] *Not Strangers but Pilgrims*: *Report of the Swanwick Conference, 31 August to 4 September 1987* (London: British Council of Churches and Catholic Truth Society for the Inter-Church Process, n.d. [1987]).

[41] *SBM* (February 1988), 12.

[42] *SBM* (March 1989), 9. Full details were published in *The Next Steps for Churches Together in Pilgrimage, Including Definite Proposals for Ecumenical Instruments*

In April Peter made a major contribution to the discussion after attending the debate on the Process in the Council of the Baptist Union of Great Britain. He set out a balanced analysis of the situation:

> It is clear that in discussing this issue men and women are governed by one of two considerations, both of which spring from their understanding of the Gospel. This is the dilemma, and it is this that makes deciding the question so difficult.
>
> On the one hand we are called upon to guard the Gospel, enshrining, as it does, the Faith once-for-all delivered to the saints. The defence of that Faith will, at times, call for the denunciation of and separation from, those who may profess that Faith but who, in our judgement, have seriously departed from it.
>
> Yet, on the other hand, our stewardship of the Gospel may call on us to take risks in sharing its truth with those who, in our judgment, are not holding to it in its apostolic wholeness. Such sharing can be a dangerous business but it has to be held in balance over against the opposite danger of writing off as unbelievers those whose experiences of Christ may be as authentic as ours, but whose expression of their faith may be quite different from our own.
>
> All of us who try to walk this tight-rope between evangelical faithfulness and brotherly openness will have felt the pain of this dilemma.

This frank admission of risk, danger and pain was not reassuring to those with doubts, but Peter felt it right to express the way he saw the issues with complete honesty. He went on to argue: 'An Ecumenical dogmatism that says everything in the Inter-Church Process garden is lovely and there are no risks or complications is deluded', but 'An Evangelical dogmatism that affirms that everything in the Inter-Church Process is bad is equally to be avoided.' He ended with a plea:

> However much we may differ in our response to the Inter-Church Process and its outcome, I trust it will be said of all of us that at least, in deciding the issue, we were fully-informed and fair-minded.[43]

The BUGB Assembly at Leicester in April 1989 voted by a large majority in favour of full participation in the next phase of the Process. The figures were: for 1035, against 364, a majority in favour of 73.4%. A two-thirds majority was required. An alternative 'wait and see' resolution advocating interim associate membership was massively rejected.[44] This was a clear result, but it is noteworthy that over a quarter of the delegates

---

(London: British Council of Churches and Catholic Truth Society for the Inter-Church Process, 1989).

[43] *SBM* (April 1989), 10.

[44] *SBM* (May 1989), 12.

were against the decision. Furthermore, thirteen churches withdrew from
the BUGB with sixty-four formally registering their dissent. In Wales later
in the year a Joint-Council of the English-speaking and Welsh-speaking
Baptists decided by a small majority to opt for full membership, but as a
result considerable tension arose between the two groups.[45] There was
strong feeling against the Process in England and Wales, just as there was
in Scotland.

In April 1989 consultations on the Process were held on Saturday
afternoons at nine venues across Scotland.[46] Because these revealed
widespread misunderstandings Peter wrote at length in the July *Magazine*
to clarify the ACTS proposals. He set out the options before
denominations: Full Membership, Participant (or Associate) Membership,
Observer Status, Non-membership. Although churches had a right to
mandate their delegates to Assembly, it had not been the customary
procedure among Scottish Baptists for several reasons, in particular:

> We have customarily seen [the Assembly] as a prayerful gathering of trusted
> delegates met in dependence on the Holy Spirit to seek the Lord's guidance in
> matters relating to our common life together as a Baptist Union of Scotland.

> We have recognised that, in seeking the Lord's will for our Union, delegates
> would speak on behalf of their churches—but not so mandated that they were
> not free to be led by the Spirit in the unfolding discussion.

He appealed finally that all should make the issue a matter for sustained
prayer, to avoid any 'party spirit' and to be fully informed.[47]

During the summer the Union published *Our Roman Catholic
Neighbours*, a booklet in the 'Viewpoint' series. It had been carefully
researched by Alf Peck and a small group. Peter wrote that its purpose
was 'to note any significant changes in Catholicism over recent years, to
highlight points of convergence and disagreement and to enable Scottish
Baptists to achieve an informed understanding of the Roman Catholic
Church'.[48]

In the October *Magazine*, just before the Assembly, Peter took two
pages to give a full description of the Baptist Union of Scotland and how
it operated. In view of statements made about churches on either end of
the ecumenical spectrum leaving the Union should the Assembly decision
not go their way, he emphasized the right of each church to dissent from
a major decision.

---

[45] Information given to the Baptist Union of Scotland Council in January 1990: *SBM*
(February 1990), 5.

[46] *SBM* (March 1989), 12.

[47] *SBM* (July 1989), 10-11.

[48] *SBM* (April 1988), 10.

However much we may disagree at times, and however strong the tensions of living together, we must not lose sight of the astonishing phenomenon our 120-year old Union represents nor of the storms we have weathered in the years of our history despite which (sometimes because of which) we have been bound together in a growing maturity.

He pointed out that Baptists had learned the delicate art of working together in the apprenticeship of local church membership:

There too we have our differences; there too there are those who cannot agree with the mind of the majority. But we remain in fellowship both as a witness to the reconciling Gospel of Christ and because we recognise that the things that unite us are far bigger and far more than the items on which we differ.

So it is in our Union. We care about each other and we are committed to each other. We rejoice in the Evangelical, Baptist principles that bind us together. We are grateful for the history that lies behind us. We recognise that we can do much more together than ever we could do apart. We find enrichment (not impoverishment) in the diversity that exists among us. We belong together.

Yet, at the same time, we recognise the right of each church to have its own view and to pursue its own policy. Suppression of opinion or coercion we find unacceptable. And this liberty we claim for ourselves we gladly extend to others.

It is this remarkable blend of committed inter-dependence and safeguarded liberty that is the genius of our Union. I trust that as we come to this year's Assembly we will again prove worthy heirs of our great heritage.[49]

Peter brought to the September Council the Executive recommendation that the Union should participate in ACTS as an associate member. He said that the motive for it was not fear but pastoral concern for all those who had strongly differing views. 'If we cannot go wholly into it, then let us keep in touch with it rather than be left in a backwater', he said. The Council accepted the motion: forty-seven in favour, fourteen against, five abstentions. Other proposals, for full membership on the one hand and observer status on the other, were heavily defeated. In seconding the proposal for full membership the Rev. T. Watson Moyes said that he wanted to see Peter Barber as a member of the Council of ACTS, first of all because of his position as General Secretary and secondly because of his own gifts and spiritual insights. This would not be possible if the Union were only an associate member.[50]

The Assembly debate took place at the Methodist Central Hall in Edinburgh on Thursday 26 October 1989. In a lengthy afternoon

---

[49] *SBM* (October 1989), 10-11.
[50] *SBM* (October 1989), 6.

session, with feelings running high, three votes were taken. Firstly a motion for full membership was rejected by 345 votes to 152. Then Peter, speaking as General Secretary, moved the Council's motion for associate membership. He argued that for thirty-four years the Union had had an honoured place on the SCC and had made a greater contribution than its numbers had merited, while losing nothing of Baptist and evangelical distinctives. On the other hand the Union did not want to damage relations among its own churches. Associate Membership would mean co-operation without commitment, participation without partnership, being in the new instruments without being answerable for them. This motion was rejected by 261 votes to 222.

The third vote was for observer status. Peter went down to the floor to support this motion, with the argument that as the Union had been willing to be full members of the SCC while the Roman Catholic Church had been observers, now that they were to be full members it was illogical for the Union not even to be prepared to be observers. There was a majority of 59.9% in favour of observer status (287 to 192) but it was less than the two-thirds required.[51]

Some delegates who themselves would have wished contact with the other denominations to be continued voted against the motions because they were afraid of a split in the Union. Many delegates had been mandated by their churches to vote against them all.

Peter must have known from previous feedback that he was fighting a losing battle, but he was deeply convinced that Baptists ought to be involved in ACTS, that the new body would be the poorer for being deprived of the Baptist perspective and that Baptists would be poorer for being cut off from the main means of contact with other denominations. Opposed to him were many who saw any official contact with Roman Catholicism (or indeed in the view of some Presbyterianism) as compromise and 'the beginning of the slippery slope'.

Sadly the battle sometimes became personal: some people expressed a lack of trust in Peter and his motives, accusing him of not standing up for Baptist churches because he wanted to be involved with other churches. This was quite unwarranted. People who were with Peter in discussions with those of other denominations know well how clearly and convincingly he explained and defended distinctive Baptist principles. Eric Watson wrote: 'Often I sat beside him in inter-church discussions as he advocated our insights and affirmed our principles with his humility, graciousness and integrity, winning the respect of all.'[52] David Coffey wrote: 'Peter should be honoured as a Scottish Baptist who was greatly respected in ecumenical circles. It should be recorded that wherever he

---

[51] *SBYB*, 1990, 172-179 (Assembly Minutes); *SBM* (December 1989), 11.
[52] *SBN*, (October 1994), 1.

was "playing away from home" he was renowned as a defender of the faith, generous in spirit, open-minded in fellowship and a wonderful ambassador for his Lord with never a hint of compromise.'[53] Peter was deeply hurt by the attacks on his motives, particularly when people he trusted believed some of the untruths that were told.

The Aftermath of the ACTS Decision

The Assembly decision necessitated a careful re-think of the Union's work, because much of it involved contact with other denominations. Peter felt keenly the isolation of the denomination and took a long time to adjust to it. Finally one morning he confided to Eric Watson that he had thought the matter through: he must accept the will of the Assembly and lead the denomination on that basis.[54] Some people had speculated that he would resign, but this was deemed to be inappropriate because the recommendation to be an Associate Member of ACTS had been a Council decision.

When he wrote his piece for the December *Magazine* he faced head-on a situation in which feelings were still running high. He said that some people were relieved, some were shocked, leaders of other churches were bewildered and sad. He warned that those who opposed ACTS should not be accused of blind bigotry:

> I am not denying that there are elements of blindness and bigotry in all of us, nor am I denying that zeal for a cause can lead any of us to use unworthy methods, but I am sure that most of those who were resistant to the Inter-Church Process were motivated by a sincere desire to defend the Gospel and to preserve the unity of the denomination. Not to see that would be to impugn false motives to our brethren in Christ.

He argued against the impression that all Scottish Baptists were anti-Catholic isolationists: it was simply not true of any of the churches that they wanted nothing to do with churches of other denominations. Some would limit such fellowship to those of a compatible theology, others shared very actively in their local council of churches. Almost 60% had voted for observer status because they had wanted some form of inter-church contact. Many informal and formal contacts with other denominations had been built up. Obviously it was not the intention of the Assembly that such contacts should be broken and such co-operation ended. Yet, in the light of the decision, there were areas of co-operation in

---

[53] *SBN* (October 1994), 2.
[54] Information from Eric Watson.

which the Union would not be free to participate if they came directly under the aegis of ACTS.[55]

Ten churches asked for their dissent from the Assembly decision to be recorded: Cupar, Hillhead (Glasgow), Leslie, Morningside (Edinburgh), Pitlochry, Rutherglen, Thomas Coats Memorial (Paisley), Canonmills (Edinburgh), Whyte's Causeway (Kirkcaldy), and Springburn (Glasgow).[56] Seven others indicated strong disagreement with the decision but stopped short of having their dissent formally minuted.[57]

Correspondence in the *Magazine* became acrimonious early in 1990 and Peter felt he ought to comment directly 'to sound a warning and make a plea'. Under the heading 'A Question of Trust' he insisted that all Scottish Baptists were committed to an evangelical understanding of the gospel. The Declaration of Principle affirmed that the Union comprised 'those who profess repentance towards God and faith in the Lord Jesus Christ'. He argued against adding to that any Statement of Faith or Credal Formula—out of respect for Christ; out of respect for the Bible; out of respect for one another.

> There's no denying that the last Assembly was a traumatic experience for the denomination. There were real and sharp differences of opinion over the ACTS issue and some strong reactions over how the Assembly conducted itself. Much as we may wish it, these differences of outlook and opinion are not likely to go away and no good will be served by pretending they are not there.

> Two facts remain, however—(i) these differences are not bigger than the basic Baptist Evangelical Principles that unite us and (ii) the people with whom we have enjoyed fellowship in Christ over the years have not changed. There has been no shift in the denomination's commitment to its evangelical position at any level—'leadership', Council or Assembly. Where we differed was in how that evangelical witness should be made.

He rebutted the claim that the Council was trying to dominate the Assembly—it had simply done what was its role to do—framed a recommendation to serve as an aid to the Assembly in tackling a very complex discussion.

> It would be ironic if, having decided not to participate in ACTS (and therefore being cut off from a section of church life in Scotland) we should now cut ourselves off from each other by giving hostage to a spirit of suspicion and acrimony.

---

[55] *SBM* (December 1989), 18.
[56] *SBM* (February 1990), 5; (June 1990), 8.
[57] *SBM* (February 1990), 5.

By all means let us openly share our differences—that is healthy. But let us do so in an atmosphere of mutual respect, trust and brotherly affection as members of one Scottish Baptist Family. If we go on biting and devouring one another nobody wins—except you know who![58]

It was made clear at the Council in May 1990 that local Baptist churches were free to join their local councils of churches (which became known as 'Churches Together in...') and that individual Scottish Baptists were free to join the Friends of ACTS. They could also be co-opted to serve on commissions or committees, but in their own right, not as representatives of the denomination.[59]

Scottish Television's *Eikon* programme featured Baptists as a denomination that had chosen not to join ACTS. There were interviews with the Rev. Colin Cameron (then at Drumchapel) in favour of that decision and the Rev. Kerr Spiers (then at Thomas Coats Memorial, Paisley) against it. Peter was also interviewed. Interspersed with the interviews was the visual metaphor of a closing door.[60]

The Evangelical Alliance

There was a strong feeling in the denomination that the Union should align itself with the Evangelical Alliance. Peter did not regard this as any substitute for a co-operative grouping with the Christian traditions as a whole, but it had, of course, his whole-hearted support. He had been one of the founders of the local EA in Torquay and he had become involved with the discussions that led to the formation of Evangelical Alliance, Scotland.

The initiative had been taken by the EA in November 1988, when the Rev. Ian Coffey had met with an invited group of leaders to discuss the possible formation of a Scottish section of the Alliance. The idea was to form a Federation of English, Welsh, Scottish and Irish Alliances. A Day Conference in October 1989 set out balanced affirmations about the kind of Evangelical Body those present favoured:

It should be Scottish, but not narrowly nationalistic; well-organised, but not bureaucratic; firmly evangelical, but not exclusive in spirit; positive in policy, not simply anti-ecumenical; alert to contemporary issues and prepared for constructive dialogue; open to the supernatural but not triumphalistic; governed by the principle—'In essentials, unity, in non-essentials, diversity; in all things love.'[61]

---

[58] *SBM* (April 1990), 10, 12.
[59] *SBM* (June 1990), 8.
[60] *SBM* (October 1990), 1.
[61] *SBM* (June 1990), 10.

Peter attended a further meeting in March 1990, when it was felt that a great deal of bridge-building still needed to be done and it was decided to form Scottish Evangelical Forum, which would meet at occasional functions.[62] This paved the way for the formation of 'Evangelical Alliance, Scotland' in 1992. Peter was appointed a member of its Council, as was John Drane.[63] The Union itself became a member of the EA by the decision of the 1997 Assembly, three years after Peter's death.

Dialogue with the Church of Scotland

The Roman Catholic Church is not the only stumbling block to Scottish Baptist co-operation with other denominations. At the Assembly in 1993 a considerable number of delegates voted against acceptance of the report of the Doctrine and Inter-Church Relations Committee because it contained a statement by the Joint Study Group of the Church of Scotland and the Baptist Union of Scotland on the mutual recognition of ministers.[64]

The first meeting of this Joint Study Group had taken place in 1984. Peter and other Union representatives took part in doctrinal discussions with representatives of the Church of Scotland on the basis of a Report of Conversations between the Baptist World Alliance and the World Alliance of Reformed Churches.[65] Peter's skill at explaining Baptist principles with clarity and grace without compromise, while listening carefully and with respect to contrary views, was remarkable. The group produced a report, which was presented to the respective Assemblies in 1986. The Baptist Union found it acceptable, but the Church of Scotland Panel on Doctrine was unhappy about some aspects of it, in particular the failure of their representatives to do justice to the Reformed doctrine of infant baptism.

Further dialogue was conducted on the relationship between the old and new covenants, the relation between grace and faith, the nature of baptism, children in the church and ministry. Peter reported that over a further four years these matters were discussed 'with candour, thoroughness and goodwill'.[66] Alf Peck conducted a joint communion service for the group on the last occasion it met. The outcome was reported to the Church of Scotland Assembly in May 1991 and to the Baptist Union Assembly in October the same year. Both Assemblies accepted this final report, though without much comment or interest.

[62] *SBM* (May 1990), 10-11; (June 1990), 10.

[63] *SBM* (February 1993), 7.

[64] *SBM* (December 1993), 8.

[65] *Baptists and Reformed in Dialogue: Documents from the Conversations Sponsored by the World Alliance of Reformed Churches and the Baptist World Alliance* (Geneva: World Alliance of Reformed Churches, 1984).

[66] *SBM* (May 1991), 12-13.

Peter was disappointed at the apathy this revealed. Most people did not bother to read the report. There was the suspicion 'Are we trying to unite?' A small group continued with a watching brief to ensure the exchange of matters of mutual interest.[67]

Listen to God and the Call to Prayer

In a provocative article in the *Magazine* in January 1990 Alistair Brown[68] asked what the real conversion impact of the denomination was on Scotland: there were more churches than twenty-five years before, but less members. Many churches had no baptisms. What was needed was renewal of the Holy Spirit.[69] In the February issue Peter accepted that the denomination's growth over the past decade had been 'to say the least, disappointing'. He commended the Denominational Conference that was to be held in June at Stirling University and explained the thinking of the committee:

If we are to match the opportunities of the next ten years we are going to have to face hard truths, learn new methods and consider costly changes. This was a challenge the committee was determined not to duck.

The committee was also aware that the denomination has experienced stress and a measure of division over the past two years because of the Inter-Church Process. They sensed how timely and necessary it was for us to come together in a *denominational* conference in which we would have time to pray, to worship, to share and to listen to God *together*. They therefore felt that within the conference there should be plenty of time for being with each other and waiting on God as we sought *his* vision for our shared future.[70]

At the first Denominational Conference in his time as General Secretary, in June 1984, which also took place in Stirling, Peter had a prominent speaking role. He kept more in the background in 1990, but he did contribute humour. The *Magazine* reported that there was lots of laughter at the conference, not least at the 'Saturday Night Live' occasion: 'the Peter Barber and George Mitchell Chat Show, which created a fun-filled atmosphere'.[71] Peter was pleased that the conference proved to be a time of healing and strengthening.[72]

---

[67] Information from Alf Peck.

[68] Then minister of the Gerrard Street Baptist Church, Aberdeen; now General Director of BMS World Mission.

[69] *SBM* (January 1990), 4-5.

[70] *SBM* (February 1990), 10.

[71] *SBM* (July 1990), 1. The Rev. Dr George Mitchell was minister of Harestanes, Kirkintilloch, at that time. He served as President of the Union 1995-96.

[72] *SBM* (November 1990), 9.

To the surprise of many the challenge that came out of the Conference was, as Peter put it, 'not a denominational programme with aims and objectives, but a searching call to "Listen to God"':

> As Baptists we are good at talking about God, not so good at talking to him and almost wholly inept at listening to him. Like Martha, we are distracted by our activism and seldom still enough to know God, or see God, or see life as God sees it.

> As long as this remains so our worship will be shallow, our approach to preaching hypercritical, our handling of Scripture academic, our approach to church meetings secular and our Christian service superficial.

> Really to listen to God is to begin to see ourselves as we really are and begin to look at life through his eyes. It makes us different people for we see the world differently. Mission really becomes mission because we are not just 'going'; we are 'being sent' to where HE wants us to go to do what HE wants us to do. We begin to care because he cares—and that makes all the difference (in more senses than one!).[73]

A 'Listen to God Group' was set up to act as a catalyst in helping people to apply the discipline of 'listening to God' in every area of church life. Over a period of about four years various retreats and study days were arranged and periods of reflection were led during Assembly sessions by members of the group. Peter expressed his excitement at the way the denomination was increasingly recognizing the need to listen to God:

> It is a difficult thing to do because in our busyness, we make so much din, or in our fear, we follow the safe dictates of tradition.

> To listen to God—really to listen—is to be set free. It is to determine as an individual to be HIS servant and as a fellowship to be HIS body. The only question we need answered is 'Lord, what will you have me to do?' and the only grace we need, is the grace to do it.[74]

A similar challenge to the denomination's spiritual life was the 'Call to Prayer'. The stimulus for this was an inspiring paper on the Cambuslang Revival given by Kenneth Roxburgh[75] at the Ministers' Conference in 1993. The Office Bearers and Executive issued to the denomination a 'Call to Prayer', which began with a ministers' day of prayer at Perth on 1 September 1993. Peter was pleased with the attendance (ninety-four)

---

[73] *SBM* (November 1990), 10.

[74] *SBM* (April 1991), 11.

[75] Then minister of the Ladywell, Livingstone congregation, later Principal of the Scottish Baptist College (1994–2002).

and with the mutual experience of waiting on God. In his piece for the October *Magazine* (written in the period after his first operation) Peter expressed his passion about prayer and revival for church and nation:

> The spirit of oneness during the Day of Prayer was almost tangible. A man's age, size of church, or theological bias was of no significance. You would never have guessed that this group of men over recent years had debated vigorously and disagreed openly over issues such as Charismatic Renewal, Women in the Ministry and the Ecumenical Movement. All of this faded into the background as the focus of the day was on the grandeur of God, the seeking of His glory, the empowering of His people, the redemption of our nation and obedience to His voice.[76]

Disappointment and Healing

Peter Barber showed remarkable courage and integrity in his approach to controversy. He made his own views clear, but was open to change them. He used a full consultation process, but there were times when bringing people together to arrive at a common mind was beyond even his skills of diplomacy.

The need to make a decision on ACTS cast a shadow over several years of his Secretaryship. He wrestled with the issues himself and thought them through with rigour and honesty. After the decision he was gracious and perceptive in urging those with strong feelings not to question the motives of those with whom they disagreed. Yet he suffered deep disappointment himself because he had not convinced a sufficient proportion of the denomination of the need for the Union to remain in contact with other churches and to engage with them, bearing its own distinctive witness. This was a time when he appreciated more than ever the support and understanding of Isobel.

There is a deep irony in Peter's story. He came from an upbringing in a 'door ajar' Brethren group into the Baptist denomination and rose to be its leader in Scotland. Even as a young man his knowledge of his adopted denomination soon embraced the world. He saw it as a world body within the Christian community and one that should relate as far as possible to other branches of the faith in accordance with the prayer of Jesus for the unity of his disciples. The denomination struggled to follow him.

In the years after the ecumenical decision a change of emphasis unexpectedly arose, especially through the Denominational Conference in 1990. There was no less concern for looking outward in mission, but for a while a special desire to reflect, to listen to God and to spend time in

---

[76] *SBM* (October 1993), 3.

corporate prayer. Peter was able to make his own contribution to this movement and was glad to record the healing of division through prayer.

CHAPTER 16

Partnership with Other Baptists in Britain

From his earliest days as a Christian Peter was keen to get to know his adopted denomination comprehensively. As General Secretary he related to Baptists in England and Wales, Europe and the World. At first his attention was focused solely on the home scene. He travelled often to London, but not so often abroad as his predecessor had done. The committee that recommended his appointment had told him not to spend too much time in travel.[1] He resisted it for a while, but it was inevitable that his talents would soon be recognized in wider Baptist circles and he began to make significant contributions to the European Baptist Federation (EBF) and the Baptist World Alliance (BWA). As Eric Watson wrote: 'He was a Christian with a world view and he wanted Scottish Baptists to realise that they were a part of a world-wide fellowship of Baptist believers and of the universal Church of Jesus Christ.'[2]

Southern Baptists of the USA

Within Scotland there was already a special relationship with the Foreign Mission Board of the Southern Baptist Convention of the USA. They had been sending missionaries and volunteers to Scotland with the full co-operation of the Union for several years. Andrew MacRae and Dr J.D. Hughey, the representative in Europe of the Foreign Mission Board, had developed this policy,[3] which Peter was keen to develop. Partnership missions, in which teams of Americans came to work in local churches, also continued. In 1985 no less than fifteen teams came.

Happy relationships were formed with the Americans. Dr Isam Ballenger, Director of the Convention's work in Europe and the Middle East, was a speaker at the 1985 Assembly.[4] Loren and Cherry Turnage lived in Scotland for ten years as the Fraternal Representatives of the

---

[1] Information from the late Dr Charles Anderson.
[2] *SBN* (October 1994), 1.
[3] *SBM* (October 1984), 11.
[4] *SBM* (December 1985), 8-9 and 10.

Foreign Mission Board and church planters of the Bridge of Don church,
Aberdeen, and the Ellon church.[5] Bob and Marsha Ford pioneered work
in south-west Scotland at Wigtown.[6] Kathie White came at first as a
volunteer to the Ayr church, and returned later as a career missionary to
the Kirkintilloch church.[7]

'The Union in the South'

While he was in Torquay Peter had experienced the fellowship of the
Devon and Cornwall Association and the BUGBI. He therefore
understood the ethos of groupings in the South and worked happily with
his counterparts, in particular with the General Secretaries of the BUGBI.
Bernard Green took up this office in 1981 and Peter recognized him as
an able and courageous leader. When he retired in April 1991 Peter was
delighted that David Coffey was appointed. He knew him personally as
his successor at Upton Vale, Torquay, and as the man who had
masterminded the evening programmes for the BWA Youth Conference
in Glasgow in 1988. For the previous three years he had been Secretary
for Evangelism in the BUGBI. Peter described him as 'a man with a heart
for mission with wide Evangelical sympathies' and 'imaginative,
innovative, gifted and keen, and a born leader'.

> He was one of the driving forces in the Mainstream movement within the
> Union in the South, a movement committed to seeking a renewal of the
> denomination in which evangelical Christians with differing approaches to
> renewal could work together.

> During his busy year as President of his Union David Coffey's great concern
> was to build bridges of reconciliation between believers of differing outlook for
> the sake of the larger good of the denomination.

Peter welcomed, too, the simultaneous appointment of David Coffey's
assistant, Keith Jones, former Secretary of the Yorkshire Baptist
Association:

> Keith is a born organiser. During his secretaryship in Leeds, he restructured the
> Association, bringing to its work a dynamic team spirit. He also helped lead
> the Baptists of Yorkshire into an effective three year programme of mission

[5] *SBM* (February 1986), 9; (November 1988), 1.
[6] *SBM* (February 1986), 9; (November 1988), 1.
[7] *SBM* (November 1988), 1.

not unlike our own Scotreach. There is no doubt he will bring an organisational flair to the work of the Union in Didcot.[8]

Peter had attended a two-day Mainstream conference in 1982, when it was three years old and shared his impressions. He described it as the brainchild of Dr Raymond Brown and the Rev. Douglas McBain. Those attending had diverse views, but one eager desire to see the quickening of the life and growth of the denomination. His own reasons for attending were 'to renew fellowship with Baptist brethren in the south, not least our exiled Scots; to express our Union's solidarity with this search for renewal; to seek stimulus for my own ministry, which is inclined to major on giving at the expense of receiving'. He commended the movement: 'Nothing but good could come out of such a conference. This Mainstream is flowing full—pray that its renewing influence may be felt in every part of the Baptist Union of Great Britain and Ireland; and that we too may taste of its freshness.'[9]

Peter took part in discussions on changing the name of the BUGBI. In the August 1985 *Magazine* he explained that as there were no affiliated Baptist churches in Ireland the omission of 'and Ireland' was obviously overdue. However, the complicated situation in Wales made it difficult to arrive at a satisfactory alternative to 'Baptist Union of Great Britain'. Most of the churches in the South Wales cities were in membership only of the BUGBI, though some were also members of the Baptist Union of Wales. That Union comprised two sections: the Welsh speaking churches, which were in the majority, and the English speaking churches, some of whom were also in membership of the BUGBI. It was difficult, therefore, to change the BUGBI to 'The Baptist Union of England' or 'The Baptist Union of England and Wales'. Moreover there were nine churches in Scotland that were affiliated to the BUGBI, though their primary link was to the Baptist Union of Scotland. Peter recognized the need for patience but set out the goal:

> Patience will only be rewarded, however, when each of the Unions in the four countries is so named that repeated misunderstandings are a thing of the past and the way opened for a fuller recognition of the independent status of each of our national Unions within a United Kingdom framework.[10]

When Bernard Green was welcomed to the May Council meeting in 1986 he acknowledged that he was embarrassed by the BUGBI name.[11]

---

[8] *SBM* (April 1991), 10. He is now the Rector of the International Baptist Theological Seminary in Prague, Czech Republic.

[9] *SBM* (March 1982), 12.

[10] *SBM* (August 1985), 10.

[11] *SBM* (June 1986), 12.

The January 1987 Council meeting was informed that no further progress had been made and the new name was to be 'Baptist Union of Great Britain'. It accepted this 'with reluctance recognising the potential misunderstanding still embodied in the title but in the hope that mutual respect and increasing co-operation between the three mainland Unions will serve to minimise any such misunderstanding'.[12]

The Baptist Missionary Society

Peter was a great supporter of the BMS. When he took office Matthew McLachlan had only a few months to serve of his twenty-four years as BMS Scottish Representative. Angus MacNeill was appointed in his place from May 1981 but almost immediately was invited to succeed H.F. Drake as the Society's Overseas Secretary (from April 1982). Peter expressed the mixed feelings of Scottish Baptists that Angus MacNeill was to serve for only eleven months, but heartily endorsed the wisdom of the choice.[13] Ron Armstrong was appointed to the Scottish post and served until his retirement in 1992. Derek Clark's post as Youth Co-ordinator for the Union was then being phased out and he was appointed to the BMS post, which he still holds.

Peter gave full support to the Bi-Centenary of the BMS in 1992. On Friday 2 October he took part in the procession at the Service of Thanksgiving at Westminster Abbey, London, in the morning and attended the Service of Thanksgiving at Fuller Baptist Church, Kettering, in the evening. Writing in the March *Magazine* he refuted the idea that William Carey was the 'Father of Modern Missions'—because others, like the Moravians, had engaged in overseas mission before him:

> The unique thing about William Carey—for which he is justly famous—is that he was the first to engage in overseas mission with the backing of a denominational society of churches.

> It was this idea that inspired other denominations such as the Church of Scotland, the Anglican Church and the Congregational Church to undertake a similar pattern of mission work.[14]

He expressed concern at the number of missions and other Christian organizations that looked to their personnel to raise their own support, because of the embarrassment this caused to them and their churches.

---

[12] *SBM* (February 1987), 4. The name was changed by the Assembly in London on 26 April 1988 (*The Baptist Union Directory, 1988–89* [London: Baptist Union, n.d.], 37).

[13] *SBM* (May 1981), p.6.

[14] *SBM* (March 1992), 10-11.

I like the BMS principle. It is based on the belief that those called and approved for overseas service from within our denomination are the responsibility of all the churches in terms of their support. It means, of course, that the smallest Baptist church can afford to have a BMS missionary as well as the large ones — which are seen as an increasing magnet to those seeking their full support from a church. It also means that the missionaries go out secure in the knowledge that they are not dependent on the good will of a number of people whom they have managed to convince to support them but rather with the support of a whole denomination that has pledged to stand behind them.[15]

He was thrilled that the main Scottish Bi-Centenary event, 'Day in Another World', at Perth High School on Saturday 5 September, proved to be 'the biggest Scottish Baptist Family Day out in the denomination's history'.[16]

The Fellowship of British Baptists

A sign of increasing co-operation between the BMS and the Unions in Britain came in 1990 when the Joint Consultative Committee was re-constituted.[17] Peter was a driving force behind the development of this into the Fellowship of British Baptists. There was a coming together of the separate bodies: they desired closer relationships, but without federalism, delegation of powers or a new super-structure. The Baptist Union of Scotland Council unanimously endorsed the idea in September 1993[18] and the framework for closer co-operation was agreed by the January 1994 Council. The independence of each participant member was to be carefully observed and financial commitments monitored. The Fellowship was felt to hold 'the promise of increased sharing in planning and joint activities'.[19] Sadly it was shortly after Peter's death that the Fellowship of British Baptists was formed, in November 1994. David Coffey wrote:

He is not the only Scottish Baptist who could have had such a vision for drawing the Baptists in these islands together in a fellowship dedicated to mission, but not every Scottish Baptist would have had the spiritual leadership necessary.

I was part of the team of six representing Wales, Scotland, England and the BMS who travelled to Russia and Ukraine in 1991 and I know that Peter caught a glimpse during that historic visit of British Baptists of what might be accomplished in the

---

[15] *SBM* (March 1992), 11.

[16] *SBM* (October 1992), 10.

[17] *SBM* (October 1990), 14: Council report.

[18] *SBM* (October 1993), 12.

[19] *SBM* (March 1994), 12.

years ahead. He recognised the moment of time when the door of the future swings open and God invites us to step through.[20]

Peter had in fact expressed his thoughts on co-operation among Baptists in Britain much earlier, when as Centenary President of the Baptist Union of Scotland he had given greetings to the BUGBI Assembly in 1970. He referred to the regular Joint Officers' Meetings of the three Unions and the BMS:

These frank and friendly meetings have been in every way worthwhile, and while they may not have gone as fast or as far as some would have wished, we must never forget there is a point and a pace beyond which hurry ceases to be progress, or movement advance.

For ourselves, as a Union, we feel deeply convinced of the value of autonomy within the Unions because of the very different situations in which we work. But at the same time we feel equally convinced of the immeasurable advantage of consultation at every appropriate level, and co-operation in every possible way.

After all, there are so many problems and opportunities we do face together and in which we may help each other. We do not subscribe to the view of the Scottish Presbyterian minister who came to London to work alongside an Anglican vicar in an early ecumenical experiment. His parting words were as amusing as they were unforgivable: 'Och well, my dear man,' said he, 'it has been most interesting to work with you and to see how you worship God in your way, and I in His!' In our Anglo-Baptist relationships (and I shall say nothing of Hampden on Saturday) we have, I think, learned better.[21]

Vision for British Baptists

Peter Barber was a highly respected Christian leader not only in Scotland but throughout Britain. He maintained a happy and co-operative relationship with the Southern Baptist Convention and encouraged the placing of their missionaries and volunteers in Scotland. There was a deep mutual respect between him and the leaders of the BUGBI and his support of the BMS was solid, just as it had been in his pastorates. He reflected often on the rationale and methods of missionary work.

He had also reflected for some years on the relationships of the various Baptist Unions in Britain and the BMS, which is supported by all of them. The formation of the Fellowship of British Baptists owed much to his

---

[20] *SBN* (October 1994), 2.
[21] Peter's notes in his BU Centenary Presidency file: 'London: B.U. Assembly'. Hampden Park in Glasgow was the venue for football matches between Scotland and England.

vision. Happily it has flourished and drawn the Baptists of Britain together in increasing co-operation in the ten years since his death.

CHAPTER 17

European Baptist Statesman

Involvement in the Federation

Peter appreciated the significance of the European Baptist Federation (EBF) long before he became General Secretary of Baptist Union of Scotland. The EBF Council met in Glasgow in September 1970 because Andrew MacRae was taking up the EBF Presidency at that Council. This was the first EBF Council meeting in Scotland. It was towards the end of Peter's year as President of the Baptist Union of Scotland and he gave the address of welcome to the delegates. The notes he made for that occasion show that he had a full grasp of the history of the EBF and the current situation in Europe.[1]

He regularly reported the interesting details of the work done by the EBF. In January 1982, the very first of his monthly pages in the *Magazine* was devoted to the activities and projects of the Federation. He described its Council meetings (and those of the BWA) as 'not just chummy re-unions or heavily accented talking-shops. They are a source of a great deal of co-operative activity.' He committed the Union to Europe, concluding:

> No doubt for months and years to come politicians (part-time and full-time) will go on debating whether or not we should be 'in Europe'. Let the politicians say what they will, as Scottish Baptists we have already made our commitment, in Church terms at least. We are in Europe, part of a very lively, stimulating and productive Federation. I hope you pray for it, know about it—and are proud to be part of it.[2]

Peter came to know the European Baptist leaders at the EBF Council in Dorfweil, West Germany, in October 1981[3] and renewed fellowship with them at Denia in South West Spain in September 1982, when he served as Chairman of the Resolutions Committee.[4]

---

[1] Notes in his BU Centenary Presidency file: 'Address of Welcome to the EBF Council, 17th Sept., 1970'.

[2] *SBM* (January 1982), 8.

[3] *SBM* (January 1982), 8.

[4] *SBM*, (November 1982), 10.

At the Seventh Congress in Hamburg, August 1984, a remarkable reconciliation in Christ took place. Pastor Günter Hitzemann made a public confession of guilt on behalf of the West German Baptist Union for remaining silent during the Nazi regime. At a later session Peter (Scotland) and David Russell (England) responded with a statement of thanks and forgiveness on behalf of the non-German members of the Congress.[5] Peter was pleased that at one of the evening rallies the Scottish Baptist Youth Choir 'did us proud by singing with great feeling and effect'.[6]

In May 1985 he attended the Executive meeting in Lisbon. There he met Dr Manuel Alexandre, who, in addition to being a University Lecturer in the Classics, was President of the Portuguese Baptist Union, Pastor of Grace Baptist Church in Lisbon and Principal of the Baptist Seminary. He regarded him as one of the most godly people he had met.[7]

In September 1985 he attended the Executive and Council meetings in Prague. At the Council he was again made Chairman of the Resolutions Committee. He described it as a bewildering task to frame resolutions in a multi-language group in rushed brief sessions between the main business: it was a miracle that they reached a common mind!

> I discovered once more what I have discovered again and again that whatever a man's language or nation, if the love of God has been shed abroad in his heart by the Holy Spirit then the concern Christ awakens will be one when it comes to looking at our needy world.[8]

It was Glasgow's turn to host the Council meeting in September 1986. Much of the preparation fell upon Peter, in consultation with Knud Wümpelmann in Denmark. About eighty leaders of the European Unions attended. The city's Provost gave a civic dinner in their honour and they spoke in various churches in southern Scotland. They enjoyed a guided tour of Edinburgh, including historic Baptist sites.[9]

Peter constantly tried to enlarge the vision of Scottish Baptists to see themselves not as a declining influence in Scottish society but as members of 'a truly international family—and a rapidly growing family at that'.[10]

---

[5] Bernard Green, *Crossing the Boundaries: A History of the European Baptist Federation* (Didcot: Baptist Historical Society, 1999), 106-107; *SBM*, (September 1984), 9.

[6] *SBM* (September 1984), 8-11.

[7] *SBM* (June 1985), 10.

[8] *SBM* (November 1985), 10.

[9] *SBM* (February 1986), 10.

[10] *SBM* (February 1986), 10.

Called to Lead the Federation

Peter was elected as Vice-President of the Federation at the Council meeting in Santa Severa near Rome in October 1987, being unanimously approved by the representatives of the twenty-six Unions. He was to serve as Vice-President for two years (1987–89), as President for two (1989–91), and as past-President for two (1991–93).

On his appointment he faced a press conference of Baptist editors and told them that he had just returned from Russia and had noted the great difference from his last visit in 1963. He felt that the new 'glasnost' (the Russian word for 'openness') in Eastern Europe was likely to bring about changes. He would like to challenge the West to support their fellow Christians out of their riches of resources and pledged himself to encourage continuing and increasing support for the International Baptist Seminary at Rüschlikon.[11] He could not have foreseen how dramatically change was to come in Eastern Europe, nor the crisis at Rüschlikon in which he was to play a key role.

During Peter's term as Vice-President the search was on for a new Secretary of the Federation in succession to Dr Knud Wümpelmann. Peter's expertise in European matters was so highly esteemed that he himself was approached, and when he declined he was approached again. He was sorely tempted to accept a post that appealed greatly to him, but family circumstances did not allow him to accept. When Bernard Green had to step down as chairman of the Search Committee due to ill health, Peter succeeded him. Karl Heinz Walter of West Germany was appointed as General Secretary from the end of 1989.[12]

Peter became President of the Federation at the Budapest Congress in July 1989. His duties over the next two years included chairing the Executive and Council meetings of the Federation, representing it at the BWA Executive and Council, and at other special events, and visiting European Baptist Unions.

The Budapest Congress was the largest one up to that time. There were 5,212 delegates compared with 2,300 in Hamburg in 1984.[13] Around 130 people from Scotland travelled to it. Peter's own account of it included appreciation for the choir of 1,000 voices, 700 from Hungary and 300 from other countries, which 'filled the arena with rich harmonies and set our spirits soaring'.

All through the Congress there were memorable moments. The one-to-one conversations as East met West; the brass band playing in the warm sunshine during the lunch breaks; the seminars and Bible study groups engaging in serious reflection and interaction; the spine-chilling youth drama on Peace as

[11] *SBM* (November 1987), 6.
[12] *SBM* (August 1989), 1.
[13] *SBM* (September 1989), 18.

the wall that divides crumbled before the cross; the challenge through preaching to be reconcilers in our home, in our church and in our community.

To be there in Budapest was to realise afresh the wonder of the European Baptist Federation. No other Regional Fellowship of the Baptist World Alliance includes within its area such a diversity of cultures, languages and political systems. Within our Federation East meets West, the rich meet the poor, and the Middle-East (such a cauldron of troubles) finds a place. It is truly incredible to see such a patchwork of life united in Christ. To be in Budapest was to marvel afresh at what God has done—and was doing in our richly diverse part of the world.[14]

As a fitting climax to the four-day Congress Billy Graham preached at a rally on the Saturday evening[15] in the Nep Stadium. The 72,000 seats were all taken. Almost 20,000 others spilled over on to the grass and other spaces. There were hundreds more in a nearby TV relay overflow. Peter was among the platform party and described what happened as a miracle:

The response exceeded all their expectations. By the close of the Rally no less than 27,000 people had come forward. The Billy Graham Team on the basis of their wide experience, had anticipated a maximum of 17,000. It had to be seen to be believed.

And all this in an East European country where just 33 years ago the cause of freedom had been forcibly crushed and where, just two or three years ago, such a public preaching of the gospel would have been banned.[16]

Challenge of the New Europe

Peter became President of the EBF at a time of cataclysmic change in the Continent of Europe, change that for many years had seemed impossible: the collapse of Communism. He was the man for the hour. Karl Heinz Walter wrote:

Peter got very excited that a new era was coming for the churches and that we could reach new people, even more once a new Europe was proclaimed. Peter had studied all of that very carefully. He was the first leader in Europe whom I remember speaking about 'the New Europe and the Kingdom of Jesus'.[17]

---

[14] *SBM* (September 1989), 18.
[15] Saturday 29 July 1989.
[16] *SBM* (September 1989), 18.
[17] *SBN* (October 1994), 2.

The Berlin Wall had, since 1961, separated West Berlin from East Berlin and the rest of East Germany, which surrounded the city. More than 500 people had been killed trying to escape to the more prosperous West between 1961 and 1989, but the wall lost its purpose that summer when Hungary and Czechoslovakia opened their borders, enabling East Germans to reach the West by a simple detour. This emigration included many Baptists and there was concern that Baptist churches in the East were losing members, especially young people.

Then, in November 1989, the East German Government opened the wall. It was breached at the Brandenberg Gate on 9 November and soon it was demolished, with scenes of jubilation shown on worldwide television. On Sunday 3 December Peter took part in a special service in Bremerhaven, West Germany. The congregation was saying farewell to Karl Heinz Walter, who had been their pastor for eleven years, and was being inducted as Secretary of the Federation.

Karl Heinz recalls that at the service Peter spoke about the task of an EBF General Secretary:

> By that time the situation had changed dramatically in Europe. The fall of Communism had changed the task of the General Secretary of the EBF as well. But nobody could really say in which way. Peter gave the direction and revealed by that his own understanding of his ministry. I fully agreed with him, as I did in the future in almost everything. He said then: 'His task will involve a number of roles. We will be looking to him as a leader who will share vision with us, as administrator who will keep the whole work smoothly operating together, as treasurer who will both challenge us in our stewardship and convey our gifts to others in need, as a pastor available to the leaders of various unions and to the pastors in their needs'. This was Peter Barber describing himself and his ministry.[18]

Peter was soon working closely together with Karl Heinz Walter as they faced unprecedented situations and found ways of meeting them. Members of the EBF Executive remember the devotional message that Peter gave at their meeting in Rüschlikon early in 1990. It was based on the prophecy of Habakkuk:

> Look at the nations and watch—and be utterly amazed. For I am going to do something in your days that you would not believe, even if you were told. (Habakkuk 1:5)

---

[18] Karl Heinz Walter in *Reflections*, a private communication with the author, 22 May 2002.

John Merritt wrote: 'It was clear in our minds that God had broken down the wall, and we praised Him for it.'[19] Karl Heinz Walter recalls that Peter used the same text to open the EBF Council in Varna, Bulgaria, in 1991: 'Everybody echoed the truth of this word and I am sure many of us preached this word in the months after the meeting.'[20] Peter's early grounding in the scriptures stood him in good stead.

Tragically the changes in Europe were not all peaceful. In Romania in December 1989 there was a brief revolution that overthrew the repressive Communist regime of Nicolai Ceausescu. There was fierce fighting in many cities, resulting in over 60,000 deaths (including some Baptists) and much destruction throughout the country. Ceausescu and his wife Elena were shot dead on Christmas Day.

Following the revolution the EBF, the BWA, various Unions, the European Baptist Convention and the Southern Baptist Convention initiated relief activities to assist their fellow Baptists and to alleviate pain and suffering throughout the country. As President of the Federation Peter, who had visited Romania for a week in October as the first visit of his presidency, issued a statement:

> Our hearts go out to our brothers and sisters at this critical time. We are conscious it is a time of immense suffering and of immense hope. Those who suffer loss of families and limbs and homes, etc., are in our thoughts and prayers.

In a letter to Romanian Baptists he stated:

> [We are very much praying] that God will give wisdom and grace to the new leadership. They play their part in the reconstruction of a new Romania. So many voices will be heard and so many competing groups will claim to be the right way for the rebuilding of this nation. Baptists have something unique to bring.[21]

In January 1990 Peter was one of thirty-four Baptist leaders from Canada, the United States, West and East Europe who met for two days in Dorfweil, West Germany, to get first-hand accounts of what was happening in Eastern Europe, so as to give the right kind of help where it was most needed. He found it 'a profoundly moving experience to listen to these Baptist leaders [from Eastern Europe]...who had held on to the Faith at great cost, speak with wonder of what God had done in bringing about the changes in their countries'.[22]

---

[19] Stanley Crabb (ed.), *Our Favourite Memories: European Baptist Federation 1949–1999* (n.p.: European Baptist Federation, 1999), 54

[20] Walter, *Reflections*.

[21] *SBM* (February 1990), 6.

[22] *SBM* (March 1990), 10.

In their work for the EBF there was a large measure of agreement between Peter and Karl Heinz Walter on policy. Karl Heinz gives an example:

> When I explained to him my ideas about future EBF meetings we agreed that they should not only be business meetings but must provide a spiritual inspiration. He accepted my wish to give Bible studies at the Council meetings so that the leaders of the unions could hopefully take something home. We both knew too well how often the leaders have to give and how seldom they were receivers at official meetings. I also wanted not only to be seen as an EBF manager.[23]

Karl Heinz appreciated and relied upon Peter's mental acuteness and literary skills:

> Peter was famous for his excellent ability to formulate important documents. This was not only understood by all non-English speakers in the EBF but it was accepted by the English delegates as well, although Peter was a Scotsman. His gift became a great help in many ways. Not only was it a great help for me. Most important documents, letters of protest to governments, statutes or paragraphs of the new constitution and bylaws were written by Peter. Whenever I had to write an official letter I first faxed it to Peter... Only after his correction we sent the letter from our office.[24]

In May 1990 Peter spent eight days ministering in Czechoslovakia. On November 17-18 the previous year an unarmed crowd in Wenceslas Square, Prague, 'by dint of their dissent and insistence on change, had brought about the overthrow of the Communist government'.

> There was certainly no comparison between the Czechoslovakia I had visited in 1985 and the country I was now visiting. The atmosphere then had been one of repression, restriction and suspicion. This time there was a light-heartedness in the air that was almost tangible, though there was also this nagging concern over the future.

One problem facing the churches was how to evangelize when for more than forty years they had not been free to do so. Peter commented: 'They think we in the West know all the techniques for such evangelism and are keen to learn from us, but I wonder...'[25]

Nationalism was in the air and there were those among the politicians and the Baptists who were arguing that Slovakia (five million people) should break away from the Czech Republic (ten million). Peter

---

[23] Walter, *Reflections*.
[24] Walter, *Reflections*.
[25] *SBM* (July 1990), 11.

commented that this would weaken the witness of the Baptists, whose total membership was 4,000.[26] The partition took place on 1 January 1993.

The EBF Council in September 1990 (held in the DeBron Conference Centre, near Zwolle in Holland) received reports on the situation in each of the East European countries to ensure that aid was being sent where it was most needed. It spent two sessions discussing 'Baptist Identity'. As East and West Europeans rediscovered each other there was an urgent need to establish the distinctives that bound them together as a Baptist family. There were more than 300 para-church groups at work in Eastern Europe. Many of these well-financed groups were evangelical without necessarily having any Baptist allegiance.

The Council was happy to welcome the affiliation of the Jordanian Baptist Union to the Federation, although no-one from that country was able to attend because of the political situation. Israel was already in membership.[27] Karl Heinz Walter comments: 'Peter Barber brought the Baptists from the Middle East into membership with the EBF. This was his great desire.'[28]

Peter and Isobel spent eight days in Israel in October 1990 as guests of the Association of Baptist Churches, which comprised nine churches and had six full-time pastors. It was the time of the Gulf Crisis, with Saddam Hussein making threats. Violence erupted in Jerusalem on Monday 8 October. In the Temple Mount area nineteen Arab demonstrators were shot dead and 200 wounded. Peter and Isobel heard the news over the public address system of a cruise boat on the Sea of Galilee. All around them were Orthodox Jews, enjoying their Succoth holiday, and beside them a Christian Arab, President of the Association of Baptists in Israel. A young Jew opposite them flew into a rage and uttered intentions of extreme violence against the Arabs in Jerusalem, but their Arab host maintained a discreet silence. Back in Nazareth (a town half Arab and half Jewish) that evening there were demonstrations. All the shops were closed for two days and riots ensued.

Peter and Isobel found out what it was like to live as Arab Christians in such an atmosphere as they visited their churches, ate in their homes and saw their school. Peter spoke at their annual residential conference. They traced little bitterness among Arab Christians, who valued their Arab heritage and wanted to preserve it, but also hoped and prayed for a growing oneness with Jewish Christians.[29]

Towards the close of their visit they spent an evening worshipping with a Jewish-Christian house-church. Peter commented:

[26] *SBM* (July 1990), 12.

[27] *SBM* (September 1990), 10; (November 1990), 6-7.

[28] Walter, *Reflections*.

[29] *SBM* (December 1990), 15.

Their deep devotion was unmistakable as we studied the Scriptures together and sang their hymns to the strong beat of Hebrew melodies. It is not easy to be a Jewish Christian in Israel. They are looked upon as traitors to their nation and become victims of harassment and discrimination. But they are there and their light is shining.[30]

In April 1991 Peter visited East Berlin. East and West Germany had been formally reunified in October 1990. He found himself at the Brandenburg Gate, remembering the last time he had been there—with Andrew MacRae in 1984 at the time of a BWA Council meeting in West Berlin. On the West side of the wall they had seen the graffiti language of protest and the crosses marking the places where those trying to escape had been killed. On the East side they had seen the wide sandy death-strip with hidden mines and booby traps making escape impossible:

But on this visit—on Sunday, April 13, 1991—it was so different. The wall was down. Men and women were passing freely from East to West and from West to East. Not a soldier in sight. Instead the streets were lined with tables full of souvenirs for sale—parts of the wall and East German soldiers' uniforms.

As I walked through the gate in the company of Mrs Irmgard Claas, widow of the former General Secretary of the BWA [Gerhard Claas], I could only praise the Lord for the change that had come about. Welcome, welcome change![31]

In May 1991 Peter spoke at the annual Assembly of the French Baptist Federation in Paris and then went on to Siegen in West Germany to represent the EBF at the act of reunification between the Baptist Unions of East and West Germany. It was a most moving occasion when men and women wept without shame. Peter reflected on the familiar phrase of the Lord's Prayer: 'Das Reich ist dein' ('Thine is the Kingdom'):

The Third Reich might have been Hitler's (I thought) and the Reich that followed in East Germany might have been Karl Marx's, but 'Das Reich ist dein'. In the end of the day, Christ is Lord. He has the last word. However strong the tyrannies men may create, at the last 'The kingdoms of this world shall become the Kingdom of our God and of his Christ. And He shall reign for ever and ever'.

This moment in Siegen became for me an eschatological moment, a glimpse of the end time, a harbinger of promise, a sign of hope.[32]

---

[30] *SBM* (December 1990), 16.
[31] *SBM* (June 1991), 10.
[32] *SBM* (July 1991), 10.

The Varna Council

It was a great joy to Peter that the last EBF Council of his Presidency, in September 1991, met in Varna in Bulgaria, a resort town on the shore of the Black Sea. This was the first EBF Council in a Communist country after the fall of Communism and 'the excitement of the new freedom at that time was overwhelming'.[33] Baptists in Bulgaria had formerly been among the most repressed in Europe. They had not been permitted to evangelize, or to attend previous meetings of the EBF.

Before the Council meetings a series of evangelistic rallies took place in six cities in Bulgaria. Each drew good attendances and large responses. Peter was a member of the evangelistic team in Michaelovgrad, a town that had been a showpiece of the Communist government. At one of the open-air rallies he preached together with Theo Angelov, then the President of the Baptist Union of Bulgaria. More than 500 people were there and when Peter made the call for decision more than eighty came forward.[34]

Together with Karl Heinz Walter and Knud Wümpelmann, Peter had meetings with the Vice-President of Bulgaria and the Director of the Commission of Religious Affairs to discuss questions of religious equality.[35] Karl Heinz recalls that the Vice-President, Mr Semerjev, had a sculpture of Christ carrying the cross on his desk. He spoke freely about his own guilt and the guilt of the Communists. He had been the military head during the Communist government. Peter immediately reacted and told him that Christ had carried the cross also for him so that he could have forgiveness and freedom from his guilt.[36]

On the Sunday before the Council a new church building was dedicated in Varna. The previous building in the centre of town, dating from 1936, had been destroyed in 1985 by the state under the pretext of building a block of flats. As a concession the church people were offered another site—but on the fringes of the town. In 1988 they got permission to erect a new building and with sacrificial giving of time, money, energy and skills, and some gifts of money from the West, the building began to take shape and was completed just in time for the Day of Dedication:

> The spirit of celebration on this big day was uncontainable. As the church bell rang out and the crowd thronged into the new building, we felt we were really ringing out a whole era of persecution and ringing in a new era of opportunity. In such a context you can imagine how meaningful I found it to preach in that

---

[33] Karl Heinz Walter, from his tribute at the Thanksgiving Service, 9 September 1994.

[34] Walter, *Reflections*; Green, *Crossing the Boundaries*, 128.

[35] Green, *Crossing the Boundaries,* 128.

[36] Walter, *Reflections*.

building the following Sunday on the text, 'I will build my Church and the gates of Hades will not overcome it'![37]

Over 100 people attended the Council, the highest number up to that time, because many new Unions were represented. Peter had the joy of welcoming delegates from the newly formed Unions of Lebanon, Estonia, Georgia, Moldavia and Hungarians in Romania. Membership had reached thirty-two Unions/Conventions in thirty countries.

At a service in the newly opened Varna church on Saturday 28 September Peter handed over the Presidency of the Federation to John Merritt, General Secretary of the European Baptist Convention. The new Vice-President was Birgit Karlsson, General Secretary of the Swedish Baptist Union, and previously Principal of the Swedish Baptist Seminary. She had been prominent in the work of the EBF and the BWA. There was no difficulty when she was appointed Vice-President of the EBF, but two years later in 1993 she was expected to become President and that was a source of controversy as a few Unions objected to a woman minister being the leader of European Baptists. Peter encouraged Birgit and smoothed the way for her. Later she wrote:

> The deep and insightful spiritual leadership of Peter Barber of Scotland will always follow me. He was one of those who played an important role during my nomination for the EBF presidency, which was about to cause a severe crisis within our Federation.[38]

After a debate of several hours in a very tense meeting with BWA and EBF leaders, she gave her very moving testimony and then offered to stand down. The meeting did not accept this. Only one Union absented itself at the following Council on grounds of conscience.

> Well, I was elected, I served my term, and I was even invited to visit Baptist Unions where my role as a woman in a pastoral leadership role was not desirable. How much I admire them for their courage and love![39]

The Rüschlikon Crisis

Two weeks after the Council meeting in Bulgaria a severe crisis arose between the EBF and the Foreign Mission Board (later called the International Mission Board) of the Southern Baptist Convention. The Convention had helped to finance the Rüschlikon Seminary from its

---

[37] *SBM* (November 1991), 11.
[38] *Our Favourite Memories*, 134.
[39] *Our Favourite Memories*, 135; see also Bernard Green, *Crossing the Boundaries*, 97-98.

inception in 1949 and had generously made over the property to European Baptists in 1989. At that time an agreement was made to continue the present level of funding (almost 40% of the Seminary's income) until 1991 and thereafter, over a period of fifteen years, work towards a zero contribution. In October 1991 the Foreign Mission Board trustees voted thirty-five to twenty-eight to defund the Seminary on the grounds that theological liberalism was taught there.

There were many protests against this action from Southern Baptists and European Baptists. Peter wrote to the Foreign Mission Board expressing regret at their breaking a solemn undertaking to continue funding. However, the decision was confirmed in December by fifty-four votes to twenty-seven. Peter wrote to re-iterate his regret and express appreciation of the support and co-operation that the Board had given to Baptist work in Europe, and Scotland in particular.

A consultation between all the Unions of the EBF met in Dorfweil, Germany, in January 1992. They agreed on five principles of Baptist partnership in Europe. The Foreign Mission Board voted to adopt the Dorfweil Statement and in September there was a consultation between EBF leaders and representatives of the Foreign Mission Board near Hamburg, Germany. After friendly but difficult discussions reconciliation was achieved and 'The Hamburg Agreement' formulated. At the consultation the Romanian Union voted against it, but its Executive Committee gave it full approval in October.

Peter took part in all the discussions as one of the Trustees of the Seminary and his wise counsel was appreciated. At the Baptist Union of Scotland Council meeting a few days later Peter 'spoke movingly about having a sense of being upheld in prayer and of the Holy Spirit being at work in the consultation. During it differences had been settled, wrongs righted and a ten-point agreement drawn up as the basis for future partnership. It had not been easy to get to that position.' Following his report the Council agreed to reactivate full partnership with the Foreign Mission Board.[40]

All the important papers during the conflict were drafted by Peter, including the 'Dorfweil Statement', the 'Hamburg Agreement',[41] which became the basis of co-operation between the International Mission Board and the EBF, and a paper in which he reported on the crucial meeting at Hamburg to the EBF Council.[42] He was also appreciated for

---

[40] *SBM* (November 1991), 1; (January 1992), 2; (February 1992), 12-13; (September 1992), 10-11; (October 1992), 13; see also Green, *Crossing the Boundaries*, 190-193.

[41] John W. Merritt, 'Merritt's Musings', in the magazine *Highlights: A Publication of the European Baptist Convention* (September–October 1994), [2] (Peter's EBF file).

[42] Walter, *Reflections*. A full account of the Rüschlikon crisis and subsequent developments is given in John W. Merritt, *The Betrayal of Southern Baptist*

guidelines that he and Paul Fiddes drew up for the later relocation of Rüschlikon. It moved to Prague in 1995. However, the future of Rüschlikon was the one subject on which Peter and Karl Heinz Walter disagreed:

> Peter was a member of the Board of Trustees of the International Baptist Theological Seminary then still in Rüschlikon Switzerland. We were confronted with the fact that we had to make dramatic changes for this institution. Several reasons forced us to think in this direction. Most of the BOT meetings became very sensitive. One night after our meetings we were sitting together in the kitchen of the building which formerly had been the President's home. At that time it was used by the Institute for Mission and Evangelism. We were Peter Barber, John Merritt, then President of the EBF, and myself. We were discussing the future. My proposal was the most radical, but I am still convinced that it would have been a real option. I told the two others that we should celebrate in a meeting the wonderful history of the seminary. We would invite as many alumni as possible and all the leaders and friends in Europe. Then we should sell the place and invest the money in two ways. One part should go into the development of theological seminaries mainly in Eastern Europe. At that time all the new unions had plans for that and buildings and places were very cheap compared to later years. The other part should go into an endowment fund from which in coming years, students and theological teachers could receive scholarships for whatever would be helpful for theological education in Europe. Peter's immediate 'No, you cannot do this' was echoed by John Merritt. Whenever I dared to propose something like that I was left absolutely alone.[43]

Peter was also involved in the planning of the International Lay Academy in Budapest, which was opened in July 1990. He was happy that in a very short time it became an effective institution.[44]

One country that Peter had not been able to visit during his EBF Presidency was Poland. He remedied this omission in April 1992 when he spent seven days with the Baptists there. He was impressed with the numbers of young people in the churches and found that many of the pastors were young men who made up in zeal what they lacked in experience.[45]

After recuperating from his first operation Peter was able to attend the EBF Council meetings in Kishinev, the capital of Moldova, in September 1993. He spoke at the Central Baptist Church in the city, the membership of which was 1,500. He found the experience deeply moving. In response

---

Missionaries by Southern Baptist Leaders 1979–2004 (n.p.: privately published, 2004), pp. 56-107 (chs 3 and 4) and 199-200.

   [43] Walter, *Reflections*.
   [44] Karl Heinz Walter, *SBN* (October 1994), 2.
   [45] *SBM* (June 1992), 10.

to an appeal after his sermon five people came forward in tears and knelt in repentance, surrendering their lives to God.[46]

Planning for Lillehammer

The EBF Congress in 1994 was held in Norway. The location originally planned was Oslo, but had to be moved to Lillehammer, where the 1994 Winter Olympics had been held, because of a 44% rise in hall hire charges in Oslo. Peter was the Chairman of the Program Committee. The planning was hampered by the loss of two members of the organizing group. Per Midteide had demitted office as General Secretary of the Baptist Union of Norway and transferred to an Inter-Church Aid Agency and Asbjorn Bakkevoll, who had been a key figure in planning the BWA Youth Conference in Glasgow in 1988, tragically died on 29 January 1993, just short of his thirty-seventh birthday, leaving a wife, Marit, and a six year old daughter, Eli.[47] This meant that Peter became more involved in the administration of the Congress, though sadly because of his terminal illness he was unable to attend it.

Karl Heinz Walter recalls that he met with Peter and Asbjorn at the home of David Nixon (Treasurer of the BUGB) in England to plan for Lillehammer. Karl Heinz was convinced that out of the situation in Europe God was leading them to Joshua 24, when Israel was called to a meeting in Shechem to renew their commitment to God. Peter immediately reacted in favour of this. He told them that he had prepared a closing sermon on Joshua 24 for the EBF Congress in Budapest, at the beginning of his presidency, but had not been able to preach it because the programme had got out of control and there had been no time left. He had wanted to call European Baptists in 1989 to make the commitment 'Together we will serve the Lord'. The full planning committee agreed that Joshua would be the main biblical text at Lillehammer, that the theme would be 'Together we will serve the Lord' and that Peter should preach the sermon that he had prepared for Budapest as the opening message on the first evening. Sadly the sermon was never preached.[48] Around 5,000 Baptists went to Lillehammer from all over Europe. For the first time since the Federation was formed in 1949 they were free to come as families from East and West.

Karl Heinz Walter was able to report to Peter about the Congress on 17 August, a month before he died. Peter said at the end: 'This Congress has become a great spiritual battle and I still don't know why. But it also has

[46] *SBM* (November 1993), 3
[47] *SBM* (March 1993), 15.
[48] Walter, *Reflections*.

become a great spiritual victory and therefore all the glory belongs to God alone!'[49]

Among her memories of the Lillehammer Congress, Birgit Karlsson includes the loss of Asbjorn Bakkevoll, and she describes Peter's death as 'another loss not only for his family and the Scottish Baptist Union, but also for the entire Baptist family in Europe'.[50] David Coffey wrote the following reminiscence and tribute to Peter's work for the EBF:

> During the days following the Budapest Congress, I came to appreciate in the company of many others the spiritual leadership of Peter Barber, the newly installed EBF president. His organizing skills laid the foundation for the new structures of the EBF; his drive and enthusiasm gave us a vision for the Lillehammer Congress planned for 1994; his friendship and support were crucial to Karl Heinz Walter in the early days of his ministry as general secretary. By Peter's home-call to glory in 1994 we were deprived of a pastor, preacher, and administrator of the highest order, but surely his greatest legacy was to model the life of a true disciple of Jesus Christ with joy and integrity.

> The Barber family were firm friends of ours in the British Baptist scene as I had succeeded Peter as pastor of Upton Vale Baptist Church, Torquay in 1980 when he was called to become the general secretary of the Baptist Union of Scotland. Veteran attenders of EBF gatherings are used to the sense of fun which characterizes EBF gatherings and particularly the humorous exchanges between the Scots and the English. This was true for Peter and myself in EBF Executive meetings.[51]

David Coffey gave one example of such humour at the Charlotte Chapel Thanksgiving Service:

> Peter...once announced there were three ground rules for friendship between a Scotsman and an Englishman. Rule one, when visiting Scotland you refer to England as 'down south'. Rule two, never expect a Scotsman to cheer for England in a soccer competition. Rule three, if it was your turn to pay for the meal last time—it is still your turn!

The Skills for the Task

It is quite remarkable that alongside all his responsibilities in Scotland Peter Barber was able to make such a significant contribution to European Baptist life. His administrative and literary skills were soon taken up by the EBF and his leadership ability led to the Presidency. This came at a crucial point in European history when Communism was

---

[49] Karl Heinz Walter, from his tribute at the Thanksgiving Service, 9 September 1994.
[50] Crabb (ed.), *Our Favourite Memories*, 82.
[51] Crabb (ed.), *Our Favourite Memories*, 78.

collapsing and East was meeting West. Peter was fully equipped to grasp what was going on, to see the dangers, to respond as the upheaval led to different consequences in different countries, to give encouragement and comfort, to bring East and West together. His patience and diplomacy were well employed, notably in the theological and financial crisis that overtook the Rüschlikon Seminary. Much of the burden of the arrangements for the 1994 Congress was borne by him, which made his enforced absence all the more poignant for his many friends who were there. They remember him and all he achieved with love and gratitude.

CHAPTER 18

World Baptist Statesman

Experience of Global Fellowship

Peter made many trips to Europe through his work for the EBF, but had opportunities of even wider travel through his association with the BWA. In July 1982 he travelled to Nairobi, Kenya, for the annual Council meetings, but first he visited a friend who was farming in Zambia. On his second morning in Zambia he preached at the Lusaka Baptist Church, a congregation 98% black. He wrote: 'I felt their eagerness for the Word drawing the sermon out of me. Earlier in the service I had seen six people baptised by their pastor in a ceremony that was as simple as it was moving.'

In the afternoon, following a 200 mile drive north through the bush, he found the same eager attentiveness as he addressed a room full of expatriates, plus one black man. The isolation and risk of their situation had made them more open to the gospel. He described frankly the violence and poverty present in Zambia and also in Kenya, but was deeply impressed by the exuberance of the believers.[1]

The Nairobi Council meeting was Peter's first and he found it a revelation. The work of the Alliance, particularly its aid work, assumed a new significance for him. And he met its leaders:

> Its leading figures are no longer just names—they are people, brothers and sisters in Christ whose heart beats as my heart in their love for the Saviour and their desire to share him with the peoples of our world.

> Duke McCall, the President, is now a gentle-mannered Southern Baptist whose firmness as chairman is matched by his genial good humour and kindness. Gerhard Claas is not just an efficient German administrator serving as the Alliance secretary in Washington. He is a visionary with fire in his bones, whose charisma electrifies and moves his audience.

> Archie Goldie is not some high-powered executive who sits in the Headquarters office and doles out thousands of dollars. He is an expatriate Scot with a keen

---

[1] *SBM* (September 1982), 12.

mind and a heart that weeps over the plight of the many whose despair he knows first hand.[2]

The first BWA Congress that Peter attended met in Los Angeles in July 1985. He was impressed by the way the Congress theme 'Out of Darkness into the Light of Christ' was interpreted 'not simply of the light of preaching but also of the light of compassionate caring and bold intervention'. He quoted Ex-US President Jimmy Carter and Dr Billy Graham who spoke along these lines. Seven major resolutions on international social issues were passed.

But his supreme impression was a sense of wonder at the wide range of the World Baptist Family: 'Just to meet so many brothers and sisters, to share Christ and compare notes on Baptist witness in our own country was to be greatly enriched.' He came across the motto of the North American Baptist Fellowship and thought it summed up the spirit of the BWA: 'Celebrating our Unity; Honouring our Diversity'.[3]

In July 1986 he went on a trip to the Far East, which he described as traumatic and overwhelming: he would never be the same again. He represented Scottish Baptists at the BWA Council meeting in Singapore and went on, at the invitation of the BWA and the EBF, to spend five days in China. He was one of 200 BWA representatives attending a conference with Chinese church leaders, led by Bishop Ding in Nanjing. He was thrilled to have the opportunity of finding out at first hand what had happened to the church in China since the Communist Revolution of 1949 and especially since the end of the Gang of Four's reign of terror in 1976. He was able to report that the church in China was alive and well, growing faster than the birth rate.[4]

At the invitation of the BMS he went on from China to see its work in Bangladesh and North India. He came face to face with the strength and pervasiveness of the non-Christian religions and with the squalor of poverty existing alongside great wealth. His admiration for the missionaries knew no bounds. In Bangladesh he visited the Chandraghona Hospital and saw the village work undertaken by missionaries and their national helpers. He saw these as candles shining for Christ in the surrounding darkness. In Calcutta he learned of the work of Mother Teresa and her sisters, of the social welfare work of the Episcopal Cathedral and of the Assembly of God building, where 10,000 meals were offered each day to the destitute.[5] He preached at an evening service in Circular Road Baptist Church. He visited Serampore College, eighteen

---

[2] *SBM* (October 1982), 12.
[3] *SBM* (September 1985), 10-11.
[4] *SBM* (February 1986), 8; (October 1986), 10.
[5] *SBM* (September 1986), 10.

miles north of Calcutta, which William Carey, Joshua Marshman and William Ward founded in 1818.

The BWA Council meetings in July 1987 were in Amman, Jordan. Peter wrote about Jordan, Baptist work in Jordan and the political situation in the Middle East. Many, notably in the USA, had been puzzled at the decision to hold the meetings in Amman, but Peter felt that it was right, especially because of the encouragement it gave to the members of the Jordan Baptist Convention.

> The visit also served to prove how dangerous generalisations can be. While there are unstable, trigger-happy Arab countries, this was not the experience of the Council during their time in Jordan. Instead we met a people who were kind and friendly and we felt safer in the streets of Amman late at night than we would in many cities in the United Kingdom.[6]

Many Baptists around the world were shocked by the death of Dr Gerhard Claas in a car accident in California on 21 March 1988. He had served as General Secretary/Treasurer of the BWA since 1980, before which he was the Secretary of the EBF. Less than two weeks previously Peter had attended the Executive meetings of the Alliance in Washington and with some others had dined at the home of Dr and Mrs Claas. Dr Claas was a German pastor who commended himself by his statesmanlike qualities and his sympathy with the deprived and oppressed. He left a wife, Irmgard, two daughters and a son. Peter attended his funeral in Hamburg.[7]

In the *Magazine* Peter paid a fulsome tribute to his friend in terms that no doubt mirrored his own aims in office:

> His mastery of the complex administration of the Alliance, which he served as both secretary and treasurer, was unmistakable. He was efficient without being officious and authoritative without seeming bossy. He always gave the president his place and quietly stood alongside as servant and supporter.

> Yet, in a fascinating way, the same Gerhard Claas as served with quiet efficiency in administration, could stand on a platform and electrify an audience with his passionate oratory. Wherever he went in the world he had such a noting eye and such a sensitive spirit that very little passed him. What he saw he remembered, and, better still, what he saw he was able to bring alive again as he shared it with others.

> In doing so he was truly an ambassador of Christ, drawing the Lord's people together in the one world family and, above all, drawing them to Christ.

---

[6] *SBM* (September 1987), 10.
[7] *SBM* (April 1988), 7.

That, for me, was the ultimate clue to Gerhard Claas' life. He was a Baptist, and proud of it, but supremely he was Christ's man, determined to exalt Christ and to advance his mission in the world.[8]

Youth Conference in Scotland

It was through Peter's vision and drive that Scotland was chosen to host the BWA Youth Conference in Glasgow in July 1988. Impressive competition came from the Netherlands and West Germany. Peter gathered a gifted group of professional people to put Scotland's case. In particular he approached two men he had known for a long time: Douglas Inglis, a chartered surveyor and member of the Newton Mearns church, and Rodney Beaumont, a partner in a firm of landscape architects, which had been involved in the overall design co-ordination of the Liverpool Garden Festival and had acted as advisors for the Glasgow Garden Festival. These two agreed to be co-chairmen of the Committee on Local Arrangements.[9] Dr Gerhard Claas and Dr Denton Lotz (then the Executive Secretary of the BWA responsible for youth and evangelism) came to speak to the meeting of the Baptist Union of Scotland Council in May 1985. It warmly invited the Alliance to hold the Conference in Glasgow.

Peter gave the invitation to Scotland personally at the Congress in Los Angeles at the beginning of July 1985.[10] He sat on the Core Committee responsible for the Conference and promoted it on his *Magazine* page. He urged the Scottish churches to send their young people to this once in a lifetime opportunity to meet a wide variety of young people from many countries, including Russia, Poland, Hungary, Cuba and Nagaland.[11]

The Youth Conference was held in the Scottish Exhibition and Conference Centre, Glasgow, from 27-31 July 1988. The number of delegates had been expected to be around 10,000. In the event it was 6,748, but it was still the largest youth conference so far held. Eighty-two countries were represented. The number of registered delegates from Scotland was 990. The theme was 'Jesus Christ Rules', which was explored in a series of celebrations, Bible studies and seminars.[12] The *Magazine* editorial commented:

The exuberance of singing by choirs and audience as well as solo performers was both soul stirring and nerve tingling. The widespread appreciative

---

[8] *SBM* (May 1988), 10.

[9] *Baptist Times* (August 11, 1988), 2; *SBM* (June 1985), 3; (October 1985), 4.

[10] *SBM* (July 1985), 10-11.

[11] *SBM* (June 1988), 10.

[12] *SBM* (August 1988), 1 and 8-9.

comments on community groups which examined many of the contemporary ethical and social issues from a Christian standpoint revealed a seriousness of purpose among the young participants.[13]

On the Saturday afternoon the delegates marched in procession through the streets of Glasgow to a rally in Kelvingrove Park. Graham Kendrick organized the march and Steve Chalke led the rally. The *Magazine* reported:

> The delegates came in all shapes and sizes, all colours, political affiliations and nationalities. Some delegates proceeded through the march in wheelchairs or on crutches, all united in their common bond of Christ.
>
> The Naga Indians, from a tribe of former headhunters, were toward the front of the march. In their colourful costumes, the plumes in their head-dress standing tall, their spears held firm in front of them, they too proclaimed that 'Jesus is love'.[14]

Peter felt that the most memorable highlights were the response to the appeal on Saturday evening, when more than 300 young people streamed to the front, and the Sunday morning Celebration, when everyone was carried away in a spirit of exuberant praise. He found the evening Celebrations to be 'a remarkable blend of competent professionalism and spiritual sensitivity'. Each morning he sat in on the Planning Group responsible for the Celebrations and admired the way the previous one was analysed and the next one planned to the minute.

> The 'Make Way' Procession on the Saturday afternoon had to be experienced to be appreciated. To see almost 7000 young Baptists snake their way through the streets of Glasgow, carrying their banners, singing their songs and waving cheerfully to the bystanders was great fun—and a great thrill. It certainly set the people of Glasgow talking.
>
> An overwhelming impression for me was one of team-work. For a 14,500-member Union to run a 7000-member Conference was no small undertaking and it was bound to stretch our resources to the limit. The fact that so many volunteered to help run it (we had a Task Force of around 450 people) and the happy spirit in which they co-operated made what could have been a nightmare a sheer joy.
>
> Many who came to Glasgow went home transformed. They will never be the same again—nor will the lives of those they influence. Insofar as this is true,

---

[13] *SBM* (August 1988), 1.
[14] *SBM* (September 1988), 12.

all the planning, hard work and prayer over the past three years was worth it. Something started in Glasgow 1988 that will not end.[15]

Immediately after the EBF Congress in Budapest in July 1989, when Peter became President of the Federation, he went on to the Council of the BWA in Zagreb, across the Hungarian border in Yugoslavia. It had the highest attendance on record—120 delegates and a total of 500 participants. Denton Lotz of Washington was confirmed as the Secretary and Dr Knud Wümpelmann of Denmark, who had just retired as Secretary of the EBF, as President-elect. He was the first President from the Continent of Europe (as distinct from the British Isles).[16]

In August 1990 Peter attended the BWA Congress in Seoul, South Korea, when Knud Wümpelmann succeeded Dr Noel Vose of Australia as President. Dr Vose's wife Heather had died of a brain haemorrhage in Indiana during a Baptist–Mennonite Conference on 3 June. In the *Magazine* Peter expressed everyone's regret that Heather could not have been at Noel's side at the climax of their presidential years together, and commented: 'At the same time it has been a solemn reminder to all of us that we each live a heart-beat from eternity and every moment is a precious, non-renewable gift to be cherished and used for God.'[17]

Peter was deeply impressed by the way the Koreans gave themselves to prayer. At each evening rally the congregation was asked to form into groups of four for prayer, but in fact all over the auditorium there was a crescendo of sound as the Koreans broke into simultaneous prayer. He was there at the climax of the Congress, 'the biggest service of believer's baptism in the history of the Christian Church'. In the space of about an hour over 8,000 men, women and young people were baptized. He reported that there was a certain loss of 'atmosphere' owing to the sheer scale of the event and the inevitable distractions of an open-air setting, but there was no doubting the sincerity and zeal of those baptized.[18]

At the time of his death Peter had been nominated as a Vice-President of the BWA from 1995. No doubt he would have continued to make a significant contribution to its work in his 'retirement'.

Honorary Degree

In recognition of his service to Baptists in Europe and in the World Alliance as well as in Scotland Peter was awarded the honorary degree of Doctor of Divinity by Acadia University, Nova Scotia, Canada. He was reluctant to accept it, because he did not consider himself to be worthy of

---

[15] *SBM* (September 1988), 18-19.
[16] *SBM* (September 1989), 18-19.
[17] *SBM* (September 1990), 10; (July 1990), 1.
[18] *SBM* (October 1990), 12.

it, but in every respect it was well deserved. There was no doubt of his academic and teaching ability, which he used to great effect in his work at the Scottish Baptist College, quite apart from his pastoral, administrative, leadership and diplomatic gifts.

In a letter (20 January 1992) to the Vice-Chancellor of Acadia University, the Rev. Dr J.R.C. Perkin, he wrote: 'In accepting your gracious invitation, I do so not so much because of personal abilities or achievements as on behalf of the Scottish and European Baptists it has been my privilege to serve.'

Peter and Isobel managed to have a short holiday in Canada so that he could receive the degree on Monday 11 May 1992. On the previous day he preached at the Baccalaureate service for graduates.

Andrew MacRae had become Principal of Acadia Divinity College and Dean of the Faculty of Theology of Acadia University in 1984. He read the Citation at the Graduation Ceremony, which outlined Peter's contributions in pastoral ministry and in the General Secretaryship of the Baptist Union of Scotland and went on to 'his international ministry and influence':

Mr Barber, who has served on the Council and Executive of the Baptist World Alliance, has just completed a two year term as President of the European Baptist Federation, which unites Christians in more than 25 countries, and has given outstanding leadership to the rapidly changing countries of Europe, East and West, paying numerous visits to the countries of the former Soviet bloc to meet with leaders in Church and Government. The collapse of the Communist system, and the continuing development and expansion of the European Community, have called for strong and imaginative leadership in the political, societal and religious realms. The influence of the churches has been highly significant in many situations of change, particularly in the service of communities struggling to handle the intense pressures of economic change and political upheaval.

Within the community of the European churches, the man we honour today has been a source of great encouragement and wise counsel in the midst of rising nationalisms and regional conflicts. In that setting, Peter Barber has played his part in the advocacy of a message of reconciliation, which lies at the heart of the Christian gospel, and has brought inspiration and leadership to many places...

Mr Chancellor, it is a special pleasure to present to you the Reverend Peter Barber, a churchman of distinction, clear in purpose, modest in success, able in academic achievement, convincing in communication, effective in leadership, messenger of reconciliation, and citizen of the world, that, as he represents the moral and spiritual leadership of the church in a rapidly changing Europe, he may receive honour at your hand.

Needless to say he was seldom called 'Dr Barber'; he was more comfortable with 'Mr Barber'! A humorous poem was circulated in the Union Office:

> The Reverend Peter Barber's
> a lad of many parts:
> Bachelor of Divinity
> and Master, too, in Arts.
> From there across the water
> he's got one more degree
> the College in Acadia
> have made him a D.D.
>
> So shall we call him Reverend,
> or simply Mister B?
> Is Doctor now what's ordered
> to suit his new degree?
> But all that new-found honour
> might go right to his head
> so let's just stick to Peter
> or P.H.B. instead!

CHAPTER 19

Faithful to the End

It was a deep grief to his family and all who knew him that Peter's life was (from our human perspective) cut short a year before he was due to retire. Early in 1993 he discovered that he had cancer. On Friday 2 April he had taken part in the Farewell to Eric Watson as Superintendent and the induction of Douglas Hutcheon. A blood sample had been taken from him that morning. He wrote his article for the May *Magazine* on Good Friday (9 April) on the subject of the cross.

He underwent a major operation on Friday 23 April in the Victoria Infirmary on the south side of Glasgow. His surgeon was Mr David Smith, an elder of St George's Tron Church of Scotland in Glasgow. On the day of his operation he wrote a prayer:

Dear Lord Jesus,

I begin this day in your presence—as always—and in the deep assurance of your love. Through the years, despite my changeableness, you have been so patient and so faithful. But even more, you have been gracious. You have blessed me so far beyond my deserving and even my asking.

Thank you for your love, for your presence and—at this moment—for your peace. 'My peace I give unto you'—you have sung it so often to me over these past days, Lord, and I hear the song again. Our song about your peace.

Thank you too for all the love I have known through life. It goes so far back and it is all around me now. Thank you most of all for Isobel and her sheer loyalty, selflessness, understanding and support. I could not have asked more of a life-partner and she has taught me so much about your love. Thank you for the precious relationship we have shared over nearly 28 years. It has been so precious.

And thank you for the family—for Fiona, Susan, Colin and Zoe—each so different yet each so much part of us and of each other.

Thank you too for friends—so many friends in so many places who love me with a love that never ceases to amaze me.

Thank you that today—whatever it holds—is in your hands. Underneath, all day, will be your everlasting arms and I can safely rest in them. And thank you that—today—David Smith will be in your hands and you will be in his hands as he operates on me and on all whom he will serve today.

Thank you too that the future belongs to you whether in years of fruitful fellowship and service or in your calling of me 'home'. Thank you for the faith that is mine—and that of all your children—that, whatever the future, in life or in death, we are yours.

Father, Lord Jesus, Gracious Spirit, into your keeping I commit my life. Thank you.

The operation was a success. He was unable to write an article for the June *Magazine*, but his letter of thanks for messages received was printed. He was not able to be present at the Council in May, though he contributed a draft paper on the subject of associations to it.[1]

He was unable to write his page for the July *Magazine*, but his meditation 'Walking with God' was printed.[2] The meditations that he wrote in the last few years of his life express a profound spirituality. He was well enough to contribute the page for August, in which he passed on the lessons he had learned from his two and a half months when he had been

in a kind of siding while the rest of the world had rushed on its busy schedule. As you can imagine, for one who is usually on the main line, with decided express-train tendencies, this has been for me a very different, sometimes frustrating, but decidedly enriching experience.

He said he had discovered—and almost been overwhelmed by—the blessing of Christian fellowship. He had come to recognize that the caring expressed in many ways while he was in hospital was a real commendation of the fellowship of believers to those without any church connection. He had also experienced at firsthand the power of prayer. He and Isobel had found themselves suffused with a peace they did not manufacture and could not explain. He had come to appreciate at a new level the distinctiveness of the Christian faith:

What a faith we share. It deals with the guilt of the past, assures us of the daily companionship of Jesus, bestows on us a Book full of the most amazing and unbreakable promises, confirms that, whatever life brings, our Father knows and is in control and guarantees to those who love him a place in his eternal glory with Jesus, the Lord of death.

---

[1] *SBM* (June 1993), 11.
[2] *SBM* (July 1993), 16.

He had also become more assured than ever of the Father's providential care of his children:

> He has never guaranteed that trouble will never come to us or that we will never suffer adversity or pain. I can see more clearly than ever that if Christians were immune from such afflictions or instantly cured whenever illness struck, what a damaging impact this would have on Christian witness. The world would rightly accuse God of blatant partiality and where would our witness as fellow-patients be to others without a faith if we never entered hospital alongside them?

> God does not guarantee us immunity from suffering. (Certainly not on the basis of our innocence. Did not the Most Innocent suffer worst of all?) What he does guarantee us is his presence, whatever may happen, and his grace to meet whatever needs may arise—all according to his sovereign purpose.[3]

He resumed his work and his travels, being formally welcomed back to harness at the September Council meeting at Larkhall on 7 September 1993. But a few months later he became ill again: the cancer recurred. He was readmitted to the Victoria Infirmary on 17 April 1994 on an emergency basis because of internal bleeding. This was a week short of one year after the operation. Further surgery was undertaken on 6 May, but his condition was more complex than before and there was a limit to what surgery could do. It was a bitter blow to him, his family and all who knew him that he was faced with an uncertain prognosis.

Peter wrote a 'Personal Note' on 18 May addressed to 'My dear Friends and Fellow Pilgrims' for publication in the June *Magazine*. In it he gave the full medical details, expressed his gratitude for all expressions of support and declared a firm belief in God's power to heal, but his main concern was that God should be glorified:

> I shall never understand how men and women without a faith cope with such a crisis. It becomes clearer and clearer to me that, whatever our questions and hardships at a time like this, we who are God's children have two great assets—a faith that can match every contingency, be it in life or in death, and a fellowship on whose love, loyalty and prayers we can securely depend.

> Many tell us that they are praying that God will demonstrate His healing power in my body—and with all our hearts Isobel and I believe this can come about through Him to whom all things are possible. Our primary concern, however, as best we can read our hearts, is that God will be glorified in this situation, His many-sided purposes fulfilled and evidence produced that our God can do the impossible, whatever form it takes.

---

[3] *SBM* (August 1993), 3.

'The eternal God is our Refuge and underneath are the everlasting arms.'

Yours in the security of His caring love,

Peter H. Barber[4]

He sent a letter of information and good wishes to the Council that met on 10 May. An update of his medical situation was given and time was spent in intercession for him and for world matters. Jim Bernard, a former President of the Union, quoted the words of the hymn by Dora Greenwell:

> I am not skilled to understand
> What God has willed, what God has planned;
> I only know at His right hand
> Stands One who is my Saviour![5]

Peter spent eleven days in early July with his family on the beautiful island of Colonsay, which he loved very much. Over the years they had spent many holidays there. As usual he preached in the Baptist church on the Sundays (3rd and 10th): these were his last preaching engagements. Members of his family took part with him in the services. On the first Sunday he spoke on 'Breaking the "I can't" barrier'. On the second his theme was 'Finding a purpose in life'. In the first part of the sermon ('A lost generation') he pointed to meaninglessness as characteristic of the age. In the second part ('A purpose for time and eternity') he pointed to Philippians 1:21 as the answer: '*For to me to live is Christ and to die is gain.*' In his final appeal he asked, 'What is your purpose? "For to me to live is a question mark, and to die is loss" or "For to me to live is Christ and to die is gain"?'

Peter carried on with his work, well beyond the call of duty, as long as he could. His colleagues urged him not to tire himself by writing his annual report for the 1994 Assembly, but he wrote at his usual length and with his usual comprehensiveness and depth.

He was cared for at home. In the last weeks his family and friends often gathered with him, joining hands and praying. Visitors were impressed by the atmosphere of peace and faith in the home. The family doctor said he would never forget Peter's attitude to his coming death.

His daughter Fiona is glad she was able to spend so much time with him in the last year. Shortly before he died she produced a recorded album of songs. Peter listened to and commented upon each song.

---

[4] *SBM* (June 1994), 3.
[5] *SBM* (June 1994), 5.

His brother Wilf saw Peter a month before he died. He says that even in his dying weeks he wasn't angry. His only thought was 'Will Isobel manage?—and the children?' But he came to the point when he handed all that over to God. Peter said: 'I see heaven as a busy place with loads to do.' He even sent out letters of thanks to those who took part in the Lillehammer EBF Congress. David Coffey wrote:[6]

> Many of us who participated in the Congress will cherish the letter of thanks which we received. My own letter was written two weeks before he died in which there was no mention of his illness or his weakness, simply insisting 'that the glory must go to Him.'

Karl Heinz Walter wrote of his last visit to Peter:

> 'Does the world still recognise that we as Christians are different?—and—Do we still keep the Bible as the only authority for our life and faith?'
>
> These were the two questions Peter Barber raised when I met with him two weeks before his death. We had been talking about some questions in our European Baptist Federation which had come to us after the Congress in Lillehammer. Until the very last moment we could share thoughts and I could ask for his advice. He was up-to-date even in times of his great weakness.
>
> This last meeting was a great gift to both of us and we praised God for it. For more than two hours I reported on the Congress and Peter surprised me with his questions and clear advice for the future: we knew we were seeing each other for the last time. We only knew each other for five years but these were very intensive years of a deep spiritual relationship and personal friendship.[7]

Eric Watson wrote:

> During my last visit to him on the Wednesday before he died, he was pleased that he had completed all his reports for the Assembly Papers. Like other Council members I have seen the draft of what, in the purposes of God, has proved to be his final report—I quote his last sentence—'Let me therefore plead as we close another year of service, this should be our ultimate goal to keep Christ at the centre of all we say, or do, or desire. And to Him be the glory!' That is vintage Peter.[8]

In his address at the Thanksgiving Service, Andrew MacRae referred to the way Peter reacted to his sufferings:

---

[6] *SBN* (October 1994), 2
[7] *SBN* (October 1994), 2.
[8] *SBN* (October 1994), 1.

I happen to know that being the General Secretary of the Baptist Union of Scotland is no sinecure, but a demanding and challenging call and he fulfilled it to the point of suffering. Not only so but he experienced far more physical suffering of his own than many are aware and bore it for the honour of Christ. You all saw his letter in the *Scottish Baptist Magazine* a few months ago and you must have been struck by the positive mood of gratitude it conveyed, with not a tinge of self-pity. Yet Peter has gone through some pretty critical physical crises in recent years. They've all been accepted with a spirit of trust. A year ago we all held out high hopes that the excellent surgery of that Spring would take care of the physical problem, but when it turned out to be otherwise it made no difference to Peter.

Andrew and his wife Jean 'talked with Peter about ten days before his homecall. Still not a word of self-pity, still a calm, confident, trusting acknowledgement of the goodness and the faithfulness of God.'

Peter's sister Helen found that Peter looked his illness straight in the face. He was very factual and detailed about it. He had seen others with cancer, and his other sister Jean had died of it eight years before. There was no fear. He died as he lived, calmly and patiently, waiting upon God. He believed that it was in God's power to heal, but this was for those whom he desired to touch. As so many were praying for him there was almost the thought that he must be healed, but Peter said it was all in God's plan. He was open to be healed but didn't expect it to be his right to be healed. A lot of his peace came from this submission to the divine will and it stopped him fretting.

Peter died at home with his family around him on Thursday 1 September 1994, a few days after his sixty-fourth birthday. In his Thanksgiving Service address Andrew MacRae asked:

Will you be surprised if I tell you that at the moment Peter Barber left this life to be with the Lord a recording was playing softly in the background of his room of one of his favourite hymns? Do you know what it was? It was 'Great is Thy faithfulness'. And it was to the strains of that beautiful old hymn that Peter was ushered into the Lord's presence.

The funeral service was held at the East Mains church in East Kilbride on Tuesday 6 September. Edwin Gunn led and gave a tribute. Douglas Hutcheon, Superintendent of the Union, gave the message. The hymns were: 'Be still for the presence of the Lord', 'Through all the changing scenes of life', and 'In heavenly love abiding'. Peter's body was buried in Phillips Hill Cemetery in East Kilbride in accordance with the tradition of burial in the family. The inscription Isobel chose for the stone was 'For to me to live is Christ, to die is gain'.

A large representative congregation gathered for the Thanksgiving Service on Friday 9 September in Charlotte Chapel, Edinburgh. Peter and Isobel had chosen the hymns and they all spoke of Christ: 'Crown Him with many crowns', 'Jesus shall take the highest honour', 'How sweet the name of Jesus sounds', and 'With harps and with viols'. Douglas Hutcheon led the service. Eric Watson read the scriptures and prayed. Karl Heinz Walter, David Coffey and Donald McCallum gave tributes. Alex Wright[9] prayed. Andrew MacRae gave the address, based on the faith of Paul as expressed in Philippians 3, which he related to Peter's life and faith. Kathie White sang 'People need the Lord', a favourite song of Peter's. Ian Mundie prayed the closing prayer.

In many sermons throughout his ministry Peter preached with deep conviction on the subject of death and the new life to come. He closed a sermon on the doxology of the Lord's Prayer with these words:

> We know that all death can do is usher us into the presence of the King, by his power to behold His glory. It's Dr Tozer who tells the story of a Methodist...a very prominent Methodist but when he was a young man he went to visit an elderly Christian who had only a short time to live. The young fellow was appalled at having to face this and sitting on the chair, frightened, not knowing what to say, he started to stumble out words of sympathy to this dying believer. The old Christian did not need such words and she said to the young clergyman: 'Why, God bless you young man, I'm just going to cross over the Jordan in a few minutes and my Father owns the land on both sides of the river.' That is true. Brethren, His is the Kingdom now. His will be the Kingdom then. Our Father owns the land on both sides of the river and all death can do is take us across to see the King, to rejoice in His power and to behold His glory, for ever, and ever, and ever, and ever. A Christian's prospect—the hope of glory. Tell me: is it yours today? Have you entered the kingdom by being born again? Have you felt the transforming touch of God's power in your life? Are you moving on to that day when you shall behold his glory? May it be so for His Name's sake. Amen.[10]

---

[9] Minister at Glenrothes, 1958–92.

[10] Sermon preached at Upton Vale, Torquay, on 10 July 1977. From the tape-recording of the service.

CHAPTER 20

A Man in Christ

Many people found it difficult to come to terms with Peter's death. He was a multi-gifted leader at the height of his powers, with opportunities for worldwide service opening up. David Coffey described his life as 'an unfinished symphony'.[1]

Some wondered how such an active man would have adjusted to retirement. He himself viewed the prospect with some misgiving, but had in mind the possibility of a part-time pastorate in a small church, where he could help and encourage the people, as well as fulfilling wider, international responsibilities. He would also have liked to do more writing.

Out of deep grief, but with great gratitude many people paid eloquent tributes to Peter's character and the impact he made on individuals, churches, Baptists and the wider Christian world. They are evidence of the special affection in which he was held and the love that he inspired.

His daughter Fiona remembers him as 'a good, kind, wise person, who had a way of looking at something from many angles at one time'. She is a singer and songwriter. A few months after his death she wrote a song describing him as a good, strong, kind, true, brave and honest man. His daughter Susan describes him as 'an immense diplomat' who 'behaved to everyone with the same level of interest and integrity'. His son Colin remembers his consistent personality, with fundamental principles at his heart; he had a sense of fun all the time and showed people not anger but empathy.

Peter had the ability to pursue an academic career, but felt led in a different direction—to be a pastor-teacher—and such he essentially remained. He did not seek high office, but accepted it when he was persuaded that he was the right person for the task because of his God-given gifts.

His aptitudes for evangelism, preaching, teaching and pastoral care were apparent to all. He was an encourager and an enabler, always ready to give fulsome appreciation for the work of others. But on top of these

---

[1] *SBN* (October 1994), 2; he expressed similar sentiments in his tribute at the Thanksgiving Service.

gifts he had received an astounding capacity for hard, conscientious work, with the strength to live at a tremendous pace. This enabled him to keep up the momentum of pioneering work at East Kilbride for eighteen years, to give individual attention to members in a church as large as Upton Vale, to keep abreast of denominational matters and even the welfare of individual churches in Scotland while exercising a ministry to Europe at a time of colossal upheaval and being involved with Baptists worldwide. He was single-minded in his devotion to the work of his calling, but able to switch easily from the seriousness of study to the relaxation of family life. In earlier years he loved playing with his three children and in later years with his granddaughter Zoe, who adored him.

People recognized him as genuine. What he preached he lived. He was never two-faced. He was kind-hearted and not critical. He was a perfectionist for himself, but not for others. Before he spoke he asked himself: 'Is it true? Is it kind? Is it necessary?'

He had a great reverence for God and believed in reverence in church. When he said 'Let us pray', there was a real sense of worship. At the same time, with his sense of humour and his flair for kindly mischief, he created fun wherever he went. His wit made his Christian faith all the more appealing. He never lost the common touch.

'Humility' was the word that featured in many tributes. Geoffrey Grogan, Principal of the Bible Training Institute, Glasgow, from 1969–90, wrote of his 'completely natural and unaffected humility'.[2] Peter's sister Helen prefers to call him 'modest' rather than 'humble': 'Peter really didn't think about himself. If anyone paid him a compliment he was staggered. He would never hold himself up as a special person. He did not try to develop humility—it was in him.' David Coffey linked Peter's humility with his relationship to Christ:

> I believe the secret of Peter Barber was his Christlike character and the pre-eminent characteristic of his personality was that of humility. His was a submissive humility because he knew he was at all times a man under the authority of God's word. It was a self-effacing humility, always seeking to increase the glory of Christ in his achievements, desiring the hiddenness of the messenger, which could never be read as false modesty. It was a dependent humility in that he always sought to be clothed with that power from on high. He lived according to the warning of Jesus, 'Apart from me you can do nothing.'[3]

---

[2] In a private condolence letter to Isobel.

[3] *SBN* (October 1994), 2; he expressed similar sentiments in his tribute at the Thanksgiving Service.

Andrew MacRae saw the influence of the Spirit in Peter's humility, as he made clear at the Thanksgiving Service, although, off the cuff, he remembered an amusing incident that forced some humility upon Peter!

> In all his ministry, although Peter was constantly being commended for his gifts, usually flatteringly—I do have one funny and disturbing memory of going with him one occasion to Port Seton, to the Fishermen's Bethel, and hearing him preach his heart out and sing a solo, and be greeted at the door at the end by an old man who said, 'Aye, laddie, you're a rare singer!' I didn't let him forget that one for a long time!—in all his ministry, though constantly being commended for his gifts, Peter did not succumb to the temptation to think well of himself, but always of Christ.

> I confess we used to tease each other mercilessly and did so until very, very recently, about our vain attempts to straighten out the other's theology. But Peter always knew that any sufficiency for ministry, like any goodness or righteousness in the sight of God, were the result of God's divine grace. That kept him from the mean-spiritedness that so often spoils those who think that they have a position to protect, and who believe that some of the virtue is their own. In fact, Peter reminds me of that beautiful old hymn about the Holy Spirit, in which these words are written about the Spirit of God:

> He came sweet influence to impart,
>   A gracious, willing guest,
> Where He can find one humble heart
>   Wherein to rest.

> And every virtue we possess,
>   And every victory won,
> And every thought of holiness,
>   Are His alone.[4]

Peter's humility was based on an honest assessment of himself. When Nick Mercer accepted the call to work with him at Upton Vale Peter wrote to him: 'For myself, the longer I am in the ministry the more unworthy I feel of the calling and the more amazed I become at the grace of One who can use such a weak vessel.'[5]

Many people paid tribute to Peter's Christ-likeness. One of the meditations he wrote during his last illness (in August 1993) reveals the heart of his spirituality. Its title, 'A Man in Christ', is taken from 2 Corinthians 12:2: 'I know a man in Christ...'.[6] It is written as if by Paul, but it implies that all those who claim to be living in Christ should desire

---

[4] From the hymn 'Our blest Redeemer' by Henriette Auber.

[5] Letter dated 27 January 1979.

[6] No doubt Peter also had in mind that James Stewart had used this title for his book on Paul. (London: Hodder and Stoughton, 1935).

to be entirely his. In facing the pain and uncertainty of his illness Peter found his greatest assurance and security to be the reality of his life in Christ, which included 'the sharing of His sufferings' (Philippians 3:10). These are the last two stanzas:

> In Christ who never changes,
> never falters, never fails.
> In his peace.
> In his strength.
> In his fulness.
> In HIM.
>
> My name? you ask,
> My address?
> It matters not.
> I am a man in Christ.

As he accepted physical suffering and as he accepted the hurts that his work entailed he deepened his awareness of his life in Christ. Isobel was aware that Peter did feel things deeply and there were occasions when he was badly hurt, though he would always rise above them. He would say to her: 'Look what they did to the Lord—and I'm not perfect'. When he met with opposition he never reacted with anger, though with great sadness sometimes, but always graciously trying to see where the other person was coming from. He was always ready to apologize if he was in the wrong. Douglas Hutcheon commented at the Thanksgiving Service:

> Peter would never burden others with his own needs, but he had his wounds in battle, he had his moments of darkness, his faith was one which flourished amidst adversity and shone in the dark because he knew the ministry of Jesus deep in his heart as he focused his life on him.

All admired Peter's courage as he faced the trial of his illness. There were high hopes of complete recovery after his first operation, but when these were dashed he continued to accept his increasing weakness and finally his approaching death with a spirit of trust.

Knowing Peter's own acceptance of the mystery of suffering, Andrew MacRae affirmed: 'Countless numbers of us around the world prayed for the Lord to intervene. God heard our prayer and chose in his wisdom to use his servant's suffering as part of his redemptive purpose in other lives he touched during these days of weakness. And then to call him home.'[7]

Peter sometimes quoted a poem on the theme 'Christ wants the best', which had often challenged him. The final verse reads:

---

[7] Thanksgiving Service address, 9 September 1994.

And is our best too much? Ah, friends, let us remember
How once our Lord poured forth His soul for us,
And in the prime of His mysterious manhood
Gave up His precious life upon the cross.
The Lord of Lords, by Whom the worlds were made,
Through bitter grief and tears gave us
The best He had.[8]

---

[8] *Vision* (September–October 1974), 9.

Select Bibliography

Magazines

Focus on East Kilbride Baptist Church (published from August 1969 onwards)

Forum: The Magazine of the Friends, Students and Former Students of the Baptist Theological College of Scotland

East Kilbride Baptist Church Record (published from January 1957 to June–July 1969)

Scottish Baptist Magazine (monthly; ceased publication after December 2000; referred to in some chapters as the *Magazine*)

Scottish Baptist News (October 1994)

The Scottish Baptist Year Book (published annually by the Baptist Union of Scotland, Glasgow)

Vision (the bi-monthly magazine of Upton Vale Baptist Church, Torquay, before, during and after Peter Barber's ministry there)

John W. Merritt, 'Merritt's Musings', in *Highlights: A Publication of the European Baptist Convention*, (September–October 1994)

Booklets

Baptism, Eucharist and Ministry: A Scottish Baptist Response to the Lima Document (Glasgow: Baptist Union of Scotland, 1984)

Baptists and Freemasonry (written by a Group appointed by the Council; 'Viewpoint' Series; Glasgow: Baptist Union of Scotland, 1987)

Baptist Union of Scotland, *Our Roman Catholic Neighbours* ('Viewpoint' Series; Glasgow: Baptist Union of Scotland, 1989)

Doctrine and Inter-Church Relations Committee, *Scottish Baptists and the Charismatic Renewal Movement* (mainly written by Peter Barber; 'Viewpoint' Series; Glasgow: Baptist Union of Scotland, n.d. [1980s])

Not Strangers but Pilgrims: Report of the Swanwick Conference, 31 August to 4 September 1987 (London: British Council of Churches and Catholic Truth Society for the Inter-Church Process, n.d.)

Peter H. Barber, *Jesus Christ the Only Hope: Baptist Union of Scotland Presidential Address, Edinburgh, 1969* (Glasgow: Baptist Union of Scotland, 1969)

Silver Jubilee: East Kilbride Baptist Church 25, 1954–1979 (East Kilbride: East Kilbride Baptist Church, 1979)

Souvenir Brochure to commemorate the Opening of East Kilbride Baptist Church, 9th April, 1960 (East Kilbride: East Kilbride Baptist Church, 1960)

The Next Steps for Churches Together in Pilgrimage, Including Definite Proposals for Ecumenical Instruments (London: British Council of Churches and Catholic Truth Society for the Inter-Church Process, 1989)

Women in the Ministry (Report of a Sub-committee of the Joint Ministerial Board; 'Viewpoint' Series; Glasgow: Baptist Union of Scotland, 1983)

Books

Stanley Crabb *(ed.), Our Favourite Memories: European Baptist Federation 1949–1999* (n.p.: European Baptist Federation, 1999)

Bernard Green, *Crossing the Boundaries: A History of the European Baptist Federation* (Didcot: Baptist Historical Society, 1999)

John W. Merritt, *The Betrayal of Southern Baptist Missionaries by Southern Baptist Leaders 1979–2004* (n.p.: privately published, 2004)

George J. Mitchell, *Guidance and Gumption: A Hundred Years and More of Inverness Baptist Church* (Inverness: Inverness Baptist Church, 1998)

John S. Fisher, *From Friars Lane to Castle Street: A Fragment of Inverness History* (Inverness: Inverness Baptist Church, 1983)

David Hewitt, *The Power of Love* (Basingstoke: Marshall Pickering, 1987)

W.T. Stunt *et al., Turning the World Upside Down: A Century of Missionary Endeavour* (Bath: Echoes of Service, 2nd edn, 1972)

Derek B. Murray: *The First Hundred Years* (Glasgow: Baptist Union of Scotland, 1969)

Other Material

Karl Heinz Walter: *Reflections* (a private communication with the author, 22 May 2002)

General Index

Congregational Union 78
Congregationalists 186
Cook, H. 38
Cooke, F. 128
Cornton Baptist Church, Stirling 155
Council of Churches for Britain and
  Ireland 170
Counterslip Baptist Church, Bristol
  100
Crocker, D. 94
Crocker, Vera 94
Cupar Baptist Church 176
Cutts, Abraham 101
Cutts, Aubrey 120, 128
Cutts, K. 101, 104, 123, 131, 133

Dalbeattie Baptist Church 155
Dallyn, A. 127
Darvill, R. 96
Davey, B. 114
Decade of Evangelism 154
Dedridge Baptist Congregation,
  Livingston 155, 156
Dennistoun Baptist Church 139
Devon and Cornwall Baptist
  Association 100, 114, 184
Dick, J.A. 53
Dines, J. 32
Ding, Bishop 207
divorce 104, 160-61
Dobson, R. 126, 130
Drake, H.F. 186
Drane, J. 168, 178
Drumchapel Baptist Church 177
Duke Street Baptist Church,
  Richmond 98
Dumbarton Baptist Church 34, 43
Dumfries Baptist Church 140
Duncan, G. 68
Duncan, G.B. 115

East Dartmoor Baptist Church 114
East Kilbride Baptist Church 6, 9,
  12, 29, 31-48, 49-64, 65-67, 68,
  72, 75, 79, 82, 85, 86, 87, 88, 89-
  93, 94, 95, 96, 98, 102, 114, 116,
  117, 119, 124, 127, 131, 132,
  135, 139, 144, 156, 219, 222

ecumenism/ecumenical movement
  79, 82, 88, 115, 163-77, 181, 188
Ellon Baptist Church 156, 184
English, D. 154
Episcopal Church 71, 207
Erskine Baptist Church 162
European Baptist Convention 195,
  200
European Baptist Federation 38, 86,
  143, 183, 190-205, 206, 207, 208,
  211, 212, 218
Evangelical Alliance 100, 115, 177-
  78
Evangelical Baptist Fellowship Bible
  College 33
Evangelicals/Evangelicalism 80, 84,
  115, 122, 151, 158, 171, 173,
  174, 176, 177, 184
Exclusive Brethren 15, 16

Fellowship of British Baptists 87,
  187-88
Ferguson, A. 15, 19, 20
Fiddes, P.S. 202
Free Church Council 114, 116
Freel, B. 98
Freemasonry 161-63
French Baptist Federation 198
Fuller Baptist Church, Kettering 186

Gaukroger, S. 100
George Street Baptist Church, Paisley
  147
Gerrard Street Baptist Church,
  Aberdeen 179
Gibson, A. 115
Glanton Brethren 1, 5, 15, 16, 17, 18
Glegg, L. 70
Gold Hill Baptist Church 34, 97, 124
Goldie, A. 206
Gorgie Baptist Church, Edinburgh
  19, 147
Graham, Anne 71
Graham, B. 64, 114, 152, 153, 158,
  193, 207
Graham, Betty 15
Graham, J.R.G. 27, 34, 42-43, 71,
  96

Leslie Baptist Church 176
Lipscombe, J. 126
London Bible College 24, 101
Lotz, D. 209, 211
Lunnasting Baptist Church, Shetland
147-48
Lusaka Baptist Church, Zambia 206
Lustleigh Baptist Church 114

Maclagan, D. 91
MacLeay, D.S.K. 42
MacNeill, A. 186
MacRae, A.D. 9, 15, 19, 21, 24, 26,
29, 46, 53, 57, 77, 79, 80, 83, 86,
87, 90, 92, 98, 131, 135, 148,
155, 183, 190, 198, 212, 218,
219, 220, 223, 224
MacRae, H. 19, 26, 29
MacRae, Jean 57, 135, 219
Madden, S. 118, 121
Mainstream 184, 185
Manson, P.D. 100
Marshman, J. 208
Martin, G.W. 24, 142
McBain, D. 185
McBride, Kath 124, 130
McCall, D. 206
McCallum, D. 9, 38, 70, 220
McKendrick, J. 65
McLachlan, M. 186
McLean, J. 148
McManus, V. 43, 44
McNair, Muriel 140
McNeill, G. 38, 45
Mennonites 211
Mercer, N. 100, 101, 104, 118, 223
Merritt, J.W. 195, 200, 202
Methodists/Methodism 168, 220
Midteide, P. 203
Miller, A.B. 25, 27, 28, 33, 35, 36,
50, 53
Milne, B. 98, 99, 110
Misselbrook, L. 151
Mission '77 105, 110, 111, 112, 117
Mission England 152
Mission Scotland 153, 154
Mission to London 152
Mitchell, Christine 142

Mitchell, G. 179
Montgomery, A. 147
Moore, J. 47
Moravians 186
Moretonhampstead Baptist Church
114
Morgan, P. 165
Morningside Baptist Church,
Edinburgh 176
Morton, A.R. 71
Mother Teresa 207
Movement for World Evangelisation
43, 110
Moyes, T.W. 173
Mull Baptist Church 146
Mundie, I. 140, 141, 220
Murdoch, J. 55-56, 63, 67, 87, 92
Murray, D.B. 48, 77

Nairn Baptist Church 156
Neil, D. 140
New College, Edinburgh 23, 24, 25
Newton Mearns Baptist Church 156,
157, 209
Nixon, D. 203
Norman, J.G.G. 55
North American Baptist Fellowship
207

Oakley, I. 142
Open Brethren 16
Orthodox Church/Orthodoxy 168

Palau, L. 152
Peck, A. 162, 172
Perkin, J.R.C. 212
Peters, H. 129
Pitlochry Baptist Church 176
Pittenweem Baptist Church, Fife 20
Pollock, A.J. 17
Porteous, N. 24
Port Dundas Baptist Church 34
Portstewart Keswick Convention,
Co. Londonderry 68
Portuguese Baptist Union 191
Presbyterians/Presbyterianism 2, 4,
24, 174
Purley Baptist Church 99

Also from Paternoster

Studies in Baptist History and Thought
Dates in bold are of projected publication
Volumes in this series are not always published in sequence

David Bebbington and Anthony R. Cross (eds)
Global Baptist History
(SBHT vol. 14)
This book brings together studies from the Second International Conference on Baptist Studies which explore different facets of Baptist life and work especially during the twentieth century.
2005 / 1-84227-214-4

David Bebbington (ed.)
The Gospel in the World
International Baptist Studies
(SBHT vol. 1)
This volume of essays from the First International Conference on Baptist Studies deals with a range of subjects spanning Britain, North America, Europe, Asia and the Antipodes. Topics include studies on religious tolerance, the communion controversy and the development of the international Baptist community, and concludes with two important essays on the future of Baptist life that pay special attention to the United States.
2002 / 1-84227-118-0 / xiv + 362pp

Damian Brot
Church of the Baptized or Church of Believers?
A Contribution to the Dialogue between the Catholic Church and the Free Churches with Special Reference to Baptists
(SBHT vol. 26)
The dialogue between the Catholic Church and the Free Churches in Europe has hardly taken place. This book pleads for a commencement of such a conversation. It offers, among other things, an introduction to the American and the international dialogues between Baptists and the Catholic Church and strives to allow these conversations to become fruitful in the European context as well.
2006 / 1-84227-334-5 / approx. 364pp

Dennis Bustin
Paradox and Perseverence
Hanserd Knollys, Particular Baptist Pioneer in Seventeenth-Century England
(SBHT vol. 23)
The seventeenth century was a significant period in English history during which the people of England experienced unprecedented change and tumult in all spheres of life. At the same time, the importance of order and the traditional institutions of society were being reinforced. Hanserd Knollys, born during this pivotal period, personified in his life the ambiguity, tension and paradox of it, openly seeking change while at the same time cautiously embracing order. As a founder and leader of the Particular Baptists in London and despite persecution and personal hardship, he played a pivotal role in helping shape their identity externally in society and, internally, as they moved toward becoming more formalised by the end of the century.
2006 / 1-84227-259-4 / approx. 324pp

Anthony R. Cross
Baptism and the Baptists
Theology and Practice in Twentieth-Century Britain
(SBHT vol. 3)
At a time of renewed interest in baptism, *Baptism and the Baptists* is a detailed study of twentieth-century baptismal theology and practice and the factors which have influenced its development.

2000 / 0-85364-959-6 / xx + 530pp

Anthony R. Cross and Philip E. Thompson (eds)
Baptist Sacramentalism
(SBHT vol. 5)
This collection of essays includes biblical, historical and theological studies in the theology of the sacraments from a Baptist perspective. Subjects explored include the physical side of being spiritual, baptism, the Lord's supper, the church, ordination, preaching, worship, religious liberty and the issue of disestablishment.

2003 / 1-84227-119-9 / xvi + 278pp

Anthony R. Cross and Philip E. Thompson (eds)
Baptist Sacramentalism 2
(SBHT vol. 25)
This second collection of essays exploring various dimensions of sacramental theology from a Baptist perspective includes biblical, historical and theological studies from scholars from around the world.

2006 / 1-84227-325-6

Paul S. Fiddes
Tracks and Traces
Baptist Identity in Church and Theology
(SBHT vol. 13)
This is a comprehensive, yet unusual, book on the faith and life of Baptist Christians. It explores the understanding of the church, ministry, sacraments and mission from a thoroughly theological perspective. In a series of interlinked essays, the author relates Baptist identity consistently to a theology of covenant and to participation in the triune communion of God.

2003 / 1-84227-120-2 / xvi + 304pp

Stanley K. Fowler
More Than a Symbol
The British Baptist Recovery of Baptismal Sacramentalism
(SBHT vol. 2)
Fowler surveys the entire scope of British Baptist literature from the seventeenth-century pioneers onwards. He shows that in the twentieth century leading British Baptist pastors and theologians recovered an understanding of baptism that connected experience with soteriology and that in doing so they were recovering what many of their forebears had taught.

2002 / 1-84227-052-4 / xvi + 276pp

Steven R. Harmon
Towards Baptist Catholicity
Essays on Tradition and the Baptist Vision
(SBHT vol. 27)

This series of essays contends that the reconstruction of the Baptist vision in the wake of modernity's dissolution requires a retrieval of the ancient ecumenical tradition that forms Christian identity through rehearsal and practice. Themes explored include catholic identity as an emerging trend in Baptist theology, tradition as a theological category in Baptist perspective, Baptist confessions and the patristic tradition, worship as a principal bearer of tradition, and the role of Baptist higher education in shaping the Christian vision.

2006 / 1-84227-362-0

Michael A.G. Haykin (ed.)
'At the Pure Fountain of Thy Word'
Andrew Fuller as an Apologist
(SBHT vol. 6)

One of the greatest Baptist theologians of the eighteenth and early nineteenth centuries, Andrew Fuller has not had justice done to him. There is little doubt that Fuller's theology lay behind the revitalization of the Baptists in the late eighteenth century and the first few decades of the nineteenth. This collection of essays fills a much needed gap by examining a major area of Fuller's thought, his work as an apologist.

2004 / 1-84227-171-7 / xxii + 276pp

Michael A.G. Haykin
Studies in Calvinistic Baptist Spirituality
(SBHT vol. 15)

In a day when spirituality is in vogue and Christian communities are looking for guidance in this whole area, there is wisdom in looking to the past to find untapped wells. The Calvinistic Baptists, heirs of the rich ecclesial experience in the Puritan era of the seventeenth century, but, by the end of the eighteenth century, also passionately engaged in the catholicity of the Evangelical Revivals, are such a well. This collection of essays, covering such things as the Lord's Supper, friendship and hymnody, seeks to draw out the spiritual riches of this community for reflection and imitation in the present day.

2005 / 1-84227-149-0

Brian Haymes, Anthony R. Cross and Ruth Gouldbourne
On Being the Church
Revisioning Baptist Identity
(SBHT vol. 21)

The aim of the book is to re-examine Baptist theology and practice in the light of the contemporary biblical, theological, ecumenical and missiological context drawing on historical and contemporary writings and issues. It is not a study in denominationalism but rather seeks to revision historical insights from the believers' church tradition for the sake of Baptists and other Christians in the context of the modern–postmodern context.

2006 / 1-84227-121-0

Ken R. Manley
From Woolloomooloo to 'Eternity'
A History of Baptists in Australia
(SBHT vol. 16)
From their beginnings in Australia in 1831 with the first baptisms in Woolloomoolloo Bay in 1832, this pioneering study describes the quest of Baptists in the different colonies (states) to discover their identity as Australians and Baptists. Although institutional developments are analyzed and the roles of significant individuals traced, the major focus is on the social and theological dimensions of the Baptist movement.
2005 / 1-84227-194-6

Ken R. Manley
'Redeeming Love Proclaim'
John Rippon and the Baptists
(SBHT vol. 12)
A leading exponent of the new moderate Calvinism which brought new life to many Baptists, John Rippon (1751–1836) helped unite the Baptists at this significant time. His many writings expressed the denomination's growing maturity and mutual awareness of Baptists in Britain and America, and exerted a long-lasting influence on Baptist worship and devotion. In his various activities, Rippon helped conserve the heritage of Old Dissent and promoted the evangelicalism of the New Dissent
2004 / 1-84227-193-8 / xviii + 340pp

Peter J. Morden
Offering Christ to the World
Andrew Fuller and the Revival of English Particular Baptist Life
(SBHT vol. 8)
Andrew Fuller (1754–1815) was one of the foremost English Baptist ministers of his day. His career as an Evangelical Baptist pastor, theologian, apologist and missionary statesman coincided with the profound revitalization of the Particular Baptist denomination to which he belonged. This study examines the key aspects of the life and thought of this hugely significant figure, and gives insights into the revival in which he played such a central part.
2003 / 1-84227-141-5 / xx + 202pp

Peter Naylor
Calvinism, Communion and the Baptists
A Study of English Calvinistic Baptists from the Late 1600s to the Early 1800s
(SBHT vol. 7)
Dr Naylor argues that the traditional link between 'high-Calvinism' and 'restricted communion' is in need of revision. He examines Baptist communion controversies from the late 1600s to the early 1800s and also the theologies of John Gill and Andrew Fuller.
2003 / 1-84227-142-3 / xx + 266pp

Ian M. Randall, Toivo Pilli and Anthony R. Cross (eds)
Baptist Identities
International Studies from the Seventeenth to the Twentieth Centuries
(SBHT vol. 19)
These papers represent the contributions of scholars from various parts of the world as they consider the factors that have contributed to Baptist distinctiveness in different countries and at different times. The volume includes specific case studies as well as broader examinations of Baptist life in a particular country or region. Together they represent an outstanding resource for understanding Baptist identities.
2005 / 1-84227-215-2

James M. Renihan
Edification and Beauty
The Practical Ecclesiology of the English Particular Baptists, 1675–1705
(SBHT vol. 17)
Edification and Beauty describes the practices of the Particular Baptist churches at the end of the seventeenth century in terms of three concentric circles: at the centre is the ecclesiological material in the Second London Confession, which is then fleshed out in the various published writings of the men associated with these churches, and, finally, expressed in the church books of the era.
2005 / 1-84227-251-9 / approx. 230pp

Frank Rinaldi
'The Tribe of Dan'
A Study of the New Connexion of General Baptists 1770–1891
(SBHT vol. 10)
'The Tribe of Dan' is a thematic study which explores the theology, organizational structure, evangelistic strategy, ministry and leadership of the New Connexion of General Baptists as it experienced the process of institutionalization in the transition from a revival movement to an established denomination.
2006 / 1-84227-143-1 / approx. 330pp

Peter Shepherd
The Making of a Modern Denomination
John Howard Shakespeare and the Englsh Baptists 1989–1924
(SBHT vol. 4)
John Howard Shakespeare introduced revolutionary change to the Baptist denomination. The Baptist Union was transformed into a strong central institution and Baptist ministers were brought under its control. Further, Shakespeare's pursuit of church unity reveals him as one of the pioneering ecumenists of the twentieth century.
2001 / 1-84227-046-X / xviii + 220pp

Karen Smith
The Community and the Believers
*A Study of Calvinistic Baptist Spirituality in Some Towns and Villages of Hampshire
and the Borders of Wiltshire, c.1730–1830*
(SBHT vol. 22)
The period from 1730 to 1830 was one of transition for Calvinistic Baptists. Confronted
by the enthusiasm of the Evangelical Revival, congregations within the denomination as
a whole were challenged to find a way to take account of the revival experience. This
study examines the life and devotion of Calvinistic Baptists in Hampshire and Wiltshire
during this period. Among this group of Baptists was the hymn writer, Anne Steele.
2005 / 1-84227-326-4 / approx. 280pp

Martin Sutherland
Dissenters in a 'Free Land'
Baptist Thought in New Zealand 1850–2000
(SBHT vol. 24)
Baptists in New Zealand were forced to recast their identity. Conventions of
communication and association, state and ecumenical relations, even historical
divisions and controversies had to be revised in the face of new topographies and
constraints. As Baptists formed themselves in a fluid society they drew heavily on both
international movements and local dynamics. This book traces the development of ideas
which shaped institutions and styles in sometimes surprising ways.
2006 / 1-84227-327-2 / approx. 230pp

Brian Talbot
The Search for a Common Identity
The Origins of the Baptist Union of Scotland 1800–1870
(SBHT vol. 9)
In the period 1800 to 1827 there were three streams of Baptists in Scotland: Scotch,
Haldaneite and 'English' Baptist. A strong commitment to home evangelization brought
these three bodies closer together, leading to a merger of their home missionary societies
in 1827. However, the first three attempts to form a union of churches failed, but by the
1860s a common understanding of their corporate identity was attained leading to the
establishment of the Baptist Union of Scotland.
2003 / 1-84227-123-7 / xviii + 402pp

Philip E. Thompson
The Freedom of God
Towards Baptist Theology in Pneumatological Perspective
(SBHT vol. 20)
This study contends that the range of theological commitments of the early Baptists are
best understood in relation to their distinctive emphasis on the freedom of God.
Thompson traces how this was recast anthropocentrically, leading to an emphasis upon
human freedom from the nineteenth century onwards. He seeks to recover the dynamism
of the early vision via a pneumatologically-oriented ecclesiology defining the church in
terms of the memory of God.
2005 / 1-84227-125-3

Philip E. Thompson and Anthony R. Cross (eds)
Recycling the Past or Researching History?
Studies in Baptist Historiography and Myths
(SBHT vol. 11)

Recycling the Past or Researching History? brings together an international group of Baptist scholars who explore various issues in Baptist historiography and myths. To this end, contributors examine and re-examine areas of Baptist life and thought about which little is known or the received wisdom is in need of revision. Historiographical studies include the date Oxford Baptists joined the Abingdon Association, the death of the Fifth Monarchist John Pendarves, English Baptists' responses to the French Revolution and subsequent revolutionary wars, confessional identity and denominational institutions, Baptist community, ecclesiology, the priesthood of all believers, soteriology, Baptist spirituality, Strict and Reformed Baptists, the role of women among British Baptists, while various 'myths' challenged include the nature of High-Calvinism in eighteenth-century England, baptismal anti-sacramentalism, episcopacy, and Baptists and change. The theme which ties these studies together is that research into Baptist history should deal with the primary sources and not, as has too often been the case, rely uncritically on the scholarship of previous generations.
2005 / 1-84227-122-9

Linda Wilson
Marianne Farningham
A Plain Working Woman
(SBHT vol. 18)

Marianne Farningham, of College Street Baptist Chapel, Northampton, was a household name in evangelical circles in the later nineteenth century. For over fifty years she produced comment, poetry, biography and fiction for the popular Christian press. This investigation uses her writings to explore the beliefs and behaviour of evangelical Nonconformists, including Baptists, during these years.
2006 / 1-84227-124-5

Other Paternoster titles
relating to Baptist history and thought

Paul Beasley-Murray
Fearless for Truth
A Personal Portrait of the Life of George Beasley-Murray
Without a doubt George Beasley-Murray was one of the greatest Baptists of the twentieth century. A long-standing Principal of Spurgeon's College, he wrote more than twenty books and made significant contributions in the study of areas as diverse as baptism and eschatology, as well as writing highly respected commentaries on the Book of Revelation and John's Gospel.
2002 / 1-84227-134-2 / xii + 244pp

Stephen R. Holmes
Listening to the Past
The Place of Tradition in Theology
Beginning with the question 'Why can't we just read the Bible?' Stephen Holmes considers the place of tradition in theology, showing how the doctrine of creation leads to an account of historical location and creaturely limitations as essential aspects of our existence. For we cannot claim unmediated access to the Scriptures without acknowledging the place of tradition: theology is an irreducibly communal task. *Listening to the Past* is a sustained attempt to show what listening to tradition involves, and how it can be used to aid theological work today.
2002 / 1-84227-155-5 / xiv + 168pp

Mark Hopkins
Nonconformity's Romantic Generation
Evangelical and Liberal Theologies in Victorian England
A study of the theological development of key leaders of the Baptist and Congregational denominations at their period of greatest influence, including C.H. Spurgeon and R.W. Dale, and of the controversies in which those among them who embraced and rejected the liberal transformation of their evangelical heritage opposed each other.
2004 / 1-84227-150-4 / xvi + 284pp

Galen K. Johnson
Prisoner of Conscience
John Bunyan on Self, Community and Christian Faith
This is an interdisciplinary study of John Bunyan's understanding of conscience across his autobiographical, theological and fictional writings, investigating whether conscience always deserves fidelity, and how Bunyan's view of conscience affects his relationship both to modern Western individualism and historic Christianity.
2003 / 1-84227- 151-2 / xvi + 236pp

Meic Pearse
The Great Restoration
The Religious Radicals of the 16th and 17th Centuries
Pearse charts the rise and progress of continental Anabaptism—both evangelical and heretical—through the sixteenth century. He then follows the story of those English people who became impatient with Puritanism and separated—first from the Church of England and then from one another—to form the antecedents of later Congregationalists, Baptists and Quakers.
1998 / 0-85364-800-X / xii + 320pp

Charles Price and Ian M. Randall
Transforming Keswick
Transforming Keswick is a thorough, readable and detailed history of the convention. It will be of interest to those who know and love Keswick, those who are only just discovering it, and serious scholars eager to learn more about the history of God's dealings with his people.
2000 / 1-85078-350-0 / 288pp

Jim Purves
The Triune God and the Charismatic Movement
A Critical Appraisal from a Scottish Perspective
All emotion and no theology? Or a fundamental challenge to reappraise and realign our trinitarian theology in the light of Christian experience? This study of charismatic renewal as it found expression within Scotland at the end of the twentieth century evaluates the use of Patristic, Reformed and contemporary models (including those of the Baptist Union of Scotland) of the Trinity in explaining the workings of the Holy Spirit.

2004 / 1-84227-321-3 / xxiv + 246pp

Ian M. Randall
Evangelical Experiences
A Study in the Spirituality of English Evangelicalism 1918–1939
This book makes a detailed historical examination of evangelical spirituality between the First and Second World Wars. It shows how patterns of devotion led to tensions and divisions. In a wide-ranging study, Anglican, Wesleyan, Reformed and Pentecostal-charismatic spiritualities are analysed.

1999 / 0-85364-919-7 / xii + 310pp

Ian M. Randall
One Body in Christ
The History and Significance of the Evangelical Alliance
In 1846 the Evangelical Alliance was founded with the aim of bringing together evangelicals for common action. This book uses material not previously utilized to examine the history and significance of the Evangelical Alliance, a movement which has remained a powerful force for unity. At a time when evangelicals are growing world-wide, this book offers insights into the past which are relevant to contemporary issues.

2001 / 1-84227-089-3 / xii + 394pp

Ian M. Randall
Spirituality and Social Change
The Contribution of F.B. Meyer (1847–1929)
This is a fresh appraisal of F.B. Meyer (1847–1929), a leading Free Church minister. Having been deeply affected by holiness spirituality, Meyer became the Keswick Convention's foremost international speaker. He combined spirituality with effective evangelism and socio-political activity. This study shows Meyer's significant contribution to spiritual renewal and social change.

2003 / 1-84227-195-4 / xx + 184pp

Nigel G. Wright
New Baptists, New Agenda
New Baptists, New Agenda is a timely contribution to the growing debate about the health, shape and future of the Baptists. It considers the steady changes that have taken place among Baptists in the last decade – changes of mood, style, practice and structure – and encourages us to align these current movements and questions with God's upward and future call. He contends that the true church has yet to come: the church that currently exists is an anticipation of the joyful gathering of all who have been called by the Spirit through Christ to the Father.

2002 / 1-84227-157-1 / x + 162pp